COOKING OVER THE COALS

Whatever meat you choose for your barbecue—steaks, burgers or tender ribs—follow directions carefully for cooking to get the most out of the money you spend on meat. For broiling, all meats call for glowing coals. **No flame.** Let the fire burn down till a gray-ash film covers the charcoal. If the fire's too hot, you'll dry out the meat and lose all the good juices. Use the ideas on the following pages for the beginnings of great barbecues . . . and try a little experimenting on your own, too. Then invite friends and neighbors over and get ready to collect compliments for a fabulous outdoor feast!

Bantam Cookbooks
Ask your bookseller for the books you have missed

BETTER HOMES AND GARDENS® BARBECUE BOOK

BETTER HOMES AND GARDENS ® BARBECUE BOOK

*A Bantam Book / published by arrangement with
Meredith Corporation*

PRINTING HISTORY

Meredith Corporation edition published June 1956
Revised edition published 1965

Bantam edition published April 1972

2nd printing .. September 1972	5th printing ...... July 1973
3rd printing .... January 1973	6th printing .. September 1973
4th printing .... May 1973	7th printing .. December 1973
8th printing ...... March 1974	

*Bantam Books are published by Bantam Books, Inc. Its trade-
mark, consisting of the words "Bantam Books" and the por-
trayal of a bantam, is registered in the United States Patent
Office and in other countries. Marca Registrada. Bantam
Books, Inc., 666 Fifth Avenue, New York, New York 10019.*

PRINTED IN THE UNITED STATES OF AMERICA

CONTENTS

CHAPTER 1

MEAT, POULTRY, AND FISH

In planning a meal, think first of the meat. Choose from beef, pork, or lamb, either plain or fancy, all cooked to a T and carved to perfection. If poultry is your choice spin it on the rotisserie or hang a duckling in a Chinese smoke oven to be roasted in the aromatic fumes of burning fruitwoods. Broil salmon, trout, or swordfish steaks just till done and serve with a zesty sauce or marinade.

BEEF CUTS FOR THE BARBECUE

1 *Top loin steak* is boneless. Other names: loin strip, Kansas City or New York steak.

2 *T-bone* boasts tenderloin. A T-bone with a big tenderloin is called porterhouse and makes several servings. Some markets use the names interchangeably.

3 *Club steak* has rib bone along its side, looks like a rib steak. No tenderloin, but good!

4 *Top sirloin steak* (boneless) is easy to carve, serves 2 or 3. Any steak for broiling should have a network of fat through the lean.

5 *Rib-eye steak* is boneless. You may find it sold as Delmonico or Spencer steak.

6 *Blade or chuck steak.* If from the first two ribs of chuck, it'll be tender enough to grill. Other choices: Round steak—marinate or use tenderizer. Thick slices of tenderloin (filet mignon on menus)—a real splurge!

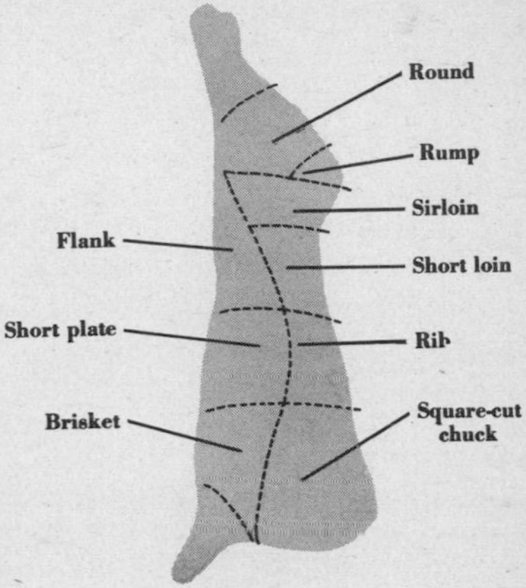

Beef Short Ribs

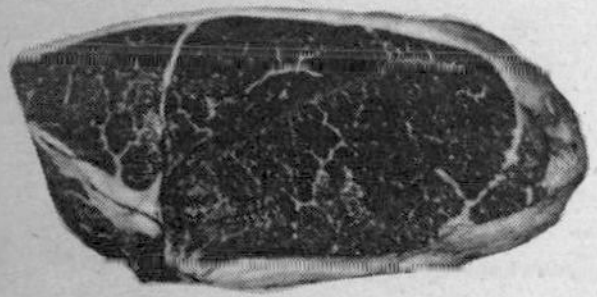

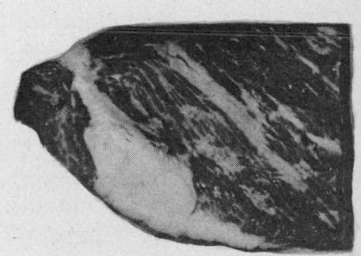

Round
Rump
Sirloin
Flank
Short loin
Short plate
Rib
Brisket
Square-cut chuck

Beef Boneless Shoulder Steak

Standing Rib Roast

Beef Boneless Fresh Brisket

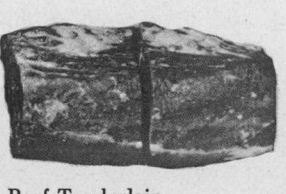

Beef Tenderloin

3

Sizzling Steaks!

MEAT BROILING TIPS

Score edges of meat—steaks, chops, ham slices, so they won't cup. Or cook in a broiler basket to keep them flat.

Trim off outer edge of fat from steaks, chops, ham slices so drippings won't blaze up too much. If drippings flare up during cooking, sprinkle the fire lightly with water to quench the blaze.

When coals are hot as blazes, tap off gray ash with fire tongs. Let grill top heat; grease it. On with the steaks!

Ready to turn? When you see little bubbles on top surface the meat is ready to turn. Heat forces the juices to the uncooked surface. Flip steaks with tongs and turner. Piercing with a fork wastes precious juices.

Time per side? When you broil steaks or burgers, broil the second side a few minutes less than the first. (Second side has a head start on heating.) Turn only once.

When to salt steak? Wait until you turn steak to salt it. Same for burgers and chops. Salt and pepper the browned side; season other side as you take the meat from the grill. If you salt uncooked meat, the juices will be drawn out and you'll lose good flavor.

Big-steak carving. It is important to know how to carve a big steak, like a porterhouse or a sirloin, so that one person doesn't rate most of the choice portions, and another person get the tag ends. First remove the bone, cutting very close to it. Now cut across the full width of the steak, making 1-inch slices and narrowing them a little on the tenderloin side. Be sure everyone gets a section of the tenderloin. If steak has a tail piece slice it last to serve for second helpings.

OUTDOOR STEAKS

Choose tender steaks, about 1 inch thick. (Rib steaks are easier on your budget than T-bones.) Slash fat edge at intervals to keep steaks flat. When coals are *hot,* tap off gray ash with fire tongs. Let grill top heat, then grease it and put on the steaks (orders for "rare" go on last). When you see little bubbles on top side of steaks they are ready to turn (heat forces the juices to the uncooked surface). Flip steaks with tongs and pancake turner—piercing with a fork wastes good meat juices. Broil second side less long than first—turn only once. For 1-inch steaks cooked medium-rare, allow 13 to 15 minutes *total* broiling time.

To season: Salt and pepper each browned side of steak right after turning, or season steaks as they come from the grill. Serve sputtering hot, with a pat of butter atop.

For char flavor: If you like steak with a deep-brown, crusty coat, try this. Sear one side by lowering grill top close to the coals for 2 to 3 minutes, then raise grill to finish same side. Turn steak, and sear second side; again raise grill and complete the cooking.

1 Fine-quality sirloin is this chef's choice, or choose club, T-bone, or porterhouse. (First marinate round or flank steak, or use meat tenderizer.) Trim excess fat so drippings won't blaze up when broiling. Steak should be evenly cut about 1½ to 2 inches thick.

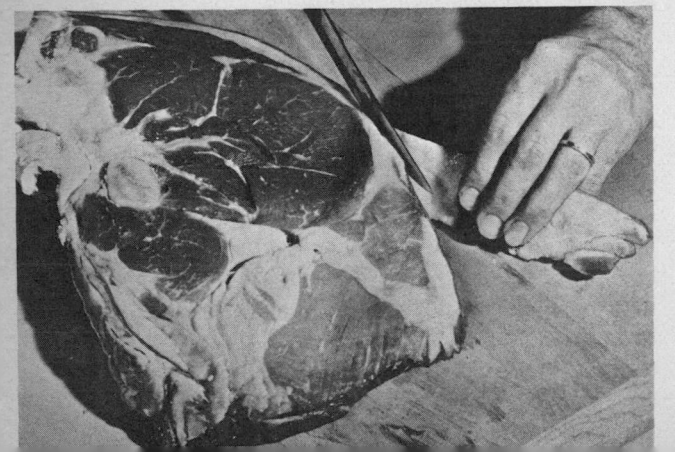

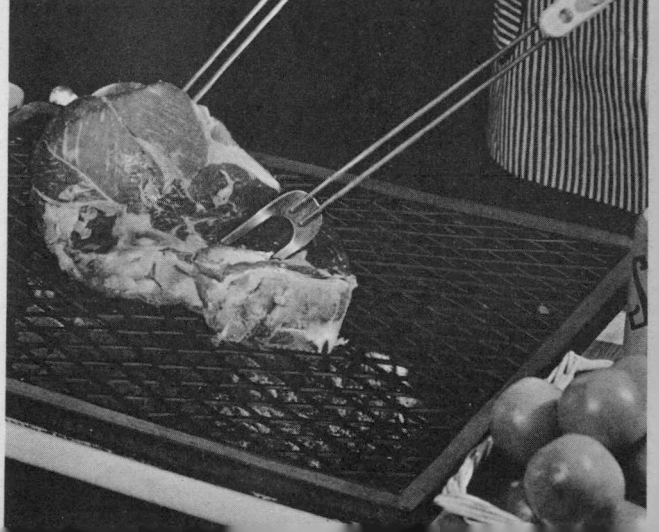

2 Next, spear some of the steak trimmings with a long-handled fork, and rub over hot grill (or broiler basket). This keeps the steak from sticking and sends up a fine aroma for kibitzers to sniff. If you like, brush steak with barbecue sauce or rub with garlic clove.

3 When coals glow with a gray film over the top, it's time to start the steak. Broil first side to a mouth-watering brown. With tongs and turner, do a neat flip. (If you use fork instead of tongs, be sure tines go in fat, not lean, or you'll lose good juices.)

4 Salt and pepper browned side to suit your taste. Continue broiling till steak is done the way you like it. (For a 2-inch cut, allow 35 to 40 minutes total broiling time for medium-rare; for 1-inch steaks allow about 15 minutes total time.) Offer sauce or mushrooms.

CRACKED-PEPPER STEAK

4 pounds chuck steak, 2½ to 3 inches thick

Instant seasoned meat tenderizer

3 tablespoons cracked or coarsely ground black pepper

Slash fat edges of steak. Sprinkle all surfaces of steak with meat tenderizer using about ½ teaspoon per pound of meat. *Do not use salt.* To insure penetration pierce all sides deeply at ½-inch intervals with a long-tined fork, working tenderizer in. Press cracked pepper into both sides of steak.

Broil steak on grill about 3 inches from coals, 35 to 50 minutes, turning frequently with tongs and a turner. To serve, slice with sharp knife diagonally across the grain of the meat, at about a 30° angle—keep the slices thin. Makes 6 to 8 servings.

FLANK STEAK BROIL

⅔ cup catsup
½ cup water
⅓ cup lemon juice
1 teaspoon celery seed
2 teaspoons
    Worcestershire
    sauce
1 bay leaf
½ teaspoon cracked or
    coarsely ground
    black pepper

¼ teaspoon crushed
    basil
Dash bottled hot pepper
    sauce
1½ pounds flank steak,
    scored

For marinade, combine all ingredients except steak. Simmer uncovered 10 minutes. Cool to room temperature. Pour over steak in shallow baking dish; let stand in refrigerator several hours or overnight, spooning sauce over occasionally.

Broil steak over *hot* coals 5 minutes; turn and broil 5 minutes more or till done. Cut *very thin* slices diagonally across the grain. Serve on buttered, toasted buns. Heat marinade and pass. Makes 6 servings.

SWANK PORTERHOUSE STEAK

Each slice of nice pink steak has a crunchy band of white onion in the center. Sensational!

1 2½- to 3-pound
    porterhouse or
    sirloin steak, about
    2 inches thick
        • • •
¾ cup finely chopped
    Bermuda onion
2 cloves garlic, minced
3 tablespoons cooking
    claret

2 tablespoons soy sauce
        • • •
¼ cup butter or
    margarine
1 3-ounce can (⅔ cup)
    broiled sliced
    mushrooms,
    drained

Slash fat edge of steak—don't cut into meat. Slitting from fat side, cut pocket in each side of lean, cutting *almost* to bone. Combine onion and garlic, seasoning with a dash of salt, pepper, and celery salt; use mixture as stuffing in steak. Mix cooking claret and soy sauce; brush on steak.

Broil over *hot* coals a total of 25 minutes or till done to your liking, turning once—brush occasionally with soy mixture. Heat butter and mushrooms in a small pan, pour over steak. Slice across grain and serve sizzling! Makes 4 servings.

TENDERED STEAK

No apologies needed when you choose a bargain steak! Give it this meat-tenderizer and kitchen-bouquet treatment, then broil!—

3 pounds 2-inch thick round steak (or rump or chuck steak)	**Instant nonseasoned meat tenderizer** **Kitchen bouquet** **Butter or margarine**

Sprinkle all sides of steak evenly with tenderizer, using about ½ teaspoon per pound. *Do not use additional salt.* To insure penetration pierce all sides deeply at ½-inch intervals with a long-tined fork.

Combine equal amounts of kitchen bouquet and butter or margarine; heat and stir to blend; brush generously over steak. (Kitchen bouquet gives nice brown to meat broiled at low temperature. And remember low-temperature broiling lessens shrinkage.) Broil on grill over coals about 12 minutes; turn and broil 10 to 15 minutes longer or till the way you like it. (Meat tenderizer cuts cooking time about one-fourth—so don't overcook.) Slice steak *diagonally, across the grain.* Makes 6 to 8 servings.

ROTISSERIE ROUND

1 2½- or 3-inch eye-of-
    round steak, about
    3 pounds
Instant nonseasoned
    meat tenderizer
        • • •
1 cup catsup

⅓ cup Worcestershire
    sauce
1 cup water
1 teaspoon chili powder
1 teaspoon salt
1 clove garlic, minced

Sprinkle all sides of steak evenly with tenderizer, using
½ teaspoon per pound. *Do not use additional salt.* To
insure penetration pierce all sides deeply at ½-inch
intervals with a long-tined fork.

Meanwhile combine remaining ingredients for sauce
and simmer slowly 30 minutes.

Center steak on spit and tie securely with cord. Roast
slowly over coals on motorized spit about 1½ hours
or to desired doneness, basting frequently with the sauce.

Meat thermometer will read 140° for rare, 160° for
medium, or 170° for well done. To serve, slice steak on
bias, across grain; pass the extra sauce. Makes 8 servings.

CHEF'S GRILLED CHUCK STEAK

½ cup chopped onion
½ cup lemon juice
¼ cup salad oil
½ teaspoon salt
½ teaspoon celery salt
½ teaspoon pepper

½ teaspoon thyme
½ teaspoon oregano
½ teaspoon rosemary
1 clove garlic, minced
2½ pounds chuck
    steak, ½-inch
    thick

Combine ingredients except steak. Marinate meat in mixture 3 hours in refrigerator, turning several times. Drain.
Broil steak on grill over *hot* coals. Cook steak to doneness you like (about 30 minutes total time), turning
once. Baste with marinade during broiling. Makes about
4 servings.

Orders for rare go on last. Some chefs like to salt and pepper each browned side right after turning; others season as they come from the grill. Serve with a pat of butter atop.

QUICK GARLIC STEAKS

Minute steaks are cooked on foil to keep them juicy, and sauced with lemon-garlic butter for an extra zip!

Tear off a sheet of heavy foil large enough to cook your minute steaks on and turn up edge ½ inch to make "pan." In it melt garlic butter (¼ cup butter mixed with 1 clove minced garlic) for 6 to 8 steaks. Dip steaks in the garlic butter to coat. Cook steaks fast on foil over *hot* coals, 1 or 2 minutes per side.

Push steaks aside and squeeze the juice of 1 lemon onto foil pan and add 2 tablespoons Worcestershire sauce, mixing with the garlic butter. Quickly swish steaks through sauce and place each atop a thin slice of toasted French bread to catch the good juices. Spoon a little pan sauce over. Salt and pepper steaks just before serving. Serve sizzling.

MARINATED HICKORY STEAKS

2 1-inch round-bone shoulder steaks, about 4 pounds total	Seasoned salt
	Pepper
	½ cup salad oil
10 small cloves garlic, peeled	½ cup wine vinegar
	1 tablespoon Worcester-shire sauce

Polka dot each steak with 5 cloves garlic. Insert tip of knife in meat and push in garlic clove as you remove knife. Sprinkle steaks generously with seasonings.

Combine salad oil, vinegar, and Worcestershire sauce for marinade. Pour over steaks in shallow dish and refrigerate overnight, or let stand several hours at room temperature, turning meat occasionally.

Broil over *hot* coals with hickory, about 15 minutes on each side, or till done to your liking; baste frequently with marinade. Heat remaining marinade and serve with steak.

CUBE-STEAK SANDWICHES

Cheese does great things for cube steak—

Arrange cube steaks in folding wire broiler basket. When fire burns to glowing coals, broil steaks briefly, first on one side, then on the other, brushing frequently with your favorite barbecue sauce. (The broiler keeps the thin steaks from curling.) Butter slices of bread and sprinkle with sharp grated cheese—have all ready to make into sandwiches.

Pop steaks between bread slices, adding relishes ad lib. Serve on paper plates with big helpings of hash-brown potatoes.

FILETS BUCKAROO

*That mustard does wonderful things—so does rolling up
slim minute steaks so they stay juicy. Any orders for
rare?—*

Flatten minute steaks and spread one side lightly with
prepared mustard. At narrow end of each, place a strip
of dill pickle or candied dill pickle, or 1 or 2 green
onions. Roll up, starting at end with pickle. Fasten with
small metal skewers or toothpicks; brush outside with
melted butter or margarine. Broil on grill over *hot* coals
10 to 15 minutes, turning once. When done to your liking,
sprinkle with salt and pepper.

STEAK SANDWICH WITH CHEF'S SAUCE

½ cup butter or
   margarine
3 tablespoons bottled
   steak sauce
2 tablespoons sliced
   green onion
1 tablespoon Worcester-
   shire sauce
¼ teaspoon salt

2 tomatoes, cut in
   1 inch slices
6 1-inch slices French
   bread
1 pound round steak,
   ¼ inch thick
Instant nonseasoned
   meat tenderizer
Freshly ground pepper

• • •

For sauce: Combine butter, steak sauce, onion, Worcestershire, and salt in small saucepan. Place on edge of
grill to heat. Arrange tomato slices in oiled foilware pan.
Heat on edge of grill while preparing sandwiches; turn
once. Toast French bread on both sides; set aside. Cut
round steak in 6 pieces. Use tenderizer according to
label directions.

Broil meat over *hot* coals 2 to 3 minutes on each side.
Sprinkle with pepper. Dip toasted French bread in
heated sauce. Arrange on platter. Top with broiled steak
and spoon remaining sauce over. Garnish with tomato
slices. Serve immediately. Serves 6.

STUFFED FLANK STEAK

Here's a hearty steak with stuffing that "meat 'n potatoes" men go for—

1 1- to 1¼-pound flank
   steak
½ teaspoon instant
   nonseasoned meat
   tenderizer
2 tablespoons prepared
   mustard
1½ cups dry bread
   cubes

⅓ cup chopped onion
⅓ cup chopped celery
3 tablespoons butter,
   melted
½ teaspoon poultry
   seasoning
¼ teaspoon salt
Garlic or clear French
   dressing

Score steak on both sides; use meat tenderizer, according to label directions. Spread one side of steak with mustard. Combine bread, onion, celery, butter and seasonings for stuffing; spread over steak.

Roll as for jellyroll; fasten meat with skewers or toothpicks; then lace with string. Balance meat on spit, insert holding forks. Attach spit and turn on motor. Baste with garlic dressing. Roast over *medium* coals about 35 minutes or till done, basting frequently with garlic dressing. Serves 4 or 5.

SALT BROILED STEAK

3 pounds (7½ cups)
   coarse-medium salt
2 pounds beef tenderloin
   (in one piece)
1 cup butter or
   margarine

2 cloves garlic, minced
1 loaf French bread,
   cut in ½-inch
   slices and toasted
   on one side

Mix just enough water (about 2¼ cups) with the salt to make it like damp sand. In a wire broiler basket, place a double thickness of paper towels, about the size of the meat. Pat out half the salt on the towels; top with meat. Completely cover meat with remaining salt, coating evenly—this keeps juices in. Now cover with double thickness paper towels, overlapping edges (don't worry, only the towel edges will burn). Close basket.

Broil tenderloin close to *hot* coals 12 to 15 minutes per side. Remove hardened cakes of salt, scraping off any that clings. Melt butter in skillet; add garlic. Dip untoasted side of bread in garlic butter and top with thin-sliced meat. Makes 8 servings.

Note: Carve the tenderloin in the skillet of garlic butter so the good beef juices blend in. And if there are any "well-doners," their meat slices can be simmered for a few minutes in this sauce.

ROLLED RIB ROAST, RESHAN

Select a 5- to 6-pound rolled rib roast. As the roast is being rolled, have meatman spread the inside with 2 cloves garlic, crushed, and ¼ to ⅓ cup prepared horseradish. (Or do this yourself, rerolling and tying roast.) Balance roast on spit, fastening with holding forks. Rub outside of roast with a cut clove of garlic and brush with additional horseradish, using some of the liquid. Insert meat thermometer. Attach spit and turn on motor (have *hot* coals at back of firebox, and a drip pan under meat).

Roast about 2 to 2½ hours for medium-rare or till done to your liking. Meat thermometer will register 140° for rare, 160° for medium, 170° for well-done. Let roast stand about 15 minutes to firm up before carving. Three servings per pound.

CHATEAUBRIAND

Carefully trim fat from the surface of 2 to 2½ pounds Chateaubriand. Make a slanting cut, 2 inches deep, the full length of the Chateaubriand with a sharp, narrow-bladed knife held at a 45-degree angle. Make another cut, just as before, along opposite side of the Chateaubriand.

Blend 4 ounces blue cheese and 1 tablespoon brandy. Spread cheese mixture in the openings formed by cuts. Skewer slashes closed with short skewers. Tie string around Chateaubriand at ends and in middle. Balance on spit; rotate over *hot* coals 1¼ to 1½ hours for medium rare. Serves 6 to 8.

ROTISSERIE ROASTING

Choose a roast weighing at least 3½ to 4 pounds so it will still be juicy when cooked. Have meatman tie roast at 1-inch intervals with heavy cord to make compact. (If meat is lean, have outside covered with a layer of fat, then trussed securely.)

Insert spit through center of roast and adjust holding forks. Test balance. If roast is off center, remount. Insert meat thermometer at slant into heaviest part of roast so tip of thermometer is in center but not touching bone, fat, or metal spit.

To carve prime ribs of beef, place the rib side to your left. Begin cutting at edge, going across to bone. Loosen slice with tip of knife. Accompany roast with baked stuffed potatoes.

Arrange *hot* coals at back of firebox, a drip pan in front of coals and under roast. The coals should be a little less hot than for broiling. (Use *slow* coals if you're cooking with hood closed.) Knock off the gray ash. Attach spit, turn on motor, and cook till meat thermometer tells you roast is done. The thermometer should read 140° for rare, 160° for medium, and 170° for well-done.

Because of the many variables in outdoor barbecuing, cooking times can be only estimates. Most roasts will cook a little faster than in a range oven. A boneless roast, such as rolled rib or rolled chuck, will require a little more cooking than a bone-in roast like standing rib roast.

When roast is done, let it firm up 15 to 20 minutes before carving. You may lower firebox to stop cooking and let roast rotate for that time, or transfer roast to platter.

RIB-EYE ROAST WITH HERB BUTTER

Select a 5- to 6-pound beef rib-eye roast. Have meatman tie roast with string at 1½-inch intervals. Center meat on spit, fastening securely with holding forks. Attach spit and turn on motor (have *hot* coals at back of firebox and drip pan under roast). Roast over coals 2 to 2½ hours for medium-rare or till done to your liking. Meat thermometer will register 140° for rare, 160° for medium, and 170° for well-done. Let roast stand about 15 minutes to firm up before carving.

Meanwhile make Herb Butter: Blend ½ cup soft butter or margarine with 2 teaspoons seasoned salt, 1 teaspoon *fines herbes*, ¼ teaspoon cracked pepper, and few drops bottled hot pepper sauce. Dab a little Herb Butter (it's potent!) on each serving of meat—it will melt deliciously. Count on three servings per pound of beef.

CHUCK'S CHUCK ROAST

Choose a 4- to 5-pound chuck pot roast, about 2 inches thick. Trim off excess fat. Slash the fat edge. Use instant meat tenderizer according to the label directions. Brown meat on grill, about 2 inches from *hot* coals, a total of 30 minutes, turning frequently. Place meat in Dutch oven or large skillet and pour Quick Bordelaise Sauce (see index listing) over; cover and cook *slowly* about 1 hour. Makes 8 to 10 servings.

For "rare" fans: Omit cooking in Dutch oven, and serve the roast directly after charcoaling. Pass Quick Bordelaise Sauce.

HICKORY BRISKET SLICES

4 pounds fresh boneless beef brisket
1¼ cups catsup
¾ cup brown sugar
¾ cup chili sauce
¾ cup wine vinegar
¾ cup water
½ cup lemon juice
¼ cup bottled steak sauce
¼ cup prepared mustard

• • •

1 tablespoon celery seed
2 tablespoons Worcestershire sauce
1 tablespoon soy sauce
1 clove garlic, minced
Dash bottled hot pepper sauce
Freshly ground black pepper to taste

Place brisket on sheet of aluminum foil on grill of barbecue smoker, away from the *hot* coals. Sprinkle meat with salt. Add some dampened hickory to the coals and close smoker hood. *Slowly* hickory-barbecue for about 4 hours or till meat is tender.

Slice brisket very thin across the grain, making ⅛-inch slices. Line up slices in shallow foilware pan. Combine remaining ingredients and simmer 30 minutes; pour over the meat. Heat 1 hour in smoker with *slow* coals. Makes 10 servings.

ROAST BEEF

Place foil drip pan in firebox with coals around pan. Place roast—standing ribs of beef or a securely tied rolled-rib roast—fat side up on grill—directly over pan. Roast slowly about 15 minutes per pound or until meat thermometer reads 140° for rare, 160° for medium, or 170° for well-done.

CAMP STEW

Elegant stew with real lusty flavor!

2 pounds boneless lean
   beef chuck or beef
   stew meat, cut in
   1-inch cubes
1½ cups water
½ cup sherry
1 8-ounce can tomato
   sauce
2 teaspoons salt
¼ teaspoon pepper
1 teaspoon Worcester-
   shire sauce

2 bay leaves
2 onions, quartered
6 carrots, cut in
   quarters
4 potatoes, pared and
   quartered
1 1-pound can (2 cups)
   green Limas,
   drained
1 8-ounce can (1 cup)
   whole kernel corn,
   drained•

In a heavy Dutch oven brown meat in small amount hot fat. Add water and next 7 ingredients; cover and simmer about 1¼ hours. Add carrots and potatoes; cook covered 30 minutes longer or till tender. Add Limas and corn; heat through. If desired, thicken with 2 tablespoons flour blended in ¼ cup cold water. Serves 8.

CORNED-BEEF ROAST WITH SPICY GLAZE

3 to 4 pounds corned-
   beef brisket
½ cup brown sugar
½ teaspoon mono-
   sodium glutamate
½ teaspoon *each* cloves
   and ginger

½ teaspoon dry
   mustard
¼ teaspoon celery salt
¼ teaspoon caraway
   seed, cracked

Barely cover corned beef with hot water; add a couple bay leaves, 1 or 2 crushed garlic cloves, and a sliced onion. Cook covered at a lazy simmer *(don't boil)*, 2 to 2½ hours; drain, then blot dry with paper towels. Blend sugar and seasonings. While meat is still warm, rub gently with sugar mixture (use a little butter on hands). Fasten in spit basket and let rotate over *slow* coals about 1 hour. To carve, cut across the grain, making thin slices. Serves 6 to 8.

HAWAIIAN SHORT RIBS

3 to 4 pounds lean beef short ribs, cut in serving pieces
Instant nonseasoned meat tenderizer
• • •

1 1-pound 4½-ounce can pineapple slices
⅓ cup soy sauce
¼ cup honey
1 tablespoon ginger

Trim excess fat from ribs. Sprinkle meat evenly on all sides with tenderizer (½ teaspoon per pound). *Don't use salt.* With long-tined fork, pierce all sides of meat deeply.

Place meat in single layer in baking dish; let stand 30 minutes at room temperature.

Drain pineapple, reserving ⅔ cup syrup. Combine syrup with remaining ingredients; pour over ribs; chill 2 to 3 hours.

Drain ribs, reserving sauce. Place bone side down on grill. Add dampened hickory to coals; close smoker hood. *Slowly* hickory-barbecue 1¾ to 2 hours or till meat is tender, brushing frequently with the sauce.

Five or ten minutes before meat is done, brush pineapple with sauce; place on grill with ribs. Heat sauce and serve with the short ribs. Makes 4 servings.

Our Best Burgers!

Fluffy Burgers. Handle hamburger like a bowl of feathers when you mix in seasonings—don't pack. Medium- or coarsely-ground beef makes for light burgers. So does juicy meat—if it's lean, have 2 or 3 ounces suet ground with each pound meat.

Same size Burgers. Use a burger press: Spoon meat for each burger onto a square of waxed paper, top with a second square. Each mound of meat goes into the jaws of burger press, paper and all. Close lid gently. Leave waxed paper in place and stack up the patties, ready to broil. Or use a bottle and a can: For even-size burgers, roll out hamburger like pie dough (except about ½ inch thick) between big sheets of waxed paper. Use a light touch, please! A bottle can double as a rolling pin. Cut out patties with large tin can (4-inch diameter) that has bottom and top removed.

Keep 'em piping: While burgers broil, heat equal parts of butter and Worcestershire sauce in skillet (enough to cover bottom). When first lot of patties is ready, slip them into skillet, turn once, broil next batch.

FAVORITE GRILLED HAMBURGERS

1½ pounds ground
    beef*
2 tablespoons finely
    chopped onion
1 teaspoon salt
Dash pepper

• • •

1 cup catsup

2 tablespoons Worces-
    tershire sauce
½ teaspoon celery salt
Dash bottled hot
    pepper sauce
6 hamburger buns,
    split, toasted, and
    buttered

Mix meat, onion, salt, and pepper. Lightly pat into 6 burgers, about ½ inch thick. Broil over *hot* coals about 6 minutes, turn and broil 4 minutes longer or till done to your liking. Meanwhile in a saucepan combine catsup, Worcestershire sauce, celery salt, and hot pepper sauce; heat on edge of grill. When burgers are done, brush both sides with the sauce and serve in hot buns. Pass extra sauce and prepared mustard.

*If meat is lean have 4 ounces suet ground with this amount. Juicier! More tender, too.

BURGER MOUNTAINS

*The difference here is sour cream—it flavors the burgers
and makes the sauce—*

1½ pounds ground
 chuck*
1 cup dairy sour cream
¼ cup Worcestershire
 sauce
1 tablespoon instant
 minced onion
1½ teaspoons salt
1 cup corn flakes
Butter or margarine
2 hamburger buns, split
1 medium tomato,
 thinly sliced

1 medium unpared
 cucumber,**
 thinly sliced
 • • •
½ cup dairy sour cream
3 tablespoons milk
1 tablespoon crumbled
 blue cheese

Combine first 5 ingredients; blend thoroughly. Crush
corn flakes slightly with hands; gently stir into meat
mixture. Let stand ½ hour. To shape burgers, divide
meat mixture in 4 portions and from each shape a 3½-
inch patty and a 3-inch patty. (Patties will be about
¾ inch thick.) Broil in a wire broiler basket over *slow*
coals, about 5 minutes per side.

Meanwhile, butter buns and toast, cut side down, on
grill. Place a large burger on each toasted bun half;
then top each with a tomato slice and 3 cucumber slices.
Add a smaller burger; spear with skewer to keep "moun-
tain" in place. Drizzle with Blue Cheese Sauce: In small
saucepan, blend ½ can sour cream, the milk, and blue
cheese; heat through, stirring constantly. Serves 4.

---

*If beef is lean, have 3 ounces suet ground with this amount of
meat.

**To flute cucumber edges, run tines of a fork down all sides of
a whole unpared cucumber.

APPETIZER MEAT BALLS

These behave—the egg keeps the meat balls intact on the grill—

Mix ½ pound ground beef, 1 egg, 1 teaspoon all-purpose flour, a little grated onion, ¾ teaspoon salt, and dash pepper. Shape in 1-inch balls (lightly roll a bit of mixture between hands). Broil in a foilware pan, that has been punctured hit and miss, over *hot* coals. Toss damp hickory chips on coals if you like smoke flavor. Serve on toothpick handles. Makes about 2 dozen.

BURGUNDY BEEFBURGERS

Burger Sophisticate, deliciously flavored with butter and wine—

2 pounds ground chuck*
1 cup soft bread crumbs
1 egg
¼ cup red cooking wine
    (not sweet)
2 tablespoons sliced
    green onions
1 teaspoon salt
Dash pepper
2 tablespoons sliced
    green onions
    and tops

½ cup butter or
    margarine
¼ cup red cooking
    wine
Butter or margarine
6 thick slices French
    bread, cut on the
    diagonal

In large bowl, toss first 7 ingredients with a fork till well mixed. Shape in 6 doughnut-shaped burgers, about 1 inch thick. For burgundy sauce, cook 2 tablespoons green onions in ½ cup butter till just tender; add ¼ cup wine. Brush burgers with the sauce.

Broil over coals about 4 inches from heat for 9 minutes, brushing frequently with sauce. Turn burgers and broil 4 minutes longer or till of desired doneness, continuing to brush with sauce. Serve on buttered Frenchbread slices. Heat remaining sauce to pass with burgers. Makes 6 servings.

---

*If beef is lean, have 4 ounces suet ground with this amount of meat.

DOUBLE-DECKER BURGERS

Two stories high and long as a coney bun—

1 pound ground beef	¼ cup catsup
1 egg	½ to ⅔ cup chopped
1 teaspoon salt	onion
Dash pepper	10 slices bacon

Combine meat, egg, seasonings, and catsup; mix well. Form into 10 thin oblong patties, the shape of coney buns. Put 2 meat patties together, sandwich-fashion, with chopped onion or pickle relish between. Press edges together; wrap each double-decker with 2 bacon slices and fasten ends with toothpicks. Broil patties on grill 3 to 5 inches from glowing coals about 5 minutes on each side. Makes 5 double patties.

PIZZA BURGERS

1½ pounds ground chuck*	Dash pepper
⅓ cup grated Parmesan cheese	1 6-ounce can (⅔ cup) tomato paste
¼ cup finely chopped onion	4 slices Mozzarella cheese, cut in half
¼ cup chopped pitted ripe olives	8 cherry tomatoes
1 teaspoon salt	8 hamburger buns, split and toasted
1 teaspoon oregano, crushed	

Combine meat with next 7 ingredients; blend. Shape meat into 8 patties. Broil on grill over *medium* coals 10 minutes. Turn and top each patty with Mozzarella slice and halved cherry tomatoes. Broil 5 minutes longer or to desired doneness. Top with additional cherry tomatoes and ripe olives.

---

*If beef is lean, have 3 ounces suet ground with this amount.

CAPER BURGERS

The most elegant big burgers you'll ever make! A brush-on of bottled brown bouquet sauce helps keep burgers plump and juicy—

¼ cup butter or
  margarine
1 tablespoon drained
  capers
   • • •
1½ pounds ground
  chuck

1 teaspoon salt
Dash pepper
Kitchen bouquet
4 thick slices French
  bread, toasted and
  buttered

Blend butter and capers. Form four mounds by pressing mixture into measuring tablespoon, then turning out on waxed paper or foil. Freeze until firm.

Meanwhile, combine ground chuck, salt, and pepper; divide in 4 portions and pat gently into oval shape. With measuring tablespoon, make a depression in the center of each burger, pressing down just to ½ inch from bottom. Place a piece of frozen caper butter in each depression and mold the meat mixture over, being sure to cover the butter *completely*. Gently form into oval burgers about 4 inches long, 3 inches wide, and 2 inches thick. Brush with kitchen bouquet and broil over *medium-hot* coals about 10 minutes. Turn carefully with tongs so that butter center does not leak; broil 10 minutes longer. Serve on toasted French bread. Makes 4 servings. Top each burger with a few additional capers, if desired.

DEVILED BEEF PATTIES

Measure in these few seasonings for burgers they'll rave about—

1 pound ground beef	1 teaspoon prepared
1 egg	horseradish
¼ cup chili sauce	1 teaspoon instant
½ teaspoon salt	minced onion
Dash pepper	1 teaspoon Worcester-
1 teaspoon prepared	shire sauce
mustard	4 hamburger buns

Combine first 9 ingredients. Shape into 4 patties. Broil over *medium* coals, 10 minutes. Turn and broil 5 minutes longer or till desired doneness. Split buns in half. Place over coals just till toasted. Makes 4 servings.

GARDENBURGERS

There's a surprise of sliced mushrooms in the center of each burger—

1½ pounds ground beef	Melted butter or
2 slightly beaten eggs	margarine
¼ cup finely chopped	6 thin slices onion,
onion	centers punched
¼ cup catsup	out
1½ teaspoons salt	6 thin slices tomato
Dash pepper	6 slices process
1 6-ounce can (⅔ cup)	American cheese
broiled sliced	
mushrooms,	
drained	

Combine meat, eggs, onion, catsup, and seasonings. Mix thoroughly. Form in 12 thin patties. Place mushrooms on half the patties, leaving border of meat. Top with remaining patties, sealing edges well.

To charcoal-broil: Broil patties slowly over *hot* coals till done the way you like, turning once. Brush with melted butter, top with onion, tomato, and cheese.

To hickory-barbecue: Place burgers on grill and top each with onion and tomato slice; brush well with butter. Following your charcoal-oven directions, smoke-cook about 45 minutes. Add cheese last 8 minutes. Serve burgers in toasted buns. Serves 6.

Note: If beef is lean, have about 3 ounces suet ground with this amount.

SQUARE BURGERS

Big square burgers for hearty appetites—

1 teaspoon instant minced onion	Dash pepper
½ cup evaporated milk	• • •
1½ pounds ground chuck*	4 slices enriched white bread, toasted and buttered
1 slightly beaten egg	
1 teaspoon salt	1 3½-ounce can onion rings *or* 1 4-ounce package frozen onion rings
¼ teaspoon monosodium glutamate	

Soak onion in evaporated milk 5 minutes; lightly mix with meat, egg, and seasonings. Place meat mixture on large sheet of waxed paper; lightly pat into a 9-inch square.

Cut meat in 4 squares. With scissors, cut through waxed paper between burgers. Place, meat side down, on grill; peel off waxed paper. Broil over coals 4 to 5 inches from heat 5 minutes; turn and broil 3 to 4 minutes longer or till of desired doneness. Meanwhile, heat onion rings according to the label directions. Place each burger on a slice of toast; top with onion rings. Pass catsup and mustard. Makes 4 servings.

*If beef is lean, have 3 ounces of suet ground with this amount of meat.

THE BIG BACON BURGER

12 to 14 slices bacon
(about ½ pound)
2 pounds ground beef
2 tablespoons lemon
juice

1 teaspoon Worcester-
shire sauce

In a wire broiler basket, line up *half* the bacon slices side by side. On waxed paper, pat the beef into a square the same size as the arranged bacon. Combine lemon juice and Worcestershire; brush *half* over ground beef and sprinkle with 1 teaspoon salt and dash of pepper. Carefully turn meat onto bacon in basket; brush top side with remaining lemon mixture and season with 1 teaspoon salt and dash of pepper. Lay remaining bacon over top. Close basket to hold meat securely.

Broil on grill over *hot* coals, turning often, 25 to 30 minutes or till bacon is crisped and meat is done. Cut in 8 squares to fit hamburger buns, or in rectangles for coney buns.

STUFFED HAMBURGERS

Butter-browned mushrooms are clapped between meat patties—

2 pounds ground beef
3 eggs
1½ tablespoons all-
purpose flour
1 medium onion, grated
1 tablespoon salt
¼ teaspoon freshly
ground pepper

2 cups mushrooms,
chopped
¼ cup butter or
margarine
8 slices bacon

• • •

Mix ground beef, eggs, flour, onion, salt, and pepper. Roll mixture into thin sheet and cut into 16 patties with large cooky cutter. Sauté mushrooms in butter and spread over 8 of the patties. Place other patties on top and pinch edges. Wrap a slice of bacon around edge of each burger and tack with toothpick. Broil over the coals, hood down about 4 minutes on each side. Serves 8.

GOURMET BEEF PATTIES

1 pound ground beef
Blue-cheese Filling:
    2 tablespoons
      crumbled blue
      cheese
    2 tablespoons snipped
      parsley *or* chopped
      onion

4 hamburger buns, split
    and toasted

Divide ground beef in 8 mounds. Flatten each between squares of waxed paper to a little less than ½ inch. Set half the patties aside for "lids." Combine cheese and parsley. Top remaining patties with Blue-cheese Filling, leaving ½-inch margin for sealing. Cover filling with "lids," sealing edges well.

Broil 3 inches from coals about 6 minutes; sprinkle with salt and pepper. Turn; broil 6 minutes more. Season second side. Slip patties into hot toasted buns. Makes 4.

SURPRISE "DOGS"

1 pound ground beef
¼ cup packaged corn-
    flake crumbs or
    finely crushed
    corn flakes
¼ cup dairy sour cream
2 tablespoons chili sauce
2 tablespoons chopped
    ripe olives

2 tablespoons chopped
    onion
1 tablespoon snipped
    parsley
½ teaspoon salt
Dash pepper
20 pitted ripe olives
5 coney buns, toasted

Combine first 9 ingredients; shape in 5 logs to fit coney buns. Press a row of olives into center of each log, molding meat around olives. Broil on grill over *hot* coals (or 3 inches from heat in range), turning occasionally, 12 to 15 minutes or till done. Serve in coney buns. Makes 5 servings.

DILLY HAMBURGERS

1 to 1½ pounds ground beef
1 cup dairy sour cream
1 teaspoon prepared mustard
1 tablespoon dill seed *or* 3 tablespoons snipped fresh dill

Lightly pat meat into 4 to 6 patties, about ¼ to ½ inch thick. Broil over *hot* coals about 9 minutes; turn, sprinkle with salt and pepper, and broil 6 minutes longer or till done "your way"; season second side. Top with Creamy Dill Sauce: Combine remaining ingredients. Makes 4 to 6 servings.

OLIVE TREASURE-BURGERS

Each burger is a pocketbook stuffed with ripe olives and cheese—

1 pound ground beef*
• • •
¼ cup chopped ripe olives
¼ cup shredded sharp process American cheese
Salt and pepper

On waxed paper, draw a 5-inch circle (use bowl or canister cover as guide). Place a fourth of the meat (½ cup) in center and pat gently to fill circle (or place waxed paper on top, too, and roll *lightly* with rolling pin). Do not press hard. Leaving a ½-inch margin for sealing, spoon about 1 tablespoon *each* of olives and cheese on half of patty. Lift point of waxed paper at the back and fold meat over filling. Press around margin to seal. (If desired, press tops with handle of wooden spoon to mark in squares.)

Brush patties with salad oil or melted margarine to keep from sticking to grill. Broil over *hot* coals about 10 to 12 minutes, turning once. Dash with salt and pepper. Pass bowl of Bar-X Barbecue Sauce (see index listing). Makes 4 servings.

---

*If meat is lean, have 2 or 3 ounces suet ground with each pound.

GRILLED FENNELBURGERS

1 pound ground beef	¼ teaspoon garlic salt
1 pound bulk pork sausage	¼ teaspoon onion salt
1 slightly beaten egg	• • •
¼ cup medium cracker crumbs	Catsup
½ teaspoon salt	Mozzarella cheese, sliced *thin*
Dash pepper	Onion slices
¼ to ½ teaspoon fennel seed	10 hamburger buns, split, toasted, and buttered
½ teaspoon crushed oregano	

Mix meats, egg, crumbs, and seasonings; pat in ten ½-inch patties. Broil over *hot* coals (or 3 or 4 inches from heat in range), turning once, 15 to 20 minutes total time or till meat is *done* (no pink inside). Brush tops with catsup. Pass catsup, Mozzarella cheese, and onion to serve with burgers in buns.

PAUL BUNYANBURGERS

2 eggs	1½ teaspoons salt
2 pounds ground beef (chuck or top sirloin)	½ teaspoon seasoned or garlic salt
	Pepper
2 tablespoons Worcestershire sauce	"Everything" (see below)

Beat eggs slightly; add ground beef and sprinkle with seasonings. Mix lightly with big wooden spoon. (Treat the meat gently.) Divide mixture in thirds.

Using a 9-inch cake pan as guide, draw a circle on waxed paper. Place a third of the meat in center and pat *gently* (or place waxed paper on top, too, and roll *lightly* with rolling pin) to fill circle. Do not press hard.

Now for the built-in filling of "everything." Leaving 1-inch margin for sealing, spread half of patty with mustard, top with chopped onion, cubed cheese, or pickle relish.

Lift point of waxed paper at the back and fold meat over filling. Press around the margin to seal in "everything." Brush top side with salad oil to keep burger from sticking to grill. Place in wire broiler basket; peel off paper. Brush other side with oil.

Broil slowly to allow "everything" to heat through, cheese to melt and flavors to intermingle. Serve on hot plate with toasted buns.

To prevent squashing burgers if using a wire broiler basket: Don't clamp handle of top rack till meat is browned on one side. Go-withs: roastin' ears, relishes, tomatoes, and coffee.

PICKLE IN A POKE

Mix 1½ pounds ground beef, 2 cups soft bread crumbs, 2 eggs, ½ cup evaporated milk, ½ cup finely chopped onion, 1 teaspoon salt, and ¼ teaspoon pepper. On a sheet of 18-inch-wide foil, shape meat in a 12-inch roll, 2 inches in diameter. Press dill pickles lengthwise into center of roll, molding meat over to cover. Wrap foil around roll; seal securely. Place on grill and cook over *hot* coals about 40 minutes, turning a quarter turn every 10 minutes.

Open foil and crush down to make "pan." Brush meat with mixture of ¼ cup *each* bottled barbecue sauce and catsup. Continue cooking, turning roll and brushing with sauce, till meat is done to your liking, about 15 minutes. Serve as a meat loaf or slice and tuck in buns. Makes about 8 servings.

FLAPJACK MEAT LOAF

Try meat loaf, grill style. Browning one side first in a skillet sets its shape—

2 pounds ground beef	1 tablespoon prepared
½ cup chopped onion	mustard
½ cup catsup	1½ teaspoons salt
½ cup medium cracker	Dash pepper
crumbs	1 recipe Spiced Catsup
1 beaten egg	

Combine first 8 ingredients, tossing with a fork till well mixed. Lightly pat mixture into a 10-inch skillet and place on grill over *hot* coals. Cook about 15 minutes; drain off fat. Then with help of pancake turner, turn meat out onto grill top. Broil 10 minutes longer or till of desired doneness. Brush with Spiced Catsup. Cut in 8 wedges.

Spiced Catsup: Combine ½ cup catsup, 2 tablespoons brown sugar, 2 teaspoons dry mustard, 2 teaspoons kitchen bouquet, and ½ teaspoon nutmeg; heat at side of grill.

MIDAS MEAT LOAF

1 celery heart, about
  2½ inches in
  diameter
1 cup grated sharp
  Cheddar cheese
2 tablespoons finely
  chopped pimiento
3 pounds ground beef
½ cup quick-cooking
  rolled oats
½ cup evaporated milk
1 tablespoon seasoned
  salt
1 teaspoon garlic
  powder

1 teaspoon Worcester-
  shire sauce
½ teaspoon chili
  powder
½ teaspoon pepper
⅛ teaspoon liquid
  smoke
2 eggs, slightly beaten
½ cup chopped green
  onion
¼ cup chopped green
  pepper
1 pound sliced bacon

Remove celery leaves and cut celery heart to about 8 or 9 inches long; wash and dry. Keep bottom of celery heart intact; do not remove the root. Gently pull branches apart and sprinkle with salt. Combine cheese and pimiento; spread generously between celery branches. Wrap heart tightly in foil and chill while preparing meat loaf.

Combine all remaining ingredients except bacon and mix. Turn meat mixture out onto a large sheet of waxed paper and pat out meat to an oval about 11x12x¾-inches. Cut off only the *very bottom of root* of celery heart; place celery on center of meat. Fold the meat up and over celery. Pat into roll shape, completely enclosing celery.

Lay bacon slices in chevron pattern over top of roll, making sure that slices overlap slightly. Gently lift roll on one side and tuck bacon ends underneath. Repeat on other side. Use wooden picks to hold bacon ends in place, if necessary. Tie roll securely with string, but not so tightly as to cut the roll. Wrap in foil; seal top with drugstore fold, but do not close ends.

Insert spit through center of celery and balance; close ends of foil around spit. Using a line of *hot* coals on each side of roll and drip pan underneath, let meat rotate 1¼ hours. Remove foil and cook 20 minutes longer. Slice to serve, removing strings and wooden picks as you carve. Makes 10 to 12 servings.

LITTLE BAR-B-Q MEAT LOAVES

2 slightly beaten eggs	1½ teaspoons salt
2 pounds ground beef	½ teaspoon dry
2 cups soft bread	mustard
crumbs	¼ cup milk
¼ cup minced onion	½ cup butter or
1 tablespoon prepared	margarine
horseradish	½ cup catsup

Combine first 8 ingredients, and mix well. Shape in 6 miniature meat loaves about 4½ inches long and 2½ inches wide. Place in wire broiler basket. Heat butter with catsup just till butter melts; brush over all sides of loaves. Broil meat loaves over *medium* coals. Turn and brush all sides frequently with sauce. Cook 40 minutes or till done. Pass remaining sauce. Makes 6 servings.

PORK CUTS FOR THE BARBECUE

Tender ribs for finger-eating, crispy skillet-fried bacon, and luscious rotisserie ham all make pork a barbecue favorite. Spareribs are one of the classics of outdoor cookery, but there are several other pork cuts that lend themselves equally well to the barbecue grill. Recipes are on following pages.

When planning to barbecue pork one must allow sufficient time and be patient. Be sure to cook fresh pork till well done—that is, no pink. A barbecue sauce for pork chops or spareribs should go easy on the fat and use plenty of chili sauce or catsup. Hold off any tomato barbecue sauce till the last 15 minutes of cooking.

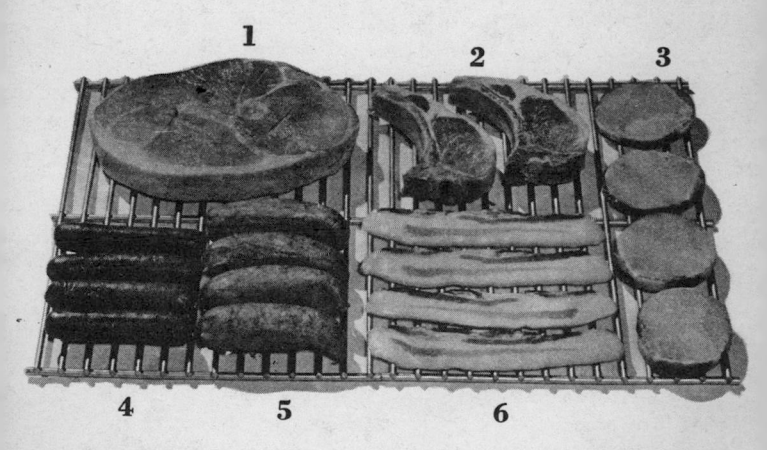

1 Center ham slice. Buy the fully cooked type of ham slice. Let it broil slowly over coals and if desired, brush with a zesty sauce during the last few minutes on the grill.

2 Pork rib chops. Lock these 1-inchers in a rotisserie basket and let 'er roll above slow coals. Or roast on a covered grill and add damp hickory chips for flavor lift.

3 Canadian style bacon. Broil slices on aluminum foil. Or roast a whole roll of bacon on a spit and baste with fruit juice.

4 Frankfurters. Score in corkscrew fashion or slit in center and fill with your favorite relish. If you prefer place them across the grill bars or in a wire broiler basket for zebra stripes. They are so easy and good.

5 Smoked sausage links. Broil until thoroughly cooked. Or broil brown-and-serves until temptingly hot. For appetizers, cut in bite-size pieces and peg on toothpicks.

6 Bacon strips. Broil on aluminum foil or in a wire broiler basket over slow coals to prevent flare-ups. For best results use the thick sliced bacon. The flavor is delicious.

Tasty Broiled Ribs!

RIB INFORMATION

Pork spareribs are rib bones from the bacon strip with little meat between. Extra-meaty loin back ribs are tops for barbecuing. Consult your meatman when buying.

Just-right ribs are crispy-brown outside, tender and juicy inside. Lean shows no pink when cut. Because they are a fat cut of meat, cook very slowly and turn frequently. For best results, long, slow cooking is required.

Canadian Style Bacon

Pork Top
Loin Chop

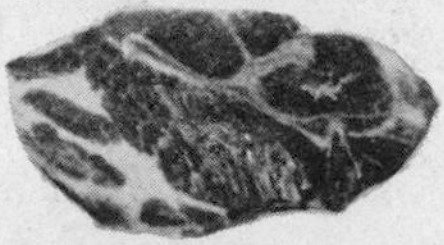

Pork Blade Steak

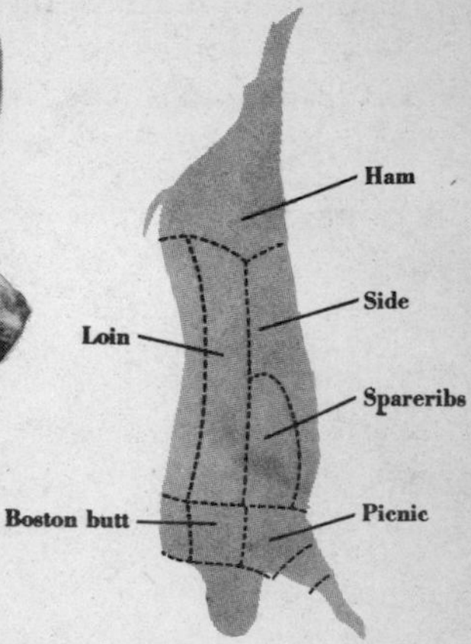

Pork Tenderloin

Ham

Side

Loin

Spareribs

Boston butt

Picnic

Pork Backribs

Pork Spareribs

Pork Arm Steak

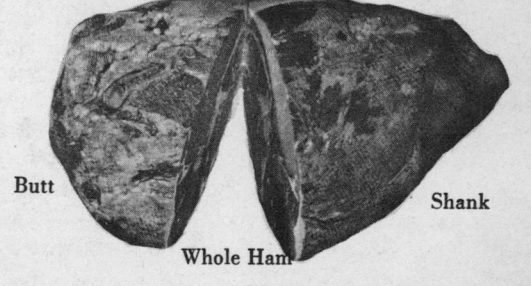

Butt

Shank

Whole Ham

BARBECUED RIBS WITH RODEO SAUCE

When you hanker for honest, cooked-outdoors flavor, you can't beat these ribs—

1 cup catsup
1 tablespoon Worcester-
    shire sauce
2 or 3 dashes bottled hot
    pepper sauce
1 cup water
¼ cup vinegar
1 tablespoon sugar

1 teaspoon salt
1 teaspoon celery seed
4 pounds pork
    spareribs
1 lemon, thinly sliced
1 large onion, thinly
    sliced

For Rodeo Sauce, combine first 8 ingredients; simmer 30 minutes. Salt ribs and place in rack over *slow* coals. Put barbecue lid on or hood down. Cook 1 hour.

Brush ribs with Rodeo Sauce and peg on slices of lemon and onion with toothpicks. Continue to cook without turning ribs, 30 to 40 minutes or till done, brushing now and then with sauce. For smoke flavor, during last half hour, toss damp hickory chips or sawdust on coals. Snip ribs in servings with scissors. Makes 4 servings.

HICKORY-SMOKED SPARERIBS

4 pounds loin back ribs
1 recipe Warren's
    Barbecue Sauce
    (see index listing)

½ lemon, thinly sliced
½ large onion, thinly
    sliced

Salt ribs and place, bone side down, on grill of barbecue-smoker, away from the coals. Add dampened hickory to *slow* coals and close smoker hood. Hickory-barbecue about 3½ hours. Last half hour baste with sauce and peg on a few slices of lemon and onion with toothpicks. Makes 4 servings.

PINEAPPLE SPARERIBS

1 cup pineapple
    preserves
	2 teaspoons Dijon-style
	    prepared mustard

1 teaspoon kitchen bouquet	• • •
2 tablespoons vinegar	3 to 4 pounds pork spareribs

For Pineapple Glaze, combine pineapple preserves, kitchen bouquet, vinegar, and mustard. Set mixture aside. Salt ribs and place the slabs, bone side down, on grill over *slow* coals. (Keep an eye on fire—ribs tend to dry out and char.) Broil about 20 minutes; then turn meat side down and broil till nicely browned, about 10 minutes.

Again turn meat side up; continue broiling without turning about 30 minutes or till meat is well-done (no pink where snipped between bones), brushing frequently with Pineapple Glaze. If you like, add hickory (in foil—see below) to coals for smoke flavor. Makes 3 or 4 servings.

Foil protector: The thinner end of spareribs is likely to get done before the thicker end. When this happens, slide a piece of foil under the thinner end and continue cooking.

Hickory in foil: Dandy technique for open-grill smoking—air is shut out, so hickory can't blaze. Wrap a fistful of dry hickory chips in foil. Puncture top of package and place on the hot coals. Smoke will puff out, continuing half an hour.

LUAU RIBS

2 4½-ounce jars or cans
    strained peaches
    (baby food)
	1 clove garlic, minced
	2 teaspoons ginger
	1 teaspoon salt

⅓ cup catsup	Dash pepper
⅓ cup cider vinegar	4 pounds meaty
2 tablespoons soy sauce	spareribs
½ cup brown sugar	

For sauce, mix all ingredients except ribs. Rub ribs on both sides with salt and pepper. Place ribs, bone side down, on grill over *slow* coals. Broil about 20 minutes; then turn meat side down and broil till nicely browned, about 10 minutes.

Again turn meat side up, brush with sauce and continue broiling without turning about 30 minutes or till meat is well done. Brush frequently with sauce. Serves 4 to 6.

BARBECUED SPARERIBS

2 tablespoons butter
   or margarine
2 cloves garlic, crushed
2 tablespoons prepared
   mustard
¼ cup brown sugar
1 cup catsup
¾ cup chili sauce
1 tablespoon celery seed
2 tablespoons Worcester-
   shire sauce

1 or 2 dashes bottled
   hot pepper sauce
½ teaspoon salt
1½ cups water
4 pounds spareribs or
   loin back ribs
1 medium onion, thinly
   sliced
1 lemon, thinly sliced

For sauce, melt butter in saucepan; add garlic and cook 4 to 5 minutes. Blend in mustard and sugar. Add catsup, chili sauce, celery seed, sauces, salt, and water; bring to boiling. Salt ribs and place bone side down on grill over *slow* coals. Broil about 20 minutes; turn meaty side down and leave briefly until nicely browned. Turn meat side up again and broil about 20 minutes longer.

Brush meat side with basting sauce and peg on slices of onion and lemon with toothpicks. Continue to broil without turning, 20 to 30 minutes, or till done, basting occasionally. At the last, brush sauce on both sides of ribs, and let broil 2 or 3 minutes on each side for a fine finish. Makes 4 servings.

CHINESE SMOKED RIBS

Ginger Sauce:
- ½ cup soy sauce
- ½ cup catsup
- ¼ cup water
- 3 tablespoons brown sugar
- 2 tablespoons grated fresh gingerroot *or* 2 teaspoons ground ginger
- 1 teaspoon mono-sodium glutamate

Barbecue Rub:
- 2 tablespoons sugar
- ½ teaspoon salt
- ¼ teaspoon *each* paprika, mono-sodium glutamate, turmeric, and celery seed
- Dash dry mustard
- 6 pounds loin back ribs *or* spareribs

For Ginger Sauce, mix first 6 ingredients and let stand overnight to mellow the flavor. For Barbecue Rub, combine sugar and seasonings. Rub the ribs with this mixture; let stand 2 hours. Brush with Ginger Sauce and let stand about 30 minutes to 1 hour.

Hang the ribs in a Chinese oven which uses wood as fuel—split logs of oak, hickory, or fruitwood. Smoke spareribs about 1½ hours or loin back ribs about 2 hours, or till done, brushing occasionally with the sauce. Keep fire at about 325°. Snip ribs in serving pieces. Makes 6 or 7 servings.

ABACUS RIBS

- 4 pounds spareribs, cut in narrow strips
- 1 cup clear French dressing
- ½ cup finely chopped onion
- ½ cup chili sauce
- 2 tablespoons brown sugar
- 2 to 3 tablespoons lemon juice
- 2 tablespoons Worcestershire sauce
- Cooked or canned small whole onions

Rub ribs with salt and pepper; place in shallow baking dishes. Combine next 6 ingredients for marinade; pour over ribs, coating all. Let stand 2 hours at room temperature or overnight in refrigerator, spooning marinade over occasionally. Drain, reserving marinade. Lace ribs on spit in accordion style, threading onions on as you weave in and out. Rotate over coals 45 minutes to 1 hour or until done, brushing frequently with marinade. Makes 4 servings.

ROYAL RIBS

This sauce turns loin back ribs into epicurean delights. Start to baste ribs 30 minutes before they're done to give just the right spunk without overpowering the juicy pork—

2 tablespoons instant minced onion
1 tablespoon brown sugar
1 tablespoon whole mustard seed
1 teaspoon monosodium glutamate
2 teaspoons paprika
1 teaspoon crushed oregano
1 teaspoon chili powder
1 teaspoon cracked pepper
½ teaspoon salt
½ teaspoon ground cloves

1 bay leaf
1 clove garlic, minced
1 cup catsup
½ cup water
¼ cup olive or salad oil
¼ cup tarragon vinegar
2 tablespoons wine vinegar
2 tablespoons Worcestershire sauce
2 or 3 drops liquid smoke
4 pounds loin back ribs or spareribs

For sauce, combine all ingredients except ribs; stir well. Heat to boiling; simmer gently 20 to 25 minutes, stirring occasionally. Remove bay leaf.

Sprinkle ribs with salt and place the slabs, bone side

down, on grill of barbecue-smoker, away from the coals.
Add dampened hickory to *slow* coals and close smoker
hood. Hickory-barbecue about 3½ hours, basting with
sauce the last half hour. Snip ribs in serving pieces.
Makes 3 or 4 servings.

HAM BARBECUE

¾ cup catsup
3 tablespoons brown
   sugar
1 to 2 tablespoons
   Dijon-style mustard
2 tablespoons Worces-
   tershire sauce
2 tablespoons lemon
   juice

2 tablespoons chili
   powder
2 ½-inch slices fully
   cooked ham
   (about 1½
   pounds)

Combine first 6 ingredients for sauce. Slash fat edge of
ham at 2-inch intervals. Brush meat liberally with sauce
and let stand 1 hour. Broil over coals 5 to 6 minutes
per side, turning once and brushing with sauce. Makes
4 to 6 servings.

ORANGE-GLAZED HAM 'N PINEAPPLE

¼ cup frozen orange-
   juice concentrate
¼ cup cooking sherry
1 teaspoon dry mustard
¼ teaspoon *fines
   herbes*

1 1-inch slice fully
   cooked ham
   (about 1½
   pounds)
4 to 6 canned pineapple
   slices

Combine first 4 ingredients for sauce; brush on ham.
Broil over *hot* coals 6 to 8 minutes on each side or till
browned, basting frequently. Last few minutes, broil
pineapple slices 2 to 3 minutes on each side or till
browned, basting frequently with sauce. Makes 4 to 6
servings.

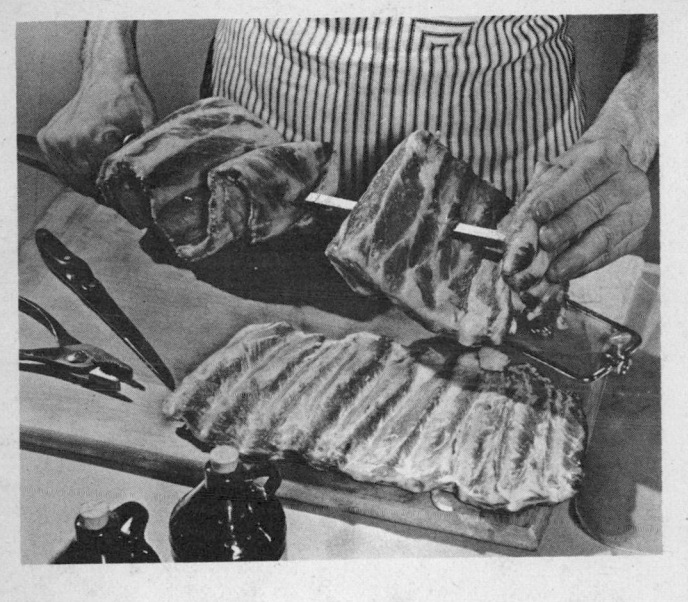

RIBS ON A SPIT

A beautiful tomato-sauce glaze with mellow seasoning. You may be sure everyone will eat a pound of ribs all by himself—

1 cup chopped onion
¼ cup salad oil
1 8-ounce can (1 cup)
    tomato sauce
¼ cup brown sugar
¼ cup water
¼ cup lemon juice
¼ cup bottled steak
    sauce

1 teaspoon salt
¼ teaspoon pepper
3 to 4 pounds loin back
    ribs, or meaty
    spareribs sawed in
    2 strips, about
    4 inches wide

For sauce, cook onion in hot oil till tender but not brown; add the next 7 ingredients. Simmer uncovered 15 minutes or until of nice sauce consistency.

Salt and pepper the ribs; lace in accordion style on

spit, securing with holding forks. Arrange hot coals at
back of firebox, a foil drip pan in front of coals and
under ribs. Attach spit, turn on motor, and lower barbecue hood. Let ribs rotate over *slow* coals 1 hour or
till meat is well done. Last 30 minutes, brush ribs frequently with sauce, and add dampened hickory (see
below) to coals for smoke flavor. Makes 3 or 4 servings.

Dampened hickory: First soak hickory hunks, crosscuts, or bark in water 1 hour. If you use sawdust, flakes,
or chips, dampen when you start the fire.

ROSY HAM SLICE

½ cup extra-hot catsup
⅓ cup orange
    marmalade
2 tablespoons finely
    chopped onion
2 tablespoons salad oil
1 tablespoon lemon
    juice

1 to 1½ teaspoons dry
    mustard
1 1-inch slice fully
    cooked ham
    (about 1½
    pounds)

Combine all ingredients except ham slice. Slash fat edge
of ham slice and broil over *slow* coals for 15 minutes,
turning once. Brush with sauce and broil 15 minutes
more, turning and basting once. Heat remaining sauce
on edge of grill; serve with ham.

BARBECUED PORK BACKS

*Absolutely delicious! The pineapple-chili-sauce glaze is
almost like tomato preserves—*

3 pounds meaty pork
    backbones, or
    spareribs, cut in
    serving pieces
1 cup chili sauce

1 12-ounce jar (1 cup)
    pineapple
    preserves
⅓ cup vinegar

Sprinkle meat with salt and broil bone side down on grill over *slow* coals about 20 minutes. Now turn and let brown (about 8 minutes). Turn ribs meaty side up again and broil about 20 minutes longer.

Combine remaining ingredients; brush on meat and continue broiling without turning 20 to 30 minutes or till done (no pink), basting occasionally with sauce. To glaze, baste both sides of pork and broil 3 or 4 minutes per side. Makes 3 or 4 servings.

ROAST CANADIAN BACON

2½ pounds fully cooked Canadian bacon
½ cup currant jelly
1 teaspoon dry mustard
¼ teaspoon finely grated orange peel

Remove outer wrap from roll of bacon. Score in 1½ inch squares, cutting about ¼ inch deep. Adjust on spit and put in place over *medium hot* coals. Have foil pan under bacon. Blend remaining ingredients for glaze. Broil about 1 hour and 15 minutes, brushing with glaze during last 10 to 15 minutes. Slice and serve. Makes 10 to 12 servings.

MARINATED PORK ROAST

The meat is permeated with the incomparable flavor of hickory—

1½ cups salad oil
¾ cup soy sauce
¼ cup Worcestershire sauce
2 tablespoons dry mustard
2¼ teaspoons salt
1 tablespoon coarse, freshly ground black pepper
½ cup wine vinegar
1½ teaspoons dried parsley flakes
2 crushed garlic cloves (optional)
⅓ cup lemon juice
4- to 5-pound pork loin roast

Combine all ingredients except pork roast and mix well. Have meatman split backbone between each rib of the pork roast. Marinate the roast overnight (or a day or two) in refrigerator, turning meat occasionally.*

Balance meat on spit. Arrange *slow* coals at rear of firebox, knock off ash. Put a foil drip pan in front of coals and under roast. Top some damp hickory on coals. Attach spit, turn on motor, lower smoker hood. Roast until meat thermometer reads 185°—pork must be cooked well done, no pink. While cooking, brush now and then with the flavorful marinade. Add more damp hickory to coals as needed. When chips catch fire and start to blaze, pick up with tongs and put out flame in water; then put chips back on coals. The way to get hickory flavor is from the smoke.

Allow about 2½ hours cooking time, but remember your only accurate guide for doneness is your meat thermometer.

---

*Marinade can be drained from meat for a second use. Store in a tightly covered container in freezer indefinitely, or in refrigerator for 1 week. Makes 3½ cups.

SPARKLING GRILLED HAM

This blond glaze shows off ham's rosy color, and adds a bit of spice—

1 1-inch slice fully
    cooked ham
    (about 1½
    pounds)

• • •

1 cup sparkling
    Catawba grape
    juice (white)
1 cup orange juice

½ cup brown sugar
3 tablespoons salad oil
1 tablespoon wine
    vinegar
2 teaspoons dry
    mustard
¾ teaspoon ginger
¼ to ½ teaspoon
    cloves

Slash the fat edge of ham. Combine remaining ingredients; pour over ham in shallow baking dish. Refrigerate overnight or let stand at room temperature 2 hours, spooning marinade over several times.

Broil ham slice over *slow* coals, about 15 minutes on each side, brushing frequently with marinade. Heat remaining marinade on edge of grill to pass. Makes 5 servings.

BIG-BANQUET BEAN POT

A great meal with rounds of warm Boston brown bread, pickles, and a green salad—

1 2- to 2½-pound smoked boneless pork shoulder butt
Prepared mustard
8 to 10 onion slices
2 No. 2½ cans (7 cups) pork and beans or baked beans

½ cup bottled barbecue sauce
2 tablespoons prepared mustard
Whole cloves
½ cup brown sugar

Place smoked pork in Dutch oven or deep kettle and pour cold water over to cover. Bring just to boiling; reduce heat and simmer covered *(do not boil)*, 45 to 60 minutes *per pound* or till meat is tender. Lift meat from water. Place meat on cutting board.

Make 4 or 5 diagonal slashes ¾ way through meat; spread cut surfaces with mustard. Insert 2 onion slices in each slash. Mix beans, barbecue sauce, and 2 tablespoons prepared mustard; pour into 3-quart casserole. Push meat into beans. Spread top of meat with mustard and stud with whole cloves. Sieve brown sugar over beans and meat. Place casserole on grill.

Bake uncovered on grill over *slow* coals with barbecue hood down at least 1 hour, adding more barbecue sauce if necessary during cooking. For smoke flavor, toss pieces of damp hickory on coals as beans bake. Makes 8 servings.

GLAZED HAM WITH CRANBERRY-RAISIN SAUCE

½ cup brown sugar
2 tablespoons
    cornstarch
Dash ground cloves
Dash salt

• • •

1½ cups bottled
    cranberry-juice
    cocktail

½ cup orange juice
½ cup seedless raisins
1 1-inch slice fully
    cooked ham
    (about 2 pounds)

Mix sugar, cornstarch, cloves, and salt. Add cranberry-juice cocktail, orange juice, and raisins. Cook and stir till mixture thickens and comes to boiling.

Slash fat edge of ham slice at 2-inch intervals. Insert whole cloves in fat if desired. Broil ham slice over *slow* coals, about 15 to 20 minutes on each side. Brush on glaze during the last 15 minutes. Brush again with glaze just before serving. Serve remaining sauce warm with ham.

ROAST PORK CHOPS

1 cup chopped onion
1 clove garlic, minced
¼ cup salad oil

• • •

1 cup water
¾ cup catsup
⅓ cup lemon juice
3 tablespoons sugar
2 teaspoons salt

2 tablespoons Worcestershire sauce
1 tablespoon prepared
    mustard
¼ teaspoon bottled hot
    pepper sauce
6 rib or loin chops,
    cut 1 to 1¼
    inches thick

For sauce: Cook onion and garlic in hot oil till tender but not brown. Add remaining ingredients except chops; simmer uncovered 15 minutes. Set aside.

Lock chops in a spit basket. Rotate over *slow* coals 45 minutes to 1 hour, or till pork is done. Baste with the sauce during the last 20 minutes of cooking.

For that wonderful charcoal flavor lock pork chops in a spit basket and let them rotate over slow coals. Another time follow the recipe for Roast Pork Chops. They are terrific! You may even want to gnaw the bones. Remember to cook pork till it is well done, no pink.

ZESTY BARBECUE PORK STEAK

Next time use this sauce on chops—

1 envelope tomato-soup mix

¼ cup dry onion-soup mix

½ cup Italian salad dressing

2 tablespoons vinegar

2 cups water

• • •

2 tablespoons brown sugar

2 teaspoons Worcestershire sauce

1 teaspoon prepared horseradish

1 teaspoon prepared mustard

6 pork steaks, ½ to ¾ inch thick

In saucepan, combine soup mixes, salad dressing, and vinegar. Gradually stir in water. Add remaining ingredients except pork steaks. Bring mixture to boiling and let simmer 10 minutes.

Slash edges of fat to keep steaks flat. Broil over *medium hot* coals for about 15 minutes. Turn and baste with sauce; broil 15 minutes longer. Baste on both sides before removing from grill. Makes 6 servings.

PEPPER PUPS

Cracked pepper turns frank bites into a sophisticated hot appetizer—

Slice 1 pound (8 to 10) frankfurters in bite-size pieces. Melt 2 tablespoons butter or margarine with 1 teaspoon coarse-cracked pepper and 1 teaspoon marjoram in foilware pan; add franks and brown in the butter, turning often (have coals *hot-hot*). Spear with toothpicks. Serves 10 to 12 nibblers.

ROTISSERIE HAM

10 pounds boneless fully cooked ham	**½ teaspoon dry mustard**
⅓ cup reserved pineapple syrup	**Whole cloves**
¼ cup brown sugar	**1 1-pound 4½-ounce can (10 slices) sliced pineapple**
½ teaspoon ground ginger	

Trim rind from ham, if any. Balance ham on spit and insert meat thermometer in lean. Arrange *hot* coals at back of firebox and a foil drip pan in front of coals and under meat. Attach spit, turn on motor, and lower barbecue hood. Let ham rotate over *medium* coals about 1½ hours without basting.

Meanwhile prepare Pineapple Basting Sauce: Combine reserved pineapple syrup, brown sugar, ginger, and dry mustard. Set aside. After 1½ hours of cooking turn off motor and remove spit from position. Score ham and insert cloves. Spoon excess fat from foil drip pan. Place canned pineapple slices in foil pan. Place spit back in position and turn on motor. Baste ham with Pineapple Basting Sauce to produce a rich glaze, cook about ½ hour longer. Meat thermometer should read 130° when ham is done. Makes about 25 to 30 servings.

PEANUT-BUTTERED PORK LOIN

5- to 6-pounds boned pork loins	¼ cup creamy peanut butter
½ cup orange juice	

Tie pork loins together at 1½-inch intervals with the fat sides out. Balance roast on spit and secure with holding forks; insert meat thermometer. Season with salt and pepper.

Arrange *medium hot* coals at rear of firebox, knock off ash. Put a foil drip pan in front of coals and under roast. Attach spit, turn on motor, and lower hood. Roast until meat thermometer reads 185°. Allow about 3½ hours cooking time.

Combine orange juice and peanut butter. When thermometer reads 185° brush the peanut butter sauce on roast and continue cooking and basting for 15 to 20 minutes. Makes about 15 servings.

SASSY FRANKS

¼ cup chopped celery	3 tablespoons vinegar
¼ cup chopped green pepper	1 tablespoon Worcestershire sauce
¼ cup butter or margarine	¼ teaspoon garlic salt
• • •	• • •
1 can condensed tomato soup	1 pound (8 to 10) frankfurters
¼ cup brown sugar	½ lemon, thinly sliced
¼ cup water	½ onion, thinly sliced

In skillet, cook celery and green pepper in the butter or margarine until almost tender. Add soup, brown sugar, water, vinegar, Worcestershire sauce, and garlic salt; simmer uncovered 15 minutes.

Meanwhile, score franks in corkscrew fashion; roast on grill top or in wire broiler basket over *hot* coals. Add lemon and onion in slices to sauce; simmer 15 minutes—drop grilled franks in to keep hot. Serves 4 or 5.

BARBECUED BOLOGNA

1 3- to 4-pound big
   Bologna, unsliced

    • • •

1 cup catsup
⅓ cup butter or
   margarine, melted
1½ tablespoons
   Worcestershire
   sauce

1½ tablespoons golden
   brown prepared
   mustard
1½ teaspoons onion
   salt

Score Bologna with diagonal lines about ¼ inch deep. Anchor on spit, attach to grill. (Place foil drip pan below, if your barbecue does not have a built-in drip catcher.) Cook on rotisserie with hood down over *medium* coals for 1¼ hours or till heated through and nicely browned.

Meanwhile, combine remaining ingredients for sauce; brush on Bologna frequently the last 15 minutes of cooking.

Slice meat about ¼ inch thick; serve between toasted hamburger buns, with remaining sauce heated and spooned over.

ROAST SUCKLING PIG

A grill with a cover lets meat roast as it would in an oven with the plus of the wonderful charcoal flavor. Plan a party and serve this delightful feast of pork—

Purchase a 12- to 14-pound suckling pig. Clean it thoroughly. Scrub with a stiff brush, rinse cavity, and pat dry. Season cavity with salt and pepper. Stuff with a sage or fruit dressing. Don't stuff it too tightly as the dressing will expand. Close openings with skewers and string; lace it closely and tightly. Truss by bringing the feet forward and tying in a kneeling position with string. Place a firm ball of foil in the pig's mouth, and cover nose, ears, and tail with foil to prevent overbrowning. Brush the skin all over with softened butter.

You will need a large covered grill with a cooking surface at least 24 inches long. Place *hot* coals at back of firebox. Place a foil pan, the same length as the suckling pig, in front of the hot coals and under the pig. Place the pig on a spit; adjust balance, and secure with holding forks *or* place the pig directly on the grill over the foil pan and lower barbecue hood. Adjust grill damper so pig will cook slowly.

Baste occasionally with a barbecue sauce or pan drippings. It will take about 2½ hours to cook a 12- to 14-pound pig. A meat thermometer inserted in the thigh, not touching spit, bone, or fat, should read 190° when pig is done. The most delicious tidbit is the crisp skin, so be sure you get it crusty and brown. If the pig is cooked directly on the grill, you may need to cover the side toward the fire with aluminum foil to prevent browning too fast.

When suckling pig is done, arrange it on a plank and remove the foil from nose, ears, and tail. Remove the ball of foil from the mouth. Decorate as you desire. Traditionally the suckling pig is decorated with a necklace of raw cranberries, two cranberries for the eyes, and an apple in the mouth.

To carve: With a sharp knife carve through the thigh joint first as you would on a turkey, removing the hams and legs first. Cut these pieces in slices. Next, start in center of pig and cut right down through the ribs. Serve two little ribs, a portion of stuffing, and a slice from the hams to each person. Makes 12 to 14 servings.

GUIDED MISSILES

2 or 3 whole dill or sweet pickles	**Count-10 Sauce**
1 pound (8 to 10) frankfurters	

Select pickles with about the same diameter as the franks. Cut pickles in 1-inch chunks. To make missile "nose cones," slice a 1½-inch piece off the end of each frank; sharpen rounded end of short piece, pencil fashion, cutting down from edge to center on 4 sides. To assemble, run the long piece of frank lengthwise on skewer. Thread on a pickle chunk crosswise, and then a nose cone. Broil on grill over *hot* coals (or in broiler), brushing with Count-10 Sauce. Makes 8 to 10. To serve, stick skewers into cabbage head. Pass toasted buns and extra sauce.

Count-10 Sauce: Cook ½ cup chopped onion in ¼ cup butter or margarine. Add one 8-ounce can tomato sauce, 1 cup water, 2 tablespoons sugar, ½ teaspoon sage, ¼ teaspoon dry mustard, dash pepper, 1 tablespoon vinegar, and 1 tablespoon Worcestershire sauce. Simmer uncovered ½ hour. Makes 1¼ cups.

SKEWER DOGS

1 pound ground beef	**6 frankfurters**
¾ cup soft bread crumbs	**1 cup catsup**
¼ cup milk	**¼ cup butter or margarine, melted**
2 tablespoons chopped onion	**¼ cup molasses**
1 slightly beaten egg	**2 tablespoons vinegar**
½ teaspoon salt	**6 slices bacon (optional)**
Dash pepper	

Combine ground beef with next 6 ingredients; mix lightly. Divide meat mixture into 6 portions. Shape meat around franks, covering completely. (Roll kabobs between waxed paper to make uniform.) Chill. Insert skewers lengthwise through frankfurters.

For Sauce: Combine catsup, butter, molasses, and vinegar; brush over kabobs. Wrap each kabob spiral-fashion with slice of bacon; secure with toothpicks. Broil 3 inches from heat about 15 minutes, turning as needed to cook bacon. Simmer sauce while kabobs are cooking; brush on kabobs just before removing from heat. Serve in toasted coney buns; pass sauce. Serves 6.

FRANKRAUTS

1 pound (8 to 10) frankfurters	¼ cup chili sauce
	1 teaspoon caraway seed
Liquid smoke	8 to 10 slices bacon

• • •

1 cup drained
   sauerkraut

Slit franks lengthwise *not quite through*. Brush cut surfaces with liquid smoke. Combine kraut, chili sauce, and caraway; stuff franks. Wrap each with strip of bacon, toothpicking in place. Grill over *hot* coals, turning so that bacon cooks crisp on all sides, about 10 to 15 minutes. Serves 4 or 5.

STUFFED CONEY ISLANDS

1 pound (8 to 10) frankfurters	½ cup chopped onion
	½ cup chopped celery
2 tablespoons prepared mustard	½ cup catsup
	½ cup water
Chopped onion	1 beef bouillon cube
8 to 10 coney buns, heated	½ teaspoon bottled steak sauce
½ pound ground beef	½ teaspoon celery seed

Slit frankfurters lengthwise, *not quite through*. Broil over *hot* coals (or in range). Smear each cut with mustard; sprinkle in chopped onion. Place in buns. Spoon on hot Coney Sauce: Brown ground beef in skillet. Add ½ cup chopped onion and the celery; cook till almost tender. Drain off excess fat. Add remaining ingredients to beef mixture and let bubble without covering till hot.

PINEAPPLE SPEARED FRANKS

1 pound (8 to 10) frankfurters	8 to 10 canned pineapple spears
Mustard and catsup	8 to 10 slices bacon

Slit frankfurters lengthwise; spread cut surfaces lightly with mustard, then catsup. Insert pineapple spears. Wrap slice of bacon around each frank; secure with toothpicks. Place cut side down on broiler rack; broil 6 inches from heat 7 to 8 minutes or till bacon is done on one side. Turn; broil 6 to 7 minutes. Remove toothpicks. Serve in warm buns, if desired. Makes 4 or 5 servings.

BEST HAMDOGS

1 cup finely chopped cooked or canned ham or luncheon meat	2 tablespoons prepared mustard
	2 tablespoons mayonnaise
3 tablespoons pickle relish	1 pound (8 to 10) frankfurters
2 tablespoons finely chopped onion	8 to 10 slices bacon
	Bottled barbecue sauce

Combine ham, seasonings, and mayonnaise. Slit franks, *cutting almost to ends and only ¾ the way through.* Stuff franks with the ham mixture; wrap with a bacon strip, anchoring ends with toothpicks. Broil over *hot* coals, brushing now and then with barbecue sauce, till filling is hot and bacon crisp. Serve in coney buns. Makes 8 to 10 servings.

FRANK WRAP-UPS

Slit frankfurters lengthwise to about ¼ inch from each end; stuff with pickle relish and wrap each with a bacon strip, anchoring ends with toothpicks. Broil over *hot* coals, turning once, till filling is hot and bacon crisped. (Remember to remove toothpicks.)

NUTTY PUPS

Broil frankfurters to suit yourself. Serve in hot toasted buns spread generously with chunk-style peanut butter. Extra great when made with Frank Wrap-ups. Pass pickle relish if desired.

FLORENTINE FRANKS

4 to 6 frankfurters	**2 tablespoons grated**
1 tomato, peeled,	**Parmesan cheese**
chopped, and	**1 small clove garlic,**
drained	**crushed**
2 tablespoons shredded	**¼ teaspoon crushed**
sharp process	**oregano**
American cheese	**4 to 6 slices bacon**

Slit franks lengthwise, *cutting almost to ends and only ¾ the way through.* Combine tomato, cheeses, and seasonings; stuff in franks. Wrap each with a bacon strip, anchoring ends with toothpicks. Place franks, filling side down, on grill. Broil over *hot* coals turning often, about 10 to 15 minutes or till filling is hot and bacon crisp. Serve in coney buns. Makes 4 to 6 servings.

CHEESE PUPS

Fix early; keep in your freezer all set to go—

Split franks and insert a strip of cheese in each. Wrap each one with a slice of bacon. Anchor with toothpicks. For each serving put two "pups" together and wrap in aluminum foil. (Be sure to push toothpicks all the way in or they might poke holes in the wrapping.) Cook now or freeze and have ready to use later.

To serve: Open a package for each person but leave the frankfurters in it. Have franks cheese side down. Broil over coals in these individual foil "pans" about 7 minutes, turning once. Serve on toasted buns.

PUPPET FRANKS

2 cups finely chopped onion
1 14-ounce bottle (1¼ cups) catsup
½ cup water
¼ cup brown sugar
¼ cup salad oil
2 tablespoons Worcestershire sauce

1 to 2 tablespoons vinegar
1 to 2 teaspoons liquid smoke
1 teaspoon salt
½ to 1 teaspoon dry mustard

• • •

24 frankfurters

Combine all ingredients except frankfurters. Simmer uncovered 15 minutes. Keep warm on edge of grill. Makes about 3 cups or enough sauce for dunking about 2 dozen frankfurters.

Slip frankfurters on cord, like stringing beads, then loop the strings over rod of a hanger for easy handling. Buy the short chubby-type franks. For each string, cut off enough cord to hold 6, 8, or 10 franks when strung lengthwise. Knot end of cord. Using skewer with eye for a needle, string franks, knotting cord each time you slip one on (otherwise they'll all tumble off when cord is cut). Tie final knot.

Slash frankfurters on both sides. Loop strings of franks, at halfway mark, twice over rod of hanger to secure. Lay franks on grill—let hanger dangle over side. Broil over *hot* coals, turning all at once.

When grilled just right pick up hanger and dunk franks into sauce. Carry franks to each guest; offer scissors so each person can snip the leash to suit his appetite. Pass the remaining sauce.

String up enough frankfurters for the crowd and corral on a hanger. Broil to a T, then sauce all with one flip of the wrist.

TANGY FRANK BARBECUE

2 tablespoons prepared
    mustard
2 8-ounce cans tomato
    sauce
½ cup dark corn syrup
⅓ cup vinegar
⅓ cup minced onion
2 tablespoons Worces-
    tershire sauce

½ teaspoon celery seed
¼ to ½ teaspoon hot
    pepper sauce
1 pound (8 to 10)
    frankfurters,
    scored diagonally

In skillet or foilware pan, blend mustard with small amount of tomato sauce; add remaining tomato sauce along with remaining ingredients, except franks. Cook over *medium* heat, stirring frequently, till mixture comes to boiling; move to side of grill and simmer gently 30 minutes. Add franks; cook till franks are hot and plumped, 7 to 8 minutes.

BROILED PORK TENDERLOIN

4 1-inch thick pork
    tenderloin steaks,
    flattened

• • •

2 tablespoons butter or
    margarine

¼ teaspoon bottled hot
    pepper sauce
Salt to season
Pepper to season

Place flattened tenderloin steaks on greased grill. Broil over *hot* coals untill browned on both sides and done, about 12 to 15 minutes. Combine butter and bottled hot pepper sauce; brush on meat. Season with salt and pepper just before removing to warmed serving platter. Makes 2 servings.

HILO FRANKS

Frankfurters are seasoned with a tangy apricot sauce. Use the sauce for glazing spitted duck or pork roast, too—

1 cup apricot preserves
½ 8-ounce can (½
    cup) tomato sauce
⅓ cup vinegar
¼ cup cooking sherry
2 tablespoons soy sauce
2 tablespoons honey
1 tablespoon salad oil

1 teaspoon salt
1 teaspoon grated fresh
    gingerroot *or* ¼
    teaspoon ground
    ginger

• • •

2 pounds frankfurters

For the sauce, combine preserves, tomato sauce, vinegar, sherry, soy sauce, honey, salad oil, salt, and grated gingerroot. Score the frankfurters on the bias.

Broil franks over *hot* coals, turning and basting often with the sauce. Broil till hot through and glazed. Heat remaining sauce on edge of grill and pass with frankfurters. Makes 8 to 10 servings.

CHEESE-FROSTED LUNCHEON MEAT

Cheese-mustard glaze perks up canned meat—

Anchor luncheon meat on spit. Blend 2 parts triple-use cheese spread and 1 part Dijon-style prepared mustard; slather on all sides of meat.

Broil over *hot* coals till golden brown. Slice and serve with dill pickle slices on toasted buns. Pass extra sauce.

MANDARIN ROASTS

Luncheon meat takes on a glamorous orange glaze. It's so easy—

1 11-ounce can (1⅓ cups) mandarin orange sections
½ cup honey
2 tablespoons finely chopped candied ginger

2 to 3 tablespoons lemon juice
2 or 3 12-ounce cans luncheon meat

· · ·

Drain orange sections, reserving ¼ cup syrup. Combine reserved syrup, honey, and candied ginger. Bring to boiling and cook 5 minutes. Add lemon juice and orange sections. Keep sauce warm on edge of grill.

Cut each loaf of meat on the diagonal to make 2 wedges. Broil on grill over *hot* coals 30 minutes, turning occasionally, and brushing the last 15 minutes with the orange sauce. To serve, garnish meat with a few orange sections (tack with toothpicks); heat remaining sauce to pass. Serves 4 to 6.

PINEAPPLE-GLAZED PORK

4 12-ounce cans luncheon meat
Whole cloves

Pineapple preserves or jam

Score each piece of meat and stud with whole cloves where scoring lines cross. Skewer meat on a long skewer and hold in place with holding forks. Let meat rotate over *medium hot* coals for 30 minutes. Baste with pineapple preserves and let rotate 5 to 10 minutes longer. Slice each can of meat in 6 to 8 slices which will give 3 to 4 servings per can of luncheon meat.

SAUSAGE APPETIZERS

1 9-ounce can (1 cup) crushed pineapple
1 cup brown sugar
2 tablespoons lemon juice

2 tablespoons prepared mustard

. . .

Precooked smoked-sausage links

Drain pineapple, reserving 2 tablespoons syrup. Combine pineapple, reserved syrup, brown sugar, lemon juice, and mustard. Cut sausage links in bite-size pieces. Let marinate 1 hour in pineapple glaze. String several chunks on individual skewers or split bamboo sticks. Broil over a few *hot* coals till heated through.

LAMB CUTS TO BARBECUE

1 *Loin chops*—the choicest cut of all. Get 1½- to 2-inchers and broil on grill or in a wire broiler basket. Serve lamb piping.

2 *Lamb patties*—best when girdled with bacon to keep them very juicy on the grill.

3 *Lamb kabobs*—let cubes of lamb steep in a tangy marinade, then line up on skewers with green pepper pieces and cherry tomatoes.

4 *Shoulder chops*—a grill bargain. We show two: the arm chop, left, and the blade-bone chop, right. For a flavor lift rub chops with pressed garlic clove or brush on bottled French dressing, if you prefer.

5 **Sirloin chops**—wonderfully meaty. Don't broil lamb too long—it is best when juicy and still a bit pink inside, yet crusty and brown on the outside. To test doneness: Cut a small slit and check the color.

6 **Rib chops**—when cut double, they are about 2 inches thick. No drying out over the coals. Serve immediately on hot plates.

7 **Saratoga chops**—a delightful gourmet delicacy. They are cut from the shoulder and tacked in rounds with wooden skewers. In the center of each chop is a nice slice of tender lamb kidney.

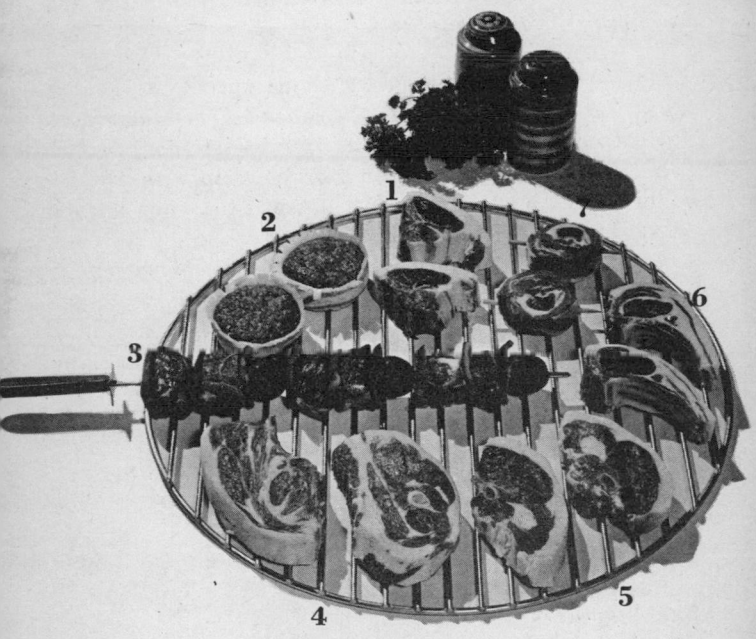

Lamb on the Grill

LAMB RACKS WITH HERB JACKETS

Select three 7-rib racks of lamb; be sure that meatman saws the chine bone between chops. (This makes for easier carving.) Balance on spit; insert meat thermometer, not touching spit, fat, or bone. Using ring of *hot* coals around meat and drip pan underneath, let meat rotate till thermometer reads 175°—about 1½ hours. Don't overcook lamb—it should have a pinkish cast.

Crush ½ cup packaged herb-seasoned stuffing to fine crumbs. Toss with 2 tablespoons snipped parsley. Sprinkle stuffing mixture over fat side of rack several times during last 15 minutes of cooking, until even "jacket" is formed. Makes 9 servings.

BROILED LAMB CHOPS

Have rib, loin, or shoulder chops cut ¾ to 1 inch thick. Cut fat in several places around edges of chops to prevent curling (or broil in a wire broiler basket).

Spear the fat trimmings or a bacon strip with a long-handled fork and rub over the hot grill or your broiler basket to prevent meat from sticking.

Arrange chops on grill above *hot* coals. When chops are brown on one side, season; turn, and brown other side. Allow total of 12 to 15 minutes for chops 1 inch thick.

LAMB CHOPS WITH PARMESAN

6 lamb chops, about
    ¾ inch thick
¼ cup shredded
    Parmesan cheese
2 tablespoons soft
    butter or
    margarine

½ teaspoon salt
Dash pepper

Broil chops 5 to 6 inches from *medium* coals for 6 to 8 minutes. Turn and broil 4 to 5 minutes or to desired doneness. Blend remaining ingredients; spread on chops. Broil 1 to 2 minutes. Makes 6 servings.

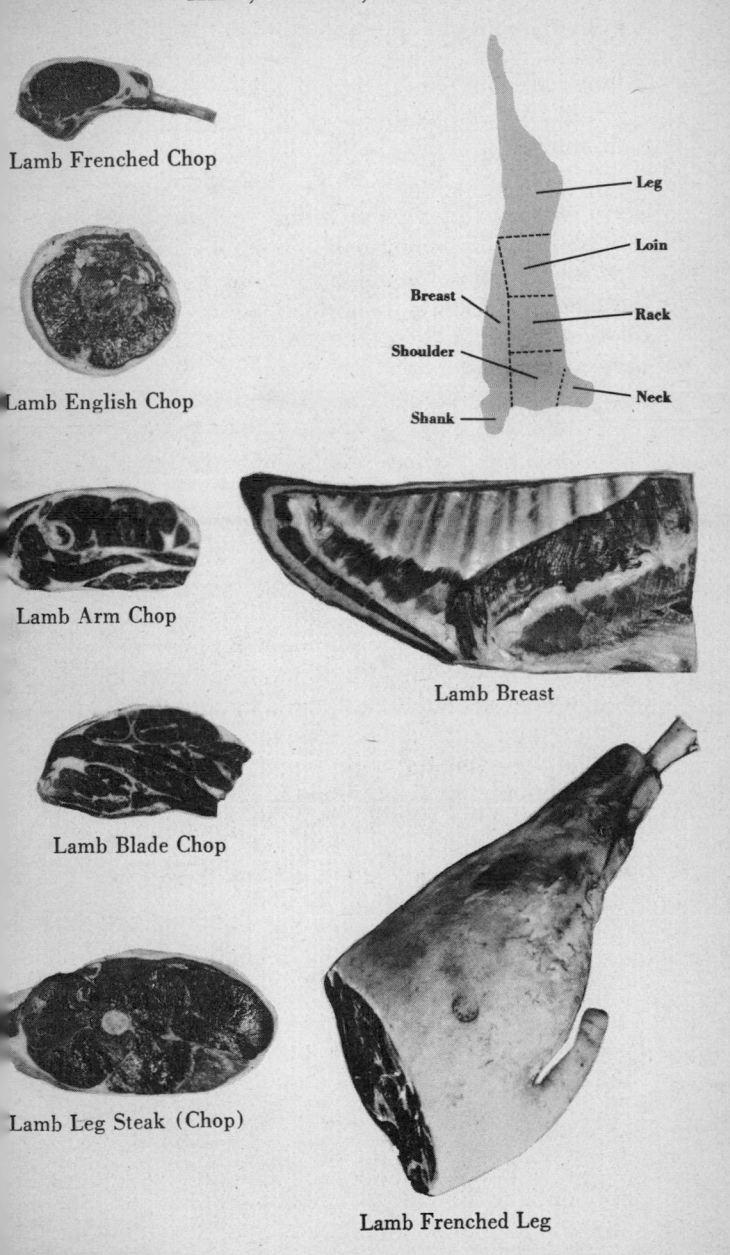

Lamb Frenched Chop

Lamb English Chop

Lamb Arm Chop

Lamb Blade Chop

Lamb Leg Steak (Chop)

Leg

Loin

Breast

Rack

Shoulder

Neck

Shank

Lamb Breast

Lamb Frenched Leg

STUFFED BREAST OF LAMB

**2 lamb breasts (about
1½ to 2 pounds
each)**

**1 recipe Rosemary
Stuffing**

Have meatman trim lamb breasts even with the longest
rib. In each, have him make a pocket with the opening
at the *wider end* (not along the side)—this will be at
the longest rib and parallel to it. (You'll probably need
to direct him, as the pockets are made differently than
usual, so stuffed roasts can rotate on rotisserie without
bumping.)

Season the pockets with salt and pepper; stuff lightly
with Rosemary Stuffing—don't pack.* Insert skewer pins
across openings; lace shut with string.

To mount first roast, push spit through center of *small*
end and on through laced opening; mount second roast,
starting at *large* end. (This places heavy part of roasts
in center of spit for better balance and even turning.)
Use 2 holding forks in each roast. Attach spit and turn
on motor. Roast over coals about 45 minutes to 1 hour.
Don't overcook—lamb is at its juicy best when roasted
medium rare to medium, and served *piping hot*. For
trencherman appetites, give everyone half a roast (cut
across between ribs). Or carve each roast in thirds.
Makes 4 generous or 6 average servings.

---

*Wrap any extra stuffing in foil and heat on edge of grill over
coals.

ROSEMARY STUFFING

To release maximum herb flavor, add a teaspoon of
boiling water to 1 teaspoon rosemary and set aside to
steep. In saucepan, combine 1 cup water, ¼ cup butter
or margarine, and 1 clove garlic, minced; bring to boiling. When butter has melted, remove from heat and add
one 8-ounce package (3½ cups) herb-seasoned stuffing,

⅔ cup snipped parsley, and the rosemary; mix lightly. Makes about 4 cups.

BROILED LAMBURGERS

1½ pounds ground lamb	⅓ cup milk
1½ teaspoons salt	• • •
	5 bacon strips

Combine lamb, salt, and milk. Shape mixture in five ¾-inch patties. Circle each with a strip of bacon and anchor ends with a toothpick. Score tops with knife handle.

Arrange meat patties on broiler or grill. Broil 12 minutes. Then turn patties. Broil 10 minutes longer or till patties are done. Makes 5 servings.

CHILI AND HOT LEG OF LAMB

Recipe name means what it says. Mighty good, but not for the "milk-toast" crowd—

1 6-pound leg of lamb, boned and flattened	1 tablespoon brown sugar
Marinade:	2 tablespoons vinegar
1 cup salad oil	1 teaspoon salt
¼ cup wine vinegar	1 teaspoon dry mustard
1 tablespoon salt	¼ teaspoon garlic powder
¼ teaspoon pepper	1 teaspoon minced canned green chiles
¼ teaspoon garlic powder	
• • •	2 teaspoons bottled hot pepper sauce
Hot Sauce:	1 bay leaf, crushed
2 cups chopped onion	
2½ cups chili sauce	
½ cup lemon juice	
⅓ cup salad oil	

Marinate lamb in mixture of first 5 ingredients 2 hours at room temperature, spooning Marinade over now and then. For Hot Sauce, combine remaining ingredients and simmer 20 minutes. Place meat flat on grill and roast about 2 hours, turning every 15 minutes and basting well with the Hot Sauce. Don't overcook lamb. Slice in thin slices across the grain. Serves 8 to 10.

LAMB SHANKS, ARMENIAN-ITALIAN

1 cup tomato juice	1 teaspoon salt
½ cup lemon juice	1 teaspoon coarse
½ cup dill-pickle juice	cracked pepper
1 large onion, finely	1 teaspoon cumin
chopped	1 teaspoon marjoram
1 green pepper, finely	6 meaty lamb shanks
chopped	

For marinade, combine first 9 ingredients; pour over lamb shanks in deep bowl and let stand 4 hours. Salt the meat. Broil over *slow* coals, brushing with marinade and turning occasionally, about 1 hour or till tender—don't overcook lamb. Heat remaining marinade; serve as a relish. Makes 6 servings.

BUTTERFLY LEG OF LAMB

1 5- to 6-pound leg of	½ teaspoon black
lamb	pepper
1 to 2 garlic cloves,	½ teaspoon thyme
minced	¼ cup grated onion
1 teaspoon salt	½ cup salad oil
1 teaspoon *fines herbes*	½ cup lemon juice

Have meatman bone leg of lamb and slit lengthwise to spread it flat like a thick steak. (Note how it takes on the butterfly shape.) Lemon-Marinade-Basting Sauce: In large glass dish or baking pan thoroughly blend remaining ingredients. Place butterfly leg in marinade. Leave at least one hour at room temperature, or overnight in the refrigerator, turning occasionally. Drain and save marinade.

Insert 2 long skewers through meat at right angles making an X or place meat in a wire broiler basket. This will make for easy turning of the meat and keep meat from "curling" during cooking. Roast over *medium* coals 1½ to 2 hours turning every 15 minutes till medium or well done. Baste frequently with reserved marinade. Place meat on carving board and remove from basket or remove skewers. Cut across grain into thin slices. Makes 8 servings.

POULTRY

Mounting Birds on a Spit

Fowl and game roasted on a spit make excellent eating. There is a crisp juiciness to a chicken done over the coals. Those who like well-done chicken may test it by bending the leg. When it moves back and forth easily, it's done just right.

Directions for trussing and mounting are the same for turkeys, ducks, and Rock Cornish game hens. Follow them carefully, add a good barbecue sauce, and you can rival the experts. Proper balance and correct timing are your keys to success as the spit roasting specialist. Follow the manufacturer's directions for your rotisserie or grill. The better you care for it, the more favorable your barbecue results.

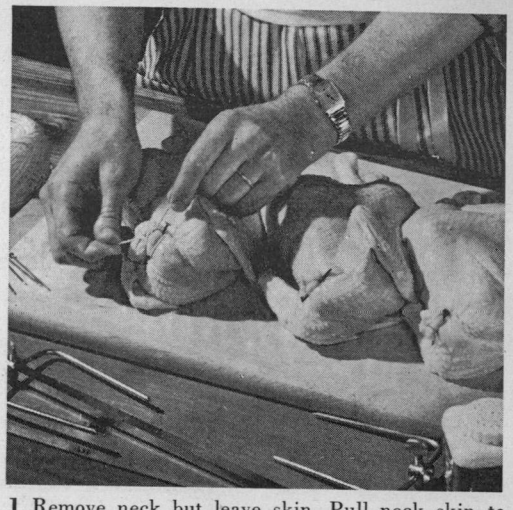

1 Remove neck but leave skin. Pull neck skin to back; fold under (trim if too long). Tack down with nail or skewer. Tie with cord to hold nail in place.

2 Salt cavity. To mount chicken on spit: Place holding fork on rod, tines toward point; insert rod through bird (pinch tines together and push firmly into the breast meat).

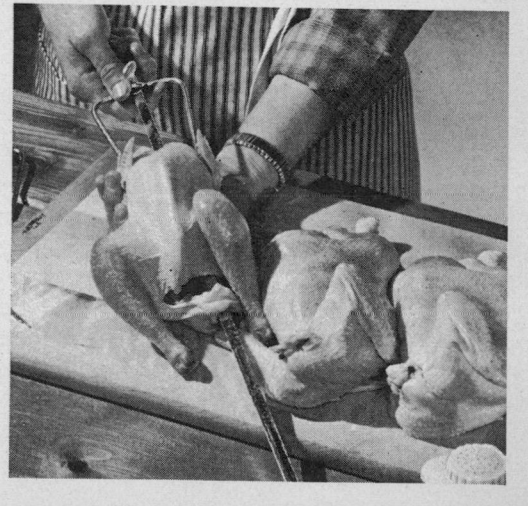

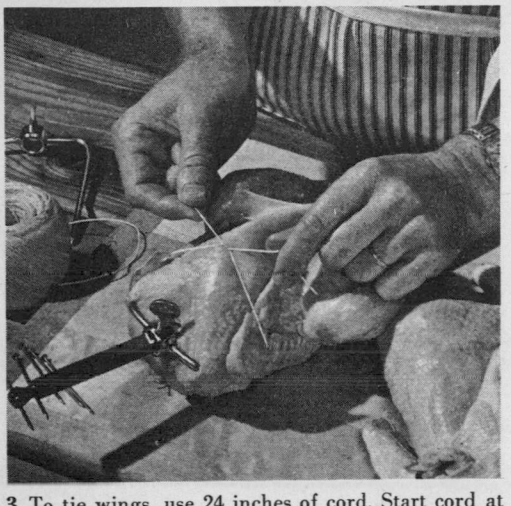

3 To tie wings, use 24 inches of cord. Start cord at back; loop around each wing tip. Make slipknots so the wings cannot straighten. Tie in center, leaving equal ends.

4 Now take an 18-inch piece of cord. Loop around the chicken's tail and then around the crossed legs as shown. Tie lightly to hold bird securely onto rod, leaving cord ends.

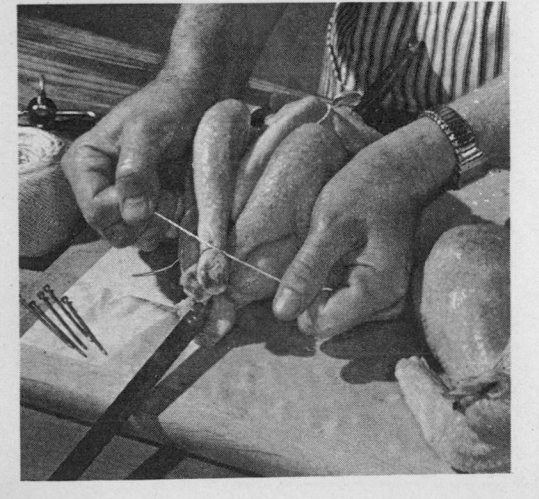

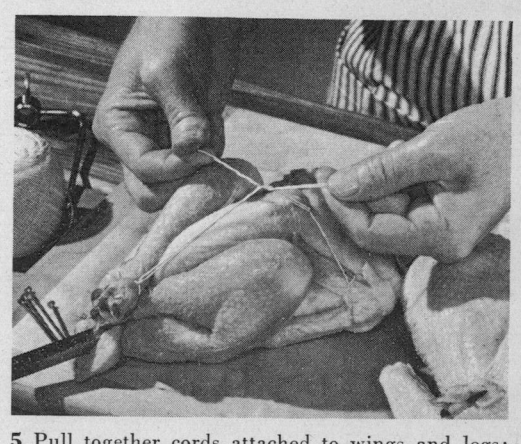

5 Pull together cords attached to wings and legs; tie tightly for compact "package." Truss the bird neatly to avoid flying drumsticks or wings—they might char.

6 If barbecuing more than one bird, fasten others on spit in same way, using holding fork for each; place the birds close together. Tighten the thumbscrews with pliers.

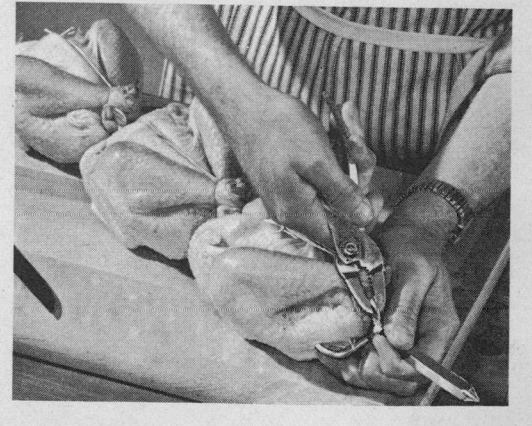

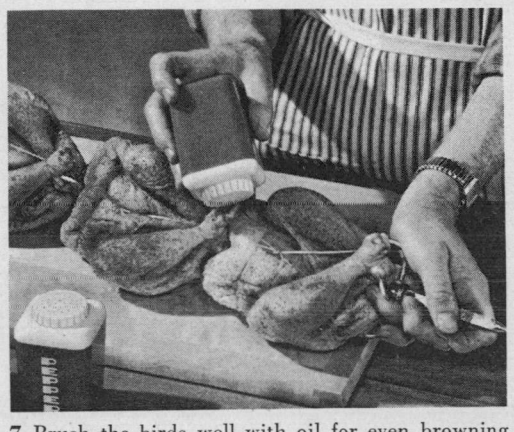

7 Brush the birds well with oil for even browning and to hold the seasonings. Sprinkle well with salt and pepper. Dust generously with paprika to give a fine, rosy finish.

Place halved broilers on grill with bony side down —the bones act as heat conductors and hurry the cooking. Baste with sauce at the last

PATIO CHICKEN BARBECUE

1 8-ounce can (1 cup) tomato sauce	1 teaspoon salt
½ cup water	¼ teaspoon pepper
¼ cup molasses	¼ teaspoon chili powder
2 tablespoons butter or margarine	• • •
2 tablespoons vinegar	2 ready-to-cook broilers (2 to 2½ pounds each), cut in half lengthwise
2 tablespoons minced onion	
1 tablespoon Worcestershire sauce	½ cup salad oil
2 teaspoons dry mustard	Salt
	Pepper

In saucepan, combine tomato sauce, water, molasses, butter or margarine, vinegar, onion, Worcestershire sauce, dry mustard, 1 teaspoon salt, pepper, and chili powder. Simmer mixture 15 to 20 minutes. Set aside.

Brush halved broilers with salad oil and season with salt and pepper. Place bone side down on grill. Broil over *slow* coals 25 minutes; turn, broil 20 minutes. Brush with sauce. Continue broiling, turning occasionally and basting with sauce 10 to 15 minutes or till tender. Makes 4 servings.

STUFFED BANTAMS

Everyone rates a whole "chicken" stuffed with crab meat. A company delicacy—

8 chicken breasts, boned but each left in one piece	1 cup packaged herb-seasoned stuffing
Salt	1 can condensed cream of mushroom soup
Monosodium glutamate	1 6½- or 7-ounce can crab meat, drained and flaked
• • •	
1 beaten egg	

¼ cup chopped green
  pepper
1 tablespoon lemon
  juice
2 teaspoons Worcester-
  shire sauce
1 teaspoon prepared
  mustard

¼ teaspoon salt
  • • •
¼ cup salad oil
1 teaspoon kitchen
  bouquet
¼ teaspoon onion juice
Dash pepper

Sprinkle inside of chicken breasts with salt and monosodium glutamate. Top with filling made of mixture of
eggs, herb-seasoned stuffing, ½ *cup of the soup*, the
crab, and next 5 ingredients. Skewer each "Bantam"
closed. Broil over *hot* coals 30 minutes or till tender,
turning frequently. Last 15 minutes, brush with Basting
Sauce: Combine remaining soup with salad oil, kitchen
bouquet, onion juice, and pepper. Serves 8.

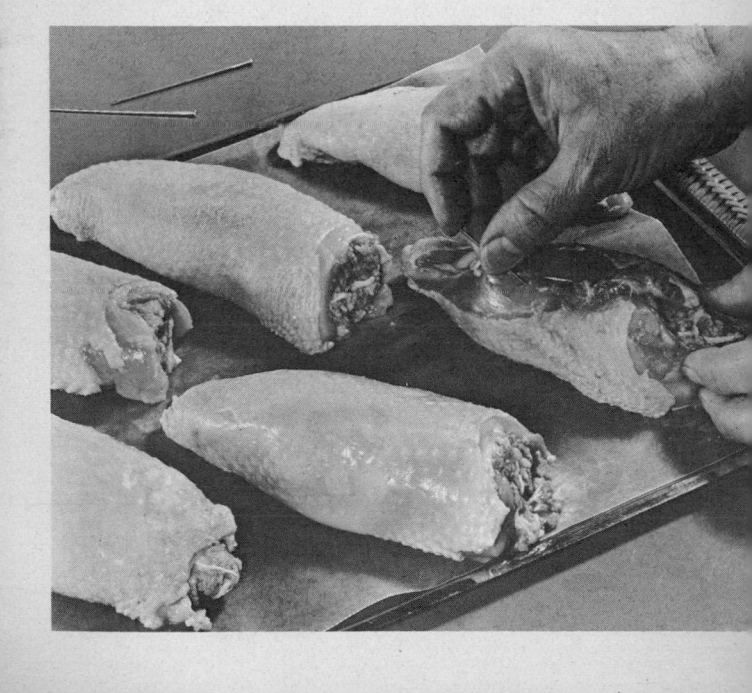

SPINNING CHICKEN

Tangy sauce gives rotisserie chicken a lovely glaze—

1 3- to 4-pound ready-to-
  cook broiler-fryer
1 teaspoon salt
Dash pepper
½ cup chopped celery
  leaves
¼ cup snipped parsley
¼ cup chopped onion
2 tablespoons butter or
  margarine, melted

¼ cup catsup
¼ cup corn syrup
2 tablespoons lemon
  juice
2 tablespoons salad oil
2 tablespoons prepared
  mustard

Rinse chicken, pat dry with paper towels. Rub body cavity with salt and pepper. Combine celery, parsley, onion, and melted butter; place in body cavity. Fasten neck skin to back with nail or skewer. Tie with cord to hold nail. To mount chicken on spit, place holding fork on rod, tines toward point; insert rod through chicken (press tines firmly into the breast meat).

To tie wings, use 24 inches of cord. Start cord at back; loop around each wing tip. Make slip knots so wings can't straighten. Tie in center, leaving equal ends. Now take an 18-inch piece of cord. Loop around tail, then around crossed legs. Tie very tightly to hold bird securely onto rod, leaving cord ends. Pull together cords attached to wings and legs; tie tightly. (If barbecuing more than one bird, fasten others on spit in same way, using holding fork for each; place birds close together.) Adjust holding forks and fasten screws tightly.

Test balance. Place chicken on rotisserie, having *medium* coals at back and front of chicken and a drip pan under revolving bird. Roast chicken for about 2 hours without barbecue hood or about 1¾ hours with the barbecue hood down.

Combine catsup, corn syrup, lemon juice, salad oil, and prepared mustard to make the tangy basting sauce. Use to baste the chicken occasionally during last 30 minutes of cooking. Makes 3 or 4 servings.

CHICKEN BROILERCUE

The jelly glaze is superb!

¼ cup salad oil
¼ cup cooking sauterne
¼ cup chicken broth
2 tablespoons lemon
   juice
2 tablespoons apple jelly
1 teaspoon salt
½ teaspoon mono-
   sodium glutamate
1 teaspoon snipped
   parsley

½ teaspoon prepared
   mustard
½ teaspoon Worcester-
   shire sauce
Dash celery seed
Dash rosemary
Dash pepper
2 ready-to-cook broilers
   (2 to 2½ pounds
   each) halved
   lengthwise

Combine all ingredients except chicken; beat out lumps of jelly with rotary beater. Brush chicken with the sauce and place bone side down on grill. Broil over *slow* coals, turning occasionally and basting frequently, about 1 hour or till meat is tender and skin is crisp and dark. Serves 4.

CHICKEN HAWAIIAN

Tender chicken with a delightful sweet-tart glaze—

2 ready-to-cook broiler-
   fryers (about 2
   pounds each), split
   in half lengthwise
½ cup salad oil
2 teaspoons salt
½ teaspoon pepper
Pineapple Glaze:
   1 9-ounce can (1 cup)
      crushed pineapple

1 cup brown sugar
2 tablespoons lemon
   juice
2 tablespoons
   prepared mustard
Dash salt

Brush birds well with oil and season with salt and pepper. Place on grill with bone side or inside nearest the coals.

Broil slowly. When bone side is well-browned, 20 to 30 minutes, turn skin side down and cook about 20 minutes longer.

Brush both sides of birds with Pineapple Glaze and broil about 10 minutes more or till tender, turning and brushing each side twice with glaze. Pass extra glaze. Serves 4.

Pineapple Glaze: Drain pineapple, reserving 2 tablespoons syrup. Combine pineapple, reserved syrup, brown sugar, lemon juice, mustard, and salt. Makes 1½ cups.

SPIT FIT

To make the most of your cooking space, mount birds efficiently. Put Rock Cornish game hens crosswise on spit, alternating front-back, front-back. Use a long holding fork for every two little biddies.

Before turning on the rotisserie, brush well with salad oil. During last 15 minutes over coals, brush with basting sauce.

STUFFED ROCK CORNISH HENS

Thaw 6 frozen Rock Cornish game hens. Stuff with Carrot Stuffing—don't pack. Truss, skewering openings. String birds crosswise on spit. Use long holding forks that secure several birds at a time. Brush before and during roasting with Soy-Butter Sauce. Roast birds on rotisserie till done, 45 to 60 minutes. Toward end of roasting, let butter-brushed mushrooms broil on the bottom of gravy pan; add a little cooking sherry. Serve everyone a hen with a spoonful of mushroom gravy. Serves 6.

SOY-BUTTER SAUCE

Combine 6 tablespoons soy sauce, 1 tablespoon melted butter, ¼ teaspoon salt, and dash *each* of pepper, marjoram, and monosodium glutamate. Baste game hens.

CARROT STUFFING

Very different and very good—

1 cup sifted all-purpose
    flour
1 teaspoon baking
    powder
½ teaspoon salt
½ teaspoon ginger
½ teaspoon nutmeg
½ cup wheat germ
1 cup dry bread crumbs,
    lightly browned in
    a little butter

½ cup chopped pecans
¼ cup butter or
    margarine
½ cup brown sugar
1 egg
1 cup finely shredded
    carrots
3 tablespoons snipped
    parsley

Sift flour with baking powder, salt, and spices; stir in wheat germ, then crumbs and nuts. Cream butter with brown sugar; add egg; mix well; add carrots and parsley. Lightly stir in sifted dry ingredients.

LUSCIOUS CORNISH HENS

4 1-pound Rock Cornish
    hens, thawed
1 cup finely chopped
    walnuts, or roasted
    Italian chestnuts
¼ cup olive oil
1 teaspoon salt
1 teaspoon celery salt

1 teaspoon poultry
    seasoning
½ teaspoon rosemary
½ cup butter or
    margarine, melted
Salt and freshly ground
    pepper

Rinse birds; pat dry with paper towels. Combine next 6 ingredients; rub *half* of mixture inside birds. Truss birds; mount on spit, securing with holding forks. Rub birds with remaining nut mixture; let stand 15 minutes. Roast over coals 1 to 1¼ hours or till tender—after 15 minutes, brush now and then with butter. Sprinkle with salt and grind pepper over; continue cooking 10 minutes. Makes 4 servings.

GRILL-BROILED GAME HENS

Split four 1-pound ready-to-cook Rock Cornish game hens in half lengthwise. Season. Broil, bone side down; brush well with melted butter. Broil slowly over *medium* coals.

When bone side is well-browned, about 20 minutes, turn skin side down. Broil about 20 to 25 minutes longer or till tender. Brush both sides with mixture of 1/4 cup consomme and 1/4 cup corn syrup. Broil 1 or 2 minutes longer to glaze. Makes 4 servings.

PINEAPPLE STUFFED ROCK CORNISH HENS

4 1-pound Rock Cornish hens, thawed	**1/2 cup butter or margarine, melted**
1 1-pound can pineapple chunks, drained	**2 tablespoons lemon juice**
1 teaspoon salt	

Rinse birds; pat dry with paper towels. Lightly salt cavities. Stuff birds with pineapple. Truss birds and tie cavity closed. Mount crosswise on spit, alternating front-back, front-back. Do not have birds touching. Secure with extra long holding forks. Combine salt, butter, and lemon; brush birds with mixture. Place on rotisserie over *medium* coals. Broil 1 to 1 1/4 hours or till done, brushing birds with lemon butter every 15 minutes. Makes 4 servings.

ROAST ROCK CORNISH HENS WITH WILD-RICE STUFFING

These tender little birds are the blondes (all light meat) of the poultry kingdom—

6 1-pound Rock Cornish hens, thawed	**1/2 cup soy sauce**
1 recipe Wild-rice Stuffing	**1/3 cup butter or margarine, melted**

Season birds inside with salt and monosodium glutamate. Skewer neck skin to back. Fill each bird with about ¼ cup stuffing; insert a flap of foil to close opening. Tie or skewer wings to body; tie legs to tail. Mount birds crosswise on spit, alternating front-back, front-back, and using a long holding fork. (Or mount lengthwise on spit as you would chickens.)

Brush with mixture of soy and melted butter. Attach spit and turn on motor (have *slow* coals at back of firebox, and a drip pan under birds). Roast over coals about 1 hour or till tender, basting frequently with soy-butter mixture.

Wild-rice Stuffing: Wash ⅓ cup wild rice; cook in boiling salted water till tender, according to package directions; drain. Add 2 tablespoons soft butter or margarine, 2 tablespoons blanched almonds, slivered and toasted, ¼ cup golden raisins, ½ teaspoon sage, and salt to taste.

CORNISH CAPONS, TANGERINE

Get acquainted with Rock Cornish capons (brothers of the dainty hens). They weigh 6 or 7 pounds each. Truss and spit-roast as you would chickens or small turkeys. During last 5 to 10 minutes of roasting time, brush with Tangerine-Currant Glaze; heat remainder on edge of grill and pass.

TANGERINE-CURRANT GLAZE

1 cup currant jelly	1 teaspoon dry mustard
1 6-ounce can frozen	Dash ginger
tangerine	Dash bottled hot pepper
concentrate	sauce

In small saucepan, break up currant jelly with fork. Stir in remaining ingredients. Heat and stir till mixture is smooth.

KOWLOON DUCKLING

Long and slow smoke cooking in a Chinese oven helps the duck stay moist and juicy. For the glorious brown color brush on a glaze of soy sauce and honey before smoking—

1 4- to 5-pounds ready-to-cook duckling	6 sprigs parsley
• • •	3 cloves garlic, quartered
1 bunch green onions (6 to 8 onions), cut up	• • •
	½ cup soy sauce
	¼ cup honey

Clean the duckling and stuff with cut green onions, parsley, and garlic. Skewer the neck and body cavities closed; tie securely. Fasten over hook through tail and over skewer that closes the body cavity. Blend the soy sauce and honey together; heat. For a beautiful brown glaze, brush duckling with this mixture every 5 minutes for 1 hour *before* hanging in the smoke oven.

Then hang duckling in 275° to 300° Chinese oven which uses wood as fuel—split logs of fruitwood, oak, or hickory. Smoke duck about 3½ hours, or until tender and a deep golden brown color.

To carve: Remove the wings, cut off leg and second joint. Make lengthwise cuts on both sides of the breastbone, cutting down to the bone. Place a knife in first cut and carve down along the breastbone to free the slices. Makes 4 servings.

SPINNING TURKEY

The tantalizing aroma of rotisseried turkey, as it turns slowly on the spit, is sure to whet hearty appetites—

Allow ½ pound ready-to-cook turkey per person. Rub inside of bird with 1 tablespoon salt. Skewer neck skin to back. Insert spit and anchor with holding forks. Check balance. Tie wings flat against the body. With another piece of cord tie the legs to the tail or use a drumstick holding fork. (Or use a rotary roast rack—no trussing needed.) Brush bird with salad oil. Adjust on rotisserie —have *slow* coals at back and sides of firebox and place an aluminum foil drip pan under revolving bird.

Roast about 15 minutes per pound. For smoke flavor, toss damp hickory on coals and roast with hood down. (If you like, brush bird with your favorite barbecue sauce during last half hour of cooking.)

About 20 minutes before turkey roasting time is up, snip cord that holds drumsticks to spit. Test doneness by moving drumstick up and down (protect hands with paper towels). When done, leg should move easily or twist out of joint. Also press thick part of drumstick— meat should feel very soft. (Meat thermometer in thickest part of thigh should register 190° to 195°.) For neat slicing, let turkey rest 15 minutes; carve.

ROTISSERIE DUCK

For a pretty golden color, sprinkle the duck with sugar during the last few minutes of roasting time. It enhances the flavor too—

1 4-pound ready-to-cook duckling	Salt
• • •	2 tablespoons sugar
	Pepper

Clean the duckling as for roasting. Rub inside with salt. Prick skin and truss well. Balance on spit securing with holding forks. Arrange *hot* coals at back and sides of firebox. Place a foil drip pan in front of coals and under the spit. (Since ducks are fat birds a large amount of fat will cook out and drip into foil pan. It may be necessary to drain fat occasionally from drip pan so that it will not get too hot and flame up.)

Attach spit, turn on motor, and lower the barbecue hood. Let duck rotate over *medium* coals about 2 hours or till done. (Maintain a temperature of 300° to 325° if the grill has a heat indicator.) The last 10 minutes of roasting time sprinkle the duck with sugar and dash pepper. Continue roasting till brown. Makes 4 servings.

TURKEY DONENESS TESTS

Shake hands with a turkey to tell when it's done. About 20 minutes before turkey roasting time is up, snip the cord that holds drumsticks to spit rod.

Grasp end of drumstick with paper towels; raise and lower to test. Leg should move easily or twist out of joint. Also press thick part of drumstick—meat should feel very soft. Do this test as a check whether you use a meat thermometer or not.

If turkey needs a few more turns over the coals, give it time to really pass the doneness test. Now that cord is snipped at drumsticks, the heat can reach all parts of bird.

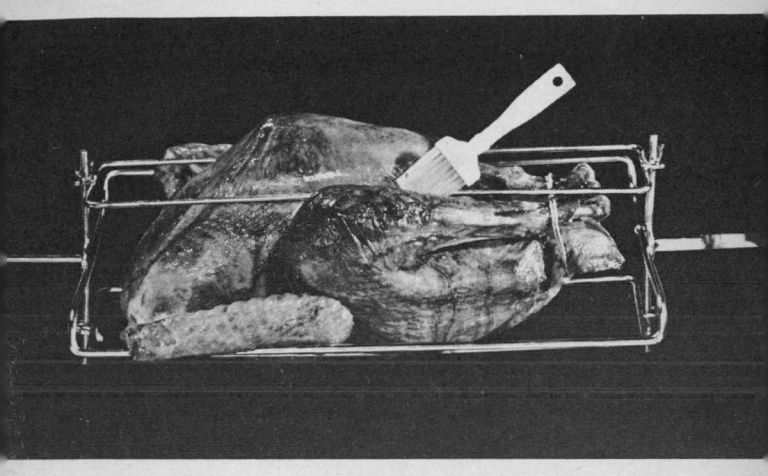

Rotary roast rack fits on rotisserie in place of the usual spit. Center the turkey in bottom rack of frame—tie drumsticks to tail. Put top section in position and tighten thumbscrews.

HICKORY SMOKED TURKEY

The meat is succulent with a subtle smoke flavor. Dusky-toned and delicious hot or cold—

Select a 10- to 12-pound ready-to-cook turkey—count on 4½ to 5 hours total roasting time. Rinse bird; pat dry with paper towels. Make a paste of ¼ cup salad oil and ½ cup salt; rub ¼ *cup* mixture over large and wishbone cavities. Truss turkey and balance on spit or use rotary roast rack; brush with salad oil.

Have slow coals at back of firebox, a drip pan under revolving bird. For moisture, place a small pan of water at one end of firebox. Roast, hood down, and at end of first hour brush bird with Basting Sauce: To remaining salt paste, add 1 cup vinegar, ¼ cup pepper, and 2 teaspoons finely chopped parsley. Also toss damp hickory chips on coals. Continue roasting, hood down, basting bird every 30 minutes or so (also check on fire, hickory, and water in pan).

About 20 minutes before roasting time is up, snip cord that holds drumsticks. Test doneness by raising drumstick up and down (protect hands with paper towels). Leg should move easily or twist out of joint. Also press thick part of drumstick—meat should feel very soft. Before carving, let turkey rest 15 minutes— easier to slice.

For charcoal oven: If you have a smoke cooker without rotisserie, follow manufacturer's directions for preparation of fire, placement of bird, and cooking time.

ROAST STUFFED TURKEY

Rinse a 10- to 12-pound ready-to-cook turkey; dry with paper towels. Brush inside with 1 teaspoon liquid smoke and rub with 1 tablespoon salt. Stuff turkey with 1 medium onion, quartered, 1 medium carrot, cut in thirds, and 2 branches celery (with tops), cut in half. Brush bird well with salad oil. Tie drumsticks to tail; tuck wing tips behind shoulder joints.

To use a meat thermometer, insert it in the center of the inside thigh muscle, adjoining cavity. (Turkey should be done when thermometer reads 195°—be sure to double check with tests below.)

If using covered barbecue kettle,* place lard on rack over drip pan with slow coals around (not under) turkey. Roast with lid on, about 3 hours or till tender, basting with salad oil after first hour, and then every half hour—no need to turn bird cooked in covered kettle since heat surrounds it.

About 20 minutes before roasting time is up, snip cord that holds drumsticks. Test doneness by raising drumstick up and down (grasp with paper towel to protect fingers). Leg should move easily. Also press thick part of drumstick—meat should feel very soft. For better carving, let turkey stand 15 minutes before slicing.

*If using rotisserie barbecue, truss turkey and balance on spit or use rotary roast rack. Have slow coals at back of barbecue, drip pan under revolving bird. Roast, hood down, about 4½ to 5 hours total roasting time.

Be firm with the turkey

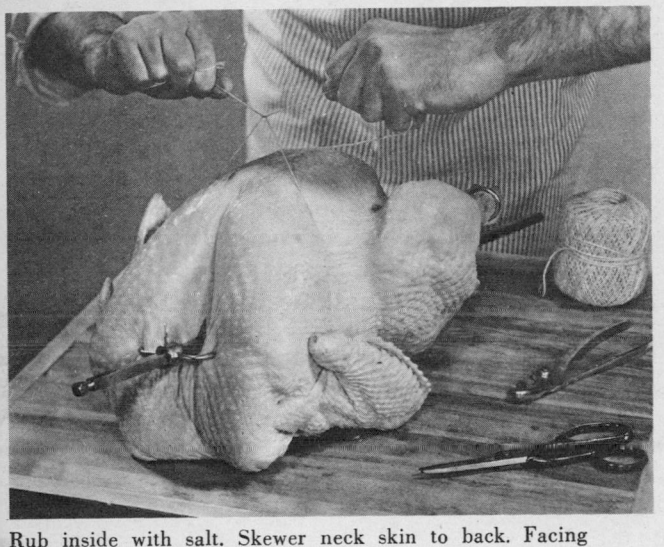

Rub inside with salt. Skewer neck skin to back. Facing
breast, insert spit at angle to avoid bone. Anchor with
holding forks. Balance.

Loop cord over right wing, around skewer, then over left
wing to hold *flat*; tie. Wrap cord around turkey and tie.
Repeat all.

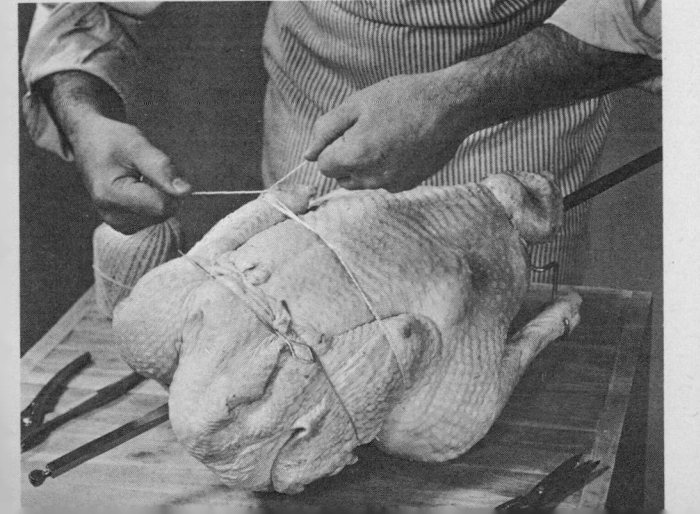

Drumstick holding fork lets heat reach inside thigh meat. Tie tail to rod—cross legs and tie on, too, if you don't have turkey bracelets.

BONELESS TURKEY ROAST

¼ cup white wine
¼ cup butter or
    margarine, melted
1 clove garlic, minced
½ teaspoon crushed
    rosemary leaves

1 5- to 6-pound boneless
    turkey roast
2 tablespoons butter or
    margarine, melted
Salt and pepper

• • •

Blend together wine, butter, garlic, and rosemary. Let mixture stand several hours at room temperature.

Thaw turkey roast. Insert spit rod through center of roast; set screws and adjust balance. Insert a meat thermometer in center of roll being careful not to touch spit with end of thermometer. Brush roast with melted butter and season with salt and pepper.

Arrange *hot* coals at back and sides of firebox. Place a foil drip pan in front of coals. Adjust spit in rotisserie and start motor. Baste with wine sauce during last 30 minutes. A 5- to 6-pound roast should be done in 2½ to 3 hours and thermometer should register 180° to 185°.

CHARCOALED TURKEY PIECES

1 6- to 7-pound ready-to-cook turkey	1 teaspoon ground ginger
• • •	1 teaspoon dry mustard
¼ cup salad oil	1 teaspoon mono-sodium glutamate
¼ cup soy sauce	
1 tablespoon honey	1 clove garlic, minced

Cut turkey in pieces as follows: 2 wings, 2 drumsticks, 2 thighs, 4 breast pieces, and 2 back pieces. Combine remaining ingredients for marinade. Place turkey pieces in marinade about 2 hours at room temperature or overnight in the refrigerator.

Place turkey pieces on grill 6 to 8 inches above *medium hot* coals. (The wings and back pieces may be added ½ hour after rest of turkey.) Broil, turning occasionally, about 1 hour. Baste with marinade and broil about 30 minutes longer. To test doneness, cut into drumstick with very sharp knife. Turkey is done when there is no pinkness near bone. Makes 10 to 12 servings.

FISH AND SEA FOOD

FISH INFORMATION

The basic rules for cooking fish and sea food are few and easy to follow, even though each type of fish has individual flavor, texture, and appearance.

If you make allowances for the fat content of fish, you can successfully use any of the cooking methods for almost all species. In other words, *lean* fish may be cooked by dry heat methods such as baking or broiling, if you baste frequently with melted butter or margarine to prevent drying. (Try combining lemon or garlic with the basting fat, or using a basting sauce.) Fish with high fat content don't have to be basted.

Avoid overcooking fish. It should be moist and tender with a delicate flavor. Overcooking causes the fish to become increasingly dry and chewy. Fish is done when the flesh is translucent and can be flaked easily with a fork.

Don't over-handle the fish during cooking and serving. Cooked fish is delicate and will flake apart easily. Turn only once during cooking and serve on a warm platter.

Never leave fresh fish soaking in water. This causes loss of flavor and makes the flesh flabby. Wash fish quickly, drain, and dry carefully on paper toweling.

Three basic cuts of fish

Dressed, or pan-dressed
Scaled, drawn with head, tail, and fins removed.

Steaked
Cross-sectional slices are cut from larger fish.

Filleted
Sides of fish are cut lengthwise along backbone.

GRILLED TROUT WITH ALMONDS

4 brook trout, cleaned
¼ cup all-purpose flour
½ teaspoon salt
Dash pepper
½ cup butter or
    margarine

2 tablespoons slivered
    almonds
¼ cup lemon juice
2 tablespoons snipped
    parsley

Remove heads from fish; wash and pat dry with paper towels. Combine flour, salt, and pepper; dip fish in seasoned flour. Place coated fish in an oiled wire broiler basket. Broil fish over *hot* coals 15 minutes or till fish flakes with a fork, turning once. Baste with ¼ cup melted butter. Melt remaining ¼ cup butter in a saucepan and add almonds. Brown almonds, stirring occasionally. Stir in lemon juice and parsley. Place grilled fish on warm platter and pour lemon sauce over. Makes 4 servings.

FISH IN CORN HUSKS

Pan fish skip the pan this time—

In the cavity of each cleaned fish place a lump of butter (cut chunks 1 inch wide from a ¼-pound stick) and give fish a generous squirt of lemon juice. Sprinkle with salt and fresh-ground or cracked pepper.

Wrap each in a whole de-silked corn husk,* and tie with string at the silk end. Place on a bed of *hot* coals; cover with more coals. Cook about 15 minutes or till fish flakes when tested with fork. Pass extra melted butter to pour over fish.

---

*If husks are quite dry, first soak in water about 5 minutes.

Fish and Bacon variation: Sprinkle fish cavity with salt and fresh-ground or cracked pepper. Place a bacon strip down each side of fish when wrapping in corn husks. Tie corn husk with string at the silk end. Continue as directed above.

CHARCOALED TROUT STEAKS

6 1-inch thick lake trout
    steaks (*or* use
    northern, young
    muskie, or salmon)

⅓ cup butter or
    margarine, melted
Salt and pepper

Brush fish with melted butter and place in an oiled wire broiler basket. Broil over *hot* coals about 2 inches from heat for 5 minutes. Turn, brush with melted butter and broil 5 minutes longer or till fish flakes. Season with salt and pepper. Serve with Caper Sauce (see index listing). Makes 6 servings.

SIMPLE SIMON FISH GRILL

When the big ones are biting, remember this recipe. Smoldering herbs flavor the fish—

1 1½- to 2-pound
    whitefish, trout, or
    similar fresh-water
    fish, cleaned
Salt

• • •

½ cup butter or
    margarine
1 teaspoon salt
1 teaspoon coriander
    seed, crushed

¼ teaspoon
    cardamom
Dash pepper
2 tablespoons lemon
    juice
1 cup yogurt

• • •

Fennel leaves or dill or
    other leafy herb

Salt the cleaned fish. Melt butter and mix in salt, crushed coriander, cardamom, pepper, lemon juice, and yogurt. Coat fish inside and out with this mixture. Place in a wire broiler basket and cook over coals till fish browns on both sides and flakes when tested with a fork, about 25 to 30 minutes. Brush fish often with sauce.

Ten minutes before the end of cooking time, make a bed of a bunch of fennel, dill, or other leafy herb on grill top and lay fish on the greens. Grill till herbs smolder and flavor the fish, turning once.

Heat remaining sauce on edge of grill to pass in bowl. Makes 4 to 6 servings.

LATE SEASON TROUT

Catch your own sea food or buy it at the store, this recipe's "worth fishing for!"

2 eggs	½ teaspoon allspice
1 tablespoon cream or milk	• • •
1 teaspoon dried parsley flakes	8 brook trout, cleaned
1 clove garlic, minced	8 or 16 strips broiled bacon

Beat to blend eggs, cream, parsley, garlic, and allspice. Coat the cleaned trout inside and out with the mixture. Put 1 to 2 strips bacon in each trout and place in an oiled wire broiler basket or on a greased hot grill. Broil fish over *hot* coals for 20 minutes or till fish flakes with fork—turn once. Serve with lemon wedges. Makes 8 servings.

FISH FRY

Coating is crusty and flavorful—

⅓ cup yellow corn meal	¼ teaspoon paprika
2 tablespoons all-purpose flour	• • •
1 teaspoon salt	1 pound fish fillets
	¼ cup salad oil

Combine corn meal, flour, salt, and paprika. Dip fish in corn meal mixture to coat. In skillet, heat oil over *hot* coals for about 10 minutes. Fry fillets till brown on one side, about 4 minutes. Turn and brown on other side. Cook till fish flakes easily when tested with a fork. Do not overcook.

Small fish may be fried whole. Larger fish are boned and cut in steaks or fillets before frying. Reduce cooking time for thin fillets. One pound fish makes 2 servings.

BROILED SALMON EPICUREAN

Beautiful pink salmon, fresh from chilly water or from the fish market, becomes a gourmet treat when teamed with the flavor of charcoal and a tangy marinade—

½ teaspoon rosemary
   leaves
¼ cup salad oil
2 tablespoons lemon
   juice
   • • •

2 pounds salmon steaks
   or fillets
   • • •
Salt
Pepper

Combine rosemary, oil, and lemon juice; shake well. Let mixture stand at room temperature for an hour or longer; strain. Dip fish in oil mixture. Sprinkle both sides of steaks with salt and pepper.

Place in an oiled wire broiler basket. Broil over *medium hot* coals about 5 to 8 minutes or until slightly brown. Baste with oil and turn carefully. Brush other side with oil and broil 5 to 8 minutes longer or until fish flakes easily with a fork. Serve immediately on warmed plates. Makes 6 servings.

GRILLED FISH FOLDOVERS

For extra-flaky and so-tender grilled fish, use sole or other thin fish fillets, fresh or thawed-frozen. Make a once-over fold in each fillet, tucking a thin slice of American cheese into fold. Brush outside with melted butter or margarine, and lemon juice; sprinkle with salt and pepper.

Arrange in a close-meshed wire broiler basket, and

broil quickly over *hot* coals, turning frequently and brushing with more butter till done—takes only a few minutes.

SMOKED FISH WITH LEMON

**6 fish steaks or fillets,
    ¾ to 1 inch thick**
Salt and pepper
2 or 3 lemons, *thinly*
    sliced

**½ cup butter or
    margarine, melted**
**1 or 2 cloves garlic,
    minced**

Sprinkle fish generously with salt and pepper. Arrange half of lemon slices in bottom of shallow baking dish; add fish in single layer. Place remaining lemon slices atop and around sides. Combine butter and garlic; pour over fish (and baste with it later). Add hickory to *slow* coals. Place baking dish on heavy-duty foil atop grill.

Close smoker hood; cook slowly, about 1 hour, turning once. Baste frequently. Serve with the cooked lemon slices and butter mixture. Makes 6 servings.

SPEEDY BROILED FISH

Soy sauce lends a surprise tingle. Use halibut or any other favorite fish—

1 pound fish fillets
Salt
Pepper
    • • •
2 teaspoons soy sauce
2 tablespoons salad oil
    • • •

**2 tablespoons lemon
    juice**
**2 tablespoons snipped
    parsley**

Cut fillets into serving pieces; season with salt and pepper. Combine soy sauce and oil. Arrange fish on an oiled grill or in an oiled wire broiler basket. If fish tends to be dry, broil on piece of heavy aluminum foil. Slit foil at regular intervals and oil lightly. Broil pieces of fish till golden brown, about 5 to 8 minutes on each side. Baste frequently with soy mixture.

Place broiled fish on a warm platter. Heat remaining soy sauce mixture; add lemon juice and parsley. Pour sauce over fish and garnish with parsley. Makes 4 servings.

FRIDAY "FRANKS"

¼ cup butter or
   margarine, melted
2 tablespoons lemon
   juice
1 8-ounce package
   frozen breaded
   fish sticks

5 coney buns, split and
   toasted
Sandwich spread
Chopped onion

• • •

Combine butter and lemon juice; quickly dip *frozen* fish sticks in mixture, coating all sides. Place fish sticks in an oiled wire broiler basket and cook over *hot* coals, brushing with lemon butter and turning once—takes about 5 minutes to brown nicely and cook through. Spread hot buns generously with sandwich spread; tuck 2 fish sticks (overlap slightly) in each bun. Pass catsup and a bowl of chopped onion to spoon over fish. Makes 5 servings.

FISH FILLETS WITH PARSLEY SAUCE

Easy as a breeze, and such flavor—

1 teaspoon salt
Dash pepper
2 tablespoons salad oil
• • •
2 1-pound packages
   frozen perch fillets
• • •

2 tablespoons prepared
   mustard
¼ cup butter or
   margarine
¼ cup chopped parsley
¼ cup lemon juice
½ teaspoon salt

Add 1 teaspoon salt and pepper to salad oil; mix. Rub mixture over fish. Broil over coals, about 4 minutes on each side, or until fillets are well browned.

Combine mustard, butter, parsley, lemon juice, and ½ teaspoon salt; spread ½ of mixture over fish. Return fish to grill till sizzling and fish flakes easily. Serve with remaining sauce. Makes 6 servings.

OYSTERS VESUVIO

12 oysters in shell
¼ cup butter or
    margarine
2 tablespoons sliced
    green onions
2 tablespoons snipped
    parsley

⅓ cup cornflake
    crumbs
⅓ cup shredded
    Parmesan cheese
Rock salt

Shuck oysters; cut in thirds. Divide oysters among 12 half-shells. Season with salt and pepper. Blend butter, onions, and parsley; dot over oysters. Mix crumbs and cheese and sprinkle over. Pour rock salt into large foil-ware pan or baking dish to 1 inch. Press shells slightly into rock salt to anchor. Broil, hood down, close to *hot* coals 20 to 30 minutes or till oysters are done and crumbs are browned. Makes 4 servings.

SHRIMP-OUT

1 pound raw shrimp,
    peeled and
    deveined
½ cup soda crackers,
    crushed

1 egg, slightly beaten
⅓ cup salad oil

Dip each shrimp in egg and coat well with cracker crumbs. Let stand in oil about 1 minute; drain shrimp slightly on paper toweling. Cook on grill over *hot* coals for 5 to 8 minutes, or till shrimp are done and crumbs are browned. Serve with hot sauce.

To prevent shrimp from falling through the grill bars, place a piece of screen wire or a cake rack over the grill top.

WINDANDSEA BARBECUE SHRIMP

⅓ cup butter or
  margarine
½ teaspoon curry
  powder
1 clove garlic, minced
½ teaspoon salt

Coarse ground black
  pepper
½ cup snipped parsley
2 pounds large raw
  shrimp, peeled
  and deveined

Cream butter with remaining ingredients except shrimp and mix well. Tear off six pieces of heavy-duty aluminum foil. Divide shrimp equally on pieces of foil. Top each with one-sixth (about 1 tablespoon) of the butter mixture. Bring foil up around shrimp; seal tightly. Place shrimp directly on *hot* coals. Cook about 5 to 7 minutes. Serve in foil packages. Serves 6.

This is the best thing that's happened to dill since pickles. Marinate shrimp overnight, then brush with more sauce while broiling.

FISHERMAN'S LUCK

Luck indeed! The savory sauce does big things for halibut—

Aluminum foil

• • •

½ cup chopped green
   pepper
½ cup chopped onion
2 tablespoons butter or
   margarine
½ cup catsup
½ teaspoon garlic salt

2 small bay leaves

• • •

1¾ pounds 1-inch
   frozen halibut
   steaks, cut in
   4 serving pieces
Salt
Pepper

For each serving, cut a 28-inch length of aluminum foil and fold it in half. Cook the green pepper and onion in butter till they are tender but not brown. Add catsup, garlic salt, and the bay leaves. Let mixture simmer 10 to 15 minutes.

For each person, place 1 serving halibut in foil, just off center; sprinkle with salt and pepper. Pour ¼ of the sauce over each serving. Bring edges of foil together and seal well with a double fold. Cook over glowing *hot* coals, turning once, until done. Serve in foil packages. Makes 4 servings.

SONORA SHRIMP

Shrimp cocktail takes on delicious "cooked-outdoors" character—

1 cup bottled barbecue
   sauce
3 tablespoons lemon
   juice
1 tablespoon Worcester-
   shire sauce

1 teaspoon dill weed

• • •

1 pound large shrimp,
   peeled and
   deveined

Combine first four ingredients for marinade and pour over shrimp; cover and let stand at least 6 hours or overnight in refrigerator, stirring occasionally.

Cook shrimp on fine wire grill over *hot* coals about 6 to 8 minutes or till done, turning once and brushing often with marinade. Don't overcook! Heat remaining marinade on edge of grill and serve with the shrimp. Or, if you prefer, pass a lemon-butter sauce jacked up with bottled hot pepper sauce and chili powder. Makes 3 to 4 servings.

SCALLOPS 'N BACON

The wonderful flavors of bacon and scallops are subtly blended over a glowing charcoal fire. Bacon is precooked slightly to prevent flaming over the grill—

1 pound fresh or frozen scallops	**½ teaspoon salt** **Dash white pepper**
• • •	• • •
¼ cup butter or margarine, melted **2 tablespoons lemon juice**	**Sliced bacon** **Paprika**

Thaw frozen scallops. Remove any shell particles and wash. Combine butter or margarine, lemon juice, salt, and pepper. Pour mixture over scallops; let stand for 30 minutes, turning once. Drain scallops.

Cut bacon slices in half lengthwise. In a skillet partially cook bacon until it begins to ruffle, but is still flexible. Drain on paper towels and let cool.

Wrap each scallop with a piece of partially cooked bacon and hold in place with a toothpick. Place the bacon-wrapped scallops in a wire broiler basket. Sprinkle top side with paprika.

Broil over *medium hot* coals for 5 minutes. Turn and sprinkle with paprika. Broil second side of scallops for 5 to 7 minutes or until bacon is crisp and brown. Serve while hot.

CHARCOAL BROILED SHRIMP

Another time use small shrimp and serve as an appetizer. Your guests won't mind waiting for the main course—

1 cup olive oil
¼ cup lemon juice
½ cup finely chopped
   onion
3 shallots, finely
   chopped
2 garlic cloves, minced

¼ cup finely snipped
   parsley
   • • •
1½ pounds large raw
   shrimp, peeled and
   deveined (about 2
   pounds in shell)

Combine olive oil, lemon juice, onion, shallots, garlic, and parsley. Marinate the shrimp in mixture in the refrigerator for several hours. Drain shrimp.

Place on aluminum foil over *medium hot* coals for about 6 to 8 minutes, on each side. Serve immediately. Serves 8 to 10.

MARINATED SWORDFISH STEAKS

A wine-flavored marinade keeps this firm-fleshed fish moist while broiling over charcoal. Brush again with marinade just before serving for added flavor—

¾ cup dry white wine
¼ cup lemon juice
½ teaspoon salt
Dash fresh ground black
   pepper
½ teaspoon dry
   mustard
   • • •

4 swordfish steaks,
   ¾ inch thick
   • • •
Salt
Pepper
2 tablespoons butter or
   margarine,
   softened

Combine wine, lemon juice, salt, pepper, and mustard. Marinate swordfish in mixture for 1 hour. Drain and reserve marinade.

Sprinkle swordfish with salt and pepper. Broil over

hot coals about 5 minutes. Turn and brush steaks with butter or margarine. Broil 5 to 7 minutes longer or until fish flakes. Brush both sides with butter or margarine. Remove to a warmed serving platter. Brush swordfish lightly with remaining marinade. Makes 4 servings.

HALIBUT HEAVEN

A delightfully different coating makes this recipe one to remember. Sour cream and sesame seeds team to make a spectacular dinner of halibut fillets—

1 1-pound package frozen halibut fillets	Pepper
• • •	• • •
	½ cup dairy sour cream
	¾ cup fine cornflake crumbs
2 tablespoons soy sauce	
1 teaspoon lemon juice	½ cup toasted sesame seeds
Salt	

Thaw halibut fillets until they come apart. Brush with mixture of soy sauce and lemon juice. Season with salt and pepper. Coat both sides of fillets with sour cream. Combine cornflake crumbs and sesame seeds. Roll fillets in crumb mixture. Place coated fillets in an oiled wire broiler basket. Broil over *medium* coals about 10 minutes, turning once. Makes 4 servings.

BARBECUED ROCK LOBSTER TAILS

The tang of orange peel and a few zippy spices make an exciting sea food sauce—

4 medium Rock lobster tails, frozen	1 teaspoon grated orange peel
• • •	Generous dash *each* ground ginger, aromatic bitters, and chili powder
¼ cup butter or margarine, melted	
2 teaspoons lemon juice	

Thaw Rock lobster tails and cut off thin undershell membrane with kitchen scissors. Bend tail back to crack shell or insert long skewers lengthwise between shell and meat to prevent curling. Combine melted butter, lemon juice, orange peel, ginger, bitters, and chili powder; brush over lobster meat.

Broil on grill over *hot* coals for about 5 minutes with meat side up. Turn shell side up, brush with sauce and continue to broil 5 to 10 minutes longer or until meat has lost its transparency and is opaque. Serve immediately. Makes 4 servings.

To broil lobster tails in range broiler: Prepare as above and place *shell side up* on broiler pan. Broil for about 5 minutes. Turn meat side up, brush with sauce, and continue to broil 5 to 10 minutes longer.

To butterfly: Partially thaw frozen lobster tails (about 30 minutes)—it's easier to cut through them while still a bit frozen. Snip through center of hard top shell with kitchen scissors. With sharp knife cut through the meat, but *not through under shell*. Spread open.

Broil with the meat side up at start; finish cooking with shell side up. While broiling, brush frequently with melted butter.

Lobster is done when you can flake it with a fork. Loosen meat: Insert fork between shell and meat. Dash with paprika before serving.

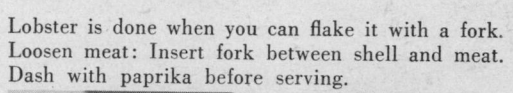

CHAPTER 2

SAUCES AND MARINADES

Compliment your favorite piece of charcoaled beef, pork, poultry, or sea food with a flavorful and colorful sauce. Select from a range of tangy tomato-spice blends to subtle sweet-sour combinations. Or choose a distinctive marinade to help tenderize a "less tender" cut of meat.

19th HOLE SAUCE

2 tablespoons instant
    onion
1 tablespoon brown
    sugar
1 tablespoon whole
    mustard seed
2 teaspoons paprika
1 teaspoon monosodium
    glutamate
1 teaspoon crushed
    oregano
1 teaspoon chili powder
1 teaspoon cracked
    pepper

½ teaspoon salt
½ teaspoon cloves
1 bay leaf
1 clove garlic, minced
1 cup catsup
½ cup water
¼ cup olive or salad oil
¼ cup tarragon vinegar
2 tablespoons wine
    vinegar
2 tablespoons Worces-
    tershire sauce
2 or 3 drops liquid
    smoke

Combine all ingredients, stirring well. Simmer gently 20 to 25 minutes or till the consistency you like. Remove bay leaf. Makes 2 cups sauce. Serve with roast pork or beef.

BAR-X BARBECUE SAUCE

Bacon is the surprise ingredient. Rich tasting with burgers or roasts—

½ pound sliced bacon
1 medium onion
1 medium green pepper
2 cans condensed
    tomato soup
⅔ cup catsup

½ cup Worcestershire
    sauce
½ cup water
1 tablespoon vinegar
1 tablespoon sugar
½ teaspoon salt

Put bacon, onion, and green pepper through food chopper, using medium blade. Add remaining ingredients and slowly bring to boiling. Simmer 2 hours. Makes 5 cups.

BARBECUE SAUCE—TEXAS STYLE

¼ cup vinegar
1 tablespoon Worcester-
    shire sauce
1 large onion, diced
2 cloves garlic, pressed
    or diced fine
Juice of 1 lemon
Grated peel of 1 lemon

½ cup catsup
½ teaspoon bottled hot
    pepper sauce
1 tablespoon salt
½ teaspoon chili
    powder
Dash sage

Combine ingredients; stir and simmer for 15 minutes.
Serve with broiled chicken or ribs.

EASY BASTING SAUCE

*Just the right flavor bite for outdoor specials, and speedy,
too! It's ready in no time—*

½ cup catsup
2 tablespoons vinegar
2 tablespoons honey
1 tablespoon prepared
    mustard

2 teaspoons kitchen
    bouquet
Dash bottled hot pepper
    sauce

Combine all ingredients; mix thoroughly. Use sauce
immediately, or store it in the refrigerator till needed.
    Use to baste burgers, steaks, chops, kabobs during
broiling. Makes ¾ cup sauce.

CHILI BARBECUE SAUCE

2 cups vinegar
2 cups catsup
½ cup sugar
1 tablespoon chili
    powder
1½ teaspoons salt

1½ teaspoons coarse
    black pepper
½ teaspoon barbecue
    spice
Bottled hot pepper
    sauce to taste

Combine all ingredients in a saucepan; simmer 30 minutes or till sauce is the consistency you prefer. Serve with franks or burgers.

QUICK BORDELAISE SAUCE '

A real chef's creation with a canned-gravy start. It does great things for a beef roast—

2 carrots, chopped fine
¼ cup butter or
    margarine
3 tablespoons instant
    minced onion
1 3-ounce can (⅔ cup)
    broiled sliced
    mushrooms,
    drained

⅓ to ½ cup cooking
    claret
1 can (1¼ cups) beef
    gravy
1 tablespoon lemon
    juice
½ teaspoon mono-
    sodium glutamate

Cook carrots in butter till tender. Add onion, mushrooms, and cooking claret. Simmer uncovered about 5 minutes. Add beef gravy, lemon juice, and monosodium glutamate; let simmer 5 minutes more.

WARREN'S BARBECUE SAUCE

For delicious ribs—it's the best sauce we've ever tasted!—

1 cup catsup
1 tablespoon Worcester-
    shire sauce
2 or 3 dashes bottled
    hot pepper sauce

1 cup water
¼ cup vinegar
1 tablespoon sugar
1 teaspoon salt
1 teaspoon celery seed

Combine all ingredients. Heat to boiling. Let simmer 30 minutes. Makes enough sauce for basting 4 pounds loin back ribs.

FRENCH QUARTER SAUCE

1 cup chopped onion
¼ cup salad oil
1 8-ounce can (1 cup)
    tomato sauce
½ cup water
¼ cup brown sugar
¼ cup lemon juice

3 tablespoons Worces-
    tershire sauce
2 tablespoons prepared
    mustard
2 teaspoons salt
¼ teaspoon pepper

Cook onion in hot oil until tender. Add remaining ingredients; simmer uncovered 15 minutes. Makes enough sauce to baste 4 pounds loin back ribs or spareribs.

CREOLE SAUCE

Adds the full, rich flavor of old Louisiana cooking—

¼ cup chopped onion
¼ cup chopped green
    pepper
2 tablespoons salad oil
        •   •   •
1 1-pound can (2 cups)
    tomatoes, drained

2 tablespoons chopped
    pimiento
1 tablespoon sugar
½ teaspoon salt
¼ teaspoon pepper

Cook onion and green pepper in salad oil till tender but not brown. Add remaining ingredients. Simmer about 20 minutes or till thick. Makes about 2 cups.

ONION SAUCE

Brown 2 tablespoons sugar in 1 tablespoon fat; add 2 medium onions, sliced; cook till almost tender. Add 1 tablespoon all-purpose flour; brown slightly.

Add 1 cup canned condensed beef broth, 1 tablespoon vinegar, salt to taste; cook till smooth. Makes about 2 cups sauce.

NO-COOK BARBECUE SAUCE

*You'll like this in winter, too, for an easy oven barbecue
—delicious with lamb—*

1 cup mayonnaise
1 6-ounce can (¾ cup)
   tomato paste
¼ cup vinegar
3 tablespoons Worces-
   tershire sauce
1 tablespoon chopped
   onion

1 tablespoon prepared
   horseradish
1 teaspoon salt
½ teaspoon pepper
½ teaspoon cayenne
¼ to ½ teaspoon
   bottled hot pepper
   sauce

Combine all ingredients; blend well. Makes 2 cups.
(This sauce may be stored several weeks in the refrigerator.)

PLANTATION HOT SAUCE

½ cup molasses
½ cup prepared
   mustard
½ cup vinegar or lemon
   juice

¼ cup Worcestershire
   sauce
2 teaspoons bottled hot
   pepper sauce
1 teaspoon salt

Blend molasses and prepared mustard; stir in remaining
ingredients. Heat to boiling. Makes enough sauce for
basting 4 pounds loin back ribs or spareribs.

SMOKY BARBECUE SAUCE

1 8-ounce can (1 cup)
   tomato sauce
1 4½-ounce bottle steak
   sauce

½ cup water
1 teaspoon celery seed
¼ teaspoon liquid
   smoke

Combine all ingredients. Makes about 2¼ cups sauce
or enough to baste about 4 pounds of spareribs.

SWEET-SOUR SAUCE

1 cup sugar
½ cup white vinegar
½ cup water
1 tablespoon chopped
  green pepper
1 tablespoon chopped
  pimiento

½ teaspoon salt
• • •
2 teaspoons cornstarch
1 tablespoon cold water
• • •
1 teaspoon paprika

In a saucepan, combine first 6 ingredients and simmer 5 minutes. Combine cornstarch and 1 tablespoon cold water; add to hot mixture, and cook and stir till sauce thickens. Cool slightly. Add paprika.

Use to baste broiled shrimp and pass extra. Makes about 1½ cups sauce.

PEPPY SEA-FOOD SAUCE

⅓ cup chili sauce
2 tablespoons lemon
  juice
1 tablespoon prepared
  horseradish

1 teaspoon Worcester-
  shire sauce
2 drops bottled hot
  pepper sauce

Combine ingredients and chill thoroughly. Serve with shrimp. Makes about ½ cup.

TARTARE SAUCE

Everyone's sea-food favorite—

1 cup mayonnaise or
  salad dressing
¼ teaspoon grated
  onion
1 tablespoon vinegar
• • •
⅓ cup sweet-pickle
  relish

⅓ cup chopped green
  olives
1 tablespoon chopped
  capers
1 teaspoon snipped
  parsley
Salt to taste

Blend mayonnaise, grated onion, and vinegar. Add remaining ingredients and blend well. Makes about 1½ cups sauce.

CAPER SAUCE

In a small mixing bowl, combine 1 cup mayonnaise and 1 tablespoon undrained capers. Serve with charcoal broiled trout.

CHICKEN BRUSH-ON SAUCE

Combine one 5-ounce bottle (⅔ cup) Worcestershire sauce, ½ cup salad oil, ¼ to ⅓ cup lemon juice, and 1 clove garlic, minced. Use as a basting sauce for chicken or turkey. Heat remaining sauce to pass in bowl. Makes about 1⅓ cups sauce.

WESTERN HOT SAUCE

In a saucepan, melt ½ cup butter or margarine. Add 1 tablespoon catsup, 2 tablespoons chopped green onion, 1 tablespoon Worcestershire sauce, 3 tablespoons steak sauce, ¼ teaspoon seasoned salt, and a dash *each* pepper and paprika. Heat sauce and serve with broiled steaks or hamburgers.

CRAN-BURGER SAUCE

Just the ticket when you want new spark for burgers or ham—

Combine one 1-pound can (2 cups) jellied cranberry sauce, ⅓ cup steak sauce, 1 tablespoon brown sugar, 1 tablespoon salad oil, and 2 teaspoons prepared mustard. Beat with electric or rotary beater (or blend in blender). Serve as is or heated.

SAVORY CHICKEN BARBECUE SAUCE

½ cup salad oil
1¼ cups water
2 tablespoons chopped
    onion
1 clove garlic, crushed
1½ teaspoons sugar
1 teaspoon salt
1 teaspoon chili powder
1 teaspoon paprika

1 teaspoon pepper
½ teaspoon dry
    mustard
Dash cayenne pepper
2 tablespoons vinegar
1 teaspoon Worcester-
    shire sauce
1 teaspoon bottled hot
    pepper sauce

Combine all ingredients. Simmer 30 minutes. As chicken broils, brush with sauce.

1-2-3 SAUCE

Barbecue flavor, lickety-split—

1 12-ounce bottle
    extra-hot catsup
2 teaspoons celery seed

3 tablespoons vinegar
1 clove garlic, halved

Combine ingredients; refrigerate for several hours. Remove garlic before serving. Makes about 1¼ cups sauce.

PIMIENTO SAUCE

½ cup mayonnaise or
    salad dressing
1 tablespoon catsup
2 teaspoons lemon juice
2 teaspoons prepared
    horseradish

½ teaspoon paprika
¼ teaspoon Worcester-
    shire sauce
2 tablespoons chopped
    pimiento

Combine ingredients and chill thoroughly. Serve with fish. Makes ¾ cup sauce.

JIFFY MUSTARD SAUCE

1 cup dairy sour cream
2 tablespoons prepared
  mustard

1 teaspoon prepared
  horseradish

Combine all ingredients. Chill till ready to serve. Makes
about 1 cup sauce.

HERB 'N HONEY BASTING SAUCE

*This sophisticated sauce has a fruit-juice base that's just
right with poultry—*

¾ cup finely chopped
  onion
1 clove garlic, minced
¼ cup salad oil or olive
  oil
1 12-ounce can pear
  nectar
½ cup white wine
  vinegar
¼ cup honey

2 tablespoons Worces-
  tershire sauce
1 teaspoon prepared
  horseradish
1 teaspoon dry mustard
1 teaspoon salt
½ teaspoon thyme
¼ teaspoon rosemary
¼ teaspoon pepper

Cook onion and garlic in hot oil till tender but not
brown. Add remaining ingredients; simmer uncovered
5 minutes. Use for marinating and basting poultry. Pass
extra sauce in a bowl. Makes 3¼ cups sauce.

HORSERADISH SAUCE

1 8-ounce package
  cream cheese
1 tablespoon sugar
2 to 3 tablespoons
  prepared horse-
  radish

1 tablespoon lemon
  juice
1 teaspoon Worcester-
  shire sauce
½ cup whipping cream,
  whipped

Soften cream cheese; blend in sugar, horseradish, lemon juice, and Worcestershire. Fold in whipped cream. Pass with ham, corned beef, and cold cuts. Makes 2 cups.

CHEESY MEAT TOPPER

Gradually add 2 tablespoons clear French dressing and 1 teaspoon Worcestershire sauce to 4 ounces (about 1 cup) blue cheese, crumbled; blend well.

Spread mixture on broiled steak or hamburger about 3 minutes before meat is done. Heat till cheese mixture bubbles; serve at once. Makes enough sauce for one 2-pound steak or 6 to 8 hamburgers.

WHIPPED ONION BUTTER

Combine ¼ cup butter or margarine, 1 teaspoon Worcestershire sauce, ¼ teaspoon dry mustard, and ¼ teaspoon cracked pepper. Cream mixture with a wooden spoon till fluffy. Stir in 2 tablespoons minced onion and 2 tablespoons finely snipped parsley. Pass at the table to spoon on piping-hot hamburgers or steaks. Makes ⅓ cup.

SAVORY ONION RELISH

Serve it with any meat—

2 cups thinly sliced onions	**2 teaspoons caraway seed**
1 cup wine vinegar	**Dash celery salt**
• • •	**½ cup mayonnaise**

Place onions in shallow dish. Pour vinegar over; chill 3 to 4 hours, turning onions frequently. Just before serving, drain off vinegar (save to use with salads later).

Sprinkle onions with caraway seed and celery salt. Add 2 tablespoons of the vinegar to mayonnaise and mix well. Mix onions and mayonnaise. Makes 8 servings.

PEPPER RELISH

2 large green peppers,
    ground
2 large sweet red
    peppers, ground
1 medium onion,
    ground

¼ cup sugar
1 teaspoon salt
1½ teaspoons mustard
    seed
⅓ cup cider vinegar

• • •

Pour boiling water over ground peppers and onions to
cover; cover with lid and let stand 20 minutes. Drain
well. Add remaining ingredients and simmer 15 minutes.
Chill well before serving. Makes 2 cups relish.

PEPPER BUTTER

Combine ½ cup softened butter or margarine, 1 tablespoon finely chopped green pepper, 1 tablespoon finely
snipped parsley, and 1 tablespoon finely chopped onion;
blend well. Form into a long roll; chill until butter is
firm. Slice and serve butter patties on broiled hamburgers
or steaks.

FRESH CHOP-CHOP

*Onto each frank pile catsup, mustard, and this crunchy
bit of garden. Yum!—*

1 cup finely chopped
    cabbage or head
    lettuce
½ cup finely diced
    tomato
¼ cup finely chopped
    onion

¼ cup finely chopped
    green pepper
¼ cup finely chopped
    celery

Combine ingredients; chill. Makes 2 cups.

GOSH AND GOLLY RELISH

Yep, it's hot!—

2 medium tomatoes,
    finely chopped and
    well drained
1 medium onion, finely
    chopped
1 small green pepper,
    finely chopped
3 or 4 small hot pickled
    Italian peppers,
    chopped (about 1
    tablespoon)

2 tablespoons sugar
½ teaspoon mustard
    seed
½ teaspoon celery seed
½ teaspoon salt

• • •

¼ cup white vinegar

Combine all ingredients except vinegar; cover with vinegar. Refrigerate for 24 hours. Makes about 2 cups relish.

SALSA

This traditional Mexican-style sauce is a must in peak tomato season. Serve as relish with meats and omelets—

4 medium firm-ripe
    tomatoes, peeled
    and finely chopped
½ cup finely chopped
    onion
½ cup finely chopped
    celery
¼ cup finely chopped
    green pepper
¼ cup olive oil or
    salad oil
2 tablespoons red wine
    vinegar

1 tablespoon mustard
    seed
1 teaspoon coriander
    seed, crushed
2 to 3 tablespoons
    drained canned
    finely chopped
    green chiles
1 teaspoon salt
Dash pepper

Mix all ingredients. Chill several hours or overnight. Makes 3 cups.

CONFETTI CORN RELISH

Fresh-tasting and bright. A snap to fix—

1 12-ounce can
    (1½ cups) whole
    kernel corn,
    drained
⅔ cup chopped celery
¼ cup French dressing
½ teaspoon salt

2 tablespoons chopped
    onion
2 tablespoons diced
    green pepper
1 tablespoon diced
    pimiento
1 tablespoon vinegar

Combine all ingredients; cover and refrigerate several hours. Makes 2 cups relish.

SUMMER RELISH

3 medium cucumbers
¼ cup grated onion
½ teaspoon pepper

1½ teaspoons salt
¼ cup cider vinegar
1 teaspoon dill seed

Put cucumbers through food chopper (medium-fine blade); drain. Add remaining ingredients; mix well. Chill in refrigerator at least 2 days before serving to let flavors blend. Makes about 2 cups relish.

TENDER-UP BEEF MARINADE

Adds a spicy flavor while a rump or chuck roast gets tender—

2½ cups vinegar
2½ cups water
3 onions, sliced
1 lemon, sliced

12 whole cloves
2 or 3 bay leaves
6 whole black peppers
1½ tablespoons salt

Combine ingredients; let stand at room temperature for 24 hours. Then add rump or chuck roast. For a mild flavor, let meat marinate 24 hours in refrigerator; for tendering action and more flavor, refrigerate in marinade 2 or 3 days.

RIPE-OLIVE RELISH

Gives flavor importance to plain burgers and frankfurters—

1 tablespoon instant minced onion	½ cup finely diced celery
1 tablespoon water	3 tablespoons salad oil
½ cup ripe olives	2 tablespoons vinegar
½ cup finely chopped dill pickle	¼ teaspoon salt
	¼ teaspoon pepper

Let instant onion stand in the water a few minutes. Cut olives in thin wedges. Combine all ingredients. For blend of flavors, let stand an hour or longer before serving. Chill if desired. Makes about 1½ cups.

FRESH CORN RELISH

4 cups (6 to 8 medium ears) fresh cut corn	½ cup chopped green pepper
2 cups chopped cabbage	2 tablespoons chopped pimiento
2 tablespoons chopped onion	
¾ cup vinegar	
½ cup water	
½ cup sugar	
½ envelope (1 tablespoon) French-style salad-dressing mix	

• • •

In a saucepan, combine first 7 ingredients. Simmer 20 minutes, stirring occasionally. Cool; add chopped pepper and pimiento. Serve cold. Makes 5 cups relish.

Marinades to Flavorize, Tenderize

The mating of a distinctive marinade with the smoky flavor of barbecued meat makes for a wonderful union. Choose any meat—beef, pork, poultry, lamb—and create a different flavor combination with each marinade you use. Flavor-wise and tender-wise a tangy marinade does great things for a less-tender (and less costly) cut of meat like rump or chuck roast. Or it makes a more special piece of meat simply exotic.

For gourmet flavor, let most marinades mellow at room temperature for 24 hours before adding meat. Marinades also make good sauces to pass with meat.

Two methods for marinating rump roast. Picture above, it's in the bag! Picture right, it's in the bowl! For this less-tender cut, marinate 2 or 3 days in the refrigerator before roasting.

ROSEMARY MARINADE

Combine ¼ cup salad oil, ¼ cup wine vinegar, 2 teaspoons salt, 2 teaspoons crushed rosemary, ½ teaspoon pepper, and ½ cup sliced onion.

Use to marinate lamb or chicken. Makes enough for 1½ to 2 pounds meat.

ARMENIAN HERB MARINADE

Combine ½ cup olive or salad oil, ¼ cup lemon juice, 1 teaspoon *each* salt, marjoram, and thyme, ½ teaspoon pepper, 1 clove garlic, minced, ½ cup chopped onion, and ¼ cup snipped parsley. Use to marinate lamb or chicken. Enough for 1½ to 2 pounds meat.

If meat is in plastic bag, twist top, knot and place on tray or shallow pan in refrigerator. If in a bowl, turn meat occasionally to tenderize and take on spicy marinade flavor.

GARLIC AND SOUR-CREAM MARINADE

1 cup dairy sour cream
1 tablespoon lemon
    juice
2 cloves garlic, crushed
¾ teaspoon white
    pepper

¾ teaspoon celery salt
½ teaspoon salt
½ teaspoon paprika
1 teaspoon Worcester-
    shire sauce

Combine ingredients. Pour over ready-to-cook broiler chicken (cut up), covering all pieces. Refrigerate overnight before broiling.

Use this marinade for extra-special steak, too. It's really delicious!

TERIYAKI MARINADE

⅔ cup soy sauce
¼ cup salad oil
6 cloves garlic, minced
2 teaspoons mono-
    sodium glutamate

2 teaspoons ginger *or*
    2 tablespoons
    grated gingerroot
2 teaspoons dry mustard
2 tablespoons molasses

Combine soy sauce, salad oil, garlic, monosodium glutamate, ginger, mustard, and molasses in a glass bowl. Let stand 24 hours at room temperature. Use to marinate lamb or tender beef. Enough for 2 pounds meat.

CHAPTER 3

THE WHOLE MEAL

Develop charcoal character in appetizers, meats, vegetables, breads, and desserts. Skewer your favorite food combinations for kabobs that are easily cooked and served. Wrap a meal in aluminum foil to heat evenly and hold in juicy goodness. Prepare sandwiches large or small and serve them piping hot from the grill.

Flavor Guide for

Meats

Poultry

Fish

Hamburger patties:
Enhance the flavor with
basil. Or try seasoning
with curry powder,
Worcestershire, garlic
salt, horseradish.

Chicken: Use paprika
with gusto. When meat is
almost done, drop a spiral
of orange or lemon peel
in the fire. Tantalizing!

Lamb chops: Sprinkle
with dill seed; broil to
perfection. Or give them
a gourmet touch with a
dash of marjoram.

Beef stew: Add subtle
flavor with basil. Or
simmer with mixed
vegetable flakes.

Fish fillets: Sprinkle
with marjoram or
tarragon before baking
or broiling.

Fish sauce: Add some
tarragon or tarragon
vinegar for a delightful
tang; stir in capers.

Salads

Vegetables

Green beans: Perk
up this old stand-by
with thyme or a pinch
of garlic salt.

Tossed salad:
Transform those greens
into a chef's delight . . .
add curry powder to an
oil-vinegar dressing (but
with caution).

Baked potatoes:
Sprinkle dill seed into
the opening of baked
potato. Or top crest of
potatoes with rosemary
or basil.

Eggplant dishes: Add
just enough basil or
thyme to enhance the
delicate eggplant flavor.

Coleslaw: For a special
treat, sprinkle with
caraway or dill seed.
Add bits of blue cheese
for wonderful flavor.

Peas: Drop in mint
flakes or leaves, a pinch
of savory, or dash of
nutmeg while they
are simmering.

Barbecue Seasonings

Eggs

Cheese

Breads

Appetizers

Desserts

Scrambled eggs:
Sprinkle lightly with
savory or tarragon.
Or season with
Worcestershire before
cooking.

**Tomato-juice
cocktail:** Try a pinch
of dill seed. Or use
a bit of oregano.

Cottage cheese: Add
onion salt, dill, or
caraway seed, as you like.

Consomme: Add dash
of allspice or savory.

Cheese spread:
Season snappy soft
cheese with thyme and
celery salt—a
complement to any
cracker.

Avocado spread: Mix
in dill seed. Serve with
potato chips.

Deviled eggs: Use
savory or tarragon and
mustard for peppy
flavor.

Grapefruit: Sprinkle
halves with ginger and
shredded coconut.

Sharp cheese: Shred
and sprinkle over hot
baked potatoes. Melts
instantly! Or use a
flavored soft cheese
spread.

Pineapple: Top slices
with cream cheese, add
a shake of cinnamon,
powdered cloves; then
broil.

Cream cheese: Blend
in basil or parsley flakes
for refreshing flavor.
Spread on rye.

Pears: Dot fresh or
canned pears with
butter; sprinkle with
sugar and cinnamon,
then broil.

(more)

Flavor Guide for

Meats

Poultry

Fish

Pork chops: Sprinkle
lightly with sage or
thyme. Or add a shake
of cinnamon.

Roast pork: Blend
marjoram and savory;
add to your basting
sauce. Or use rosemary
and a dash of garlic salt.

**Baked ham or corned
beef:** Stud with whole
cloves; or add mustard
and ground cloves to
honey for a glaze.

Salads

Vegetables

Potato salad: Season
with plenty of celery
seed. Or for subtle
flavor, cook potatoes
with onion and a bay leaf.

Acorn squash: Cut in
half; wrap in foil and bake
cut side down on grill.
Add lots of butter—
shake on cinnamon or
brown sugar.

Spinach: As it cooks,
sprinkle on rosemary,
marjoram, or tarragon.
Use fresh raw leaves
in a tossed salad.

ARMENIAN SHISH KEBAB

*Here's a traditional Near East marinade. Wonderful on
chicken halves or Rock Cornish game hens, too, for grill
broiling—*

½ cup olive or salad oil
¼ cup lemon juice
1 teaspoon salt
1 teaspoon marjoram
1 teaspoon thyme
½ teaspoon pepper
1 clove garlic, minced
½ cup chopped onion
¼ cup snipped parsley
•   •   •

2 pounds boneless
    lamb, cut in
    1½-inch cubes
•   •   •
Green peppers,
    quartered
Sweet red peppers,
    quartered
Thick onion slices

Barbecue Seasonings (continued)

Eggs

Cheese

Breads

Brown and serve rolls:
Skewer rolls to serve with
meat, vegetables, and
fruit. Makes the meal
complete.

Croutons: Toss toasted
bread cubes in melted
butter seasoned with
onion salt, marjoram,
and basil.

French bread: Slice
loaf or hard rolls; spread
on butter blended with
garlic salt, mustard, or
poultry seasoning. Wrap
in foil; heat.

Appetizers

Desserts

Baked apples: Core
and fill apples with brown
sugar and stick cinnamon.
Wrap in foil; bake over
hot coals.

Bananas: Peel and
sprinkle with brown sugar,
cinnamon, or nutmeg.
Wrap in foil and heat
over *slow* coals.

Donut holes: Cut
refrigerated biscuits (from
a tube) into fourths.
Thread on skewer or stick
and brown over coals.
Roll in cinnamon-sugar.

In deep bowl, combine first 9 ingredients for herb
marinade; mix well. Add meat cubes and stir to coat.
Refrigerate overnight or let stand at room temperature
2 or 3 hours, turning meat occasionally.

Fill skewers, alternating meat cubes with chunks of
green and red pepper and onion slices. Broil over *hot*
coals to medium rare doneness, brushing frequently with
melted butter or margarine. (Use rotating skewers or
turn often on grill.) Makes 6 servings.

LUNCH-ON-A-STICK

String 1½-inch squares of canned luncheon meat on
skewers along with quartered orange slices (cut thick
slices and leave peel on) and cooked or canned sweet
potatoes.

Broil over *slow* coals, turning frequently and brushing with Orange Glaze: Combine ½ cup brown sugar, ½ cup orange juice, ¼ cup vinegar, and 1 tablespoon prepared mustard; simmer uncovered 10 minutes.

MANDARIN DINNER

Cut canned luncheon meat in 1- to 1½-inch cubes. String on skewers with canned spiced crab apples and preserved kumquats. Broil over *slow* coals, turning frequently and brushing with Glaze: Melt 2 tablespoons butter or margarine; add ¼ cup brown sugar, ¼ cup crabapple or kumquat syrup, and 2 teaspoons lemon juice. Bring to boiling before brushing on meat and fruit.

MEXICAN BEEF KABOBS

Herbs and spices give that south-of-the-border taste to steak cubes—

½ cup chopped onion
1 tablespoon olive oil
1 cup wine vinegar
½ teaspoon salt
½ teaspoon crushed
   oregano
½ teaspoon cumin
½ teaspoon cloves

½ teaspoon cinnamon
½ teaspoon pepper
1 clove garlic, minced
1½ pounds round
   steak, cut in
   1½-inch cubes
Instant nonseasoned
   meat tenderizer

For sauce: Cook onion in hot oil until tender, but not brown. Add vinegar and seasonings; cover and simmer 20 minutes; cool.

Meanwhile sprinkle all surfaces of steak cubes with meat tenderizer as you would salt. *Do not use salt.* With fork, pierce deeply on all sides to work tenderizer in. Let stand 5 minutes at room temperature. Skewer meat; brush with sauce. Broil over *hot* coals, about 12 to 15 minutes for medium rare, turning frequently and basting often with sauce. Makes 4 or 5 servings.

SEA-FOOD SWORD

Two favorite shellfish take on that good soy flavor. Serve French fries and tomato salad—

¼ cup soy sauce
¼ cup salad oil
¼ cup lemon juice
¼ cup snipped parsley
½ teaspoon salt
Dash pepper

Fresh or frozen shrimp
Fresh or frozen scallops
Large stuffed green
  olives
Lemon wedges

• • •

Combine first 6 ingredients for basting sauce. Peel and devein shrimp, leaving last section of shell and tail intact. Add shrimp and scallops to basting sauce; let stand 1 hour at room temperature, stirring now and then. On skewers, alternate shrimp (put shrimp on skewers in pairs, turning the second one upside down and reversing direction), scallops, olives, and lemon. Broil over *hot* coals, turning and brushing sea food frequently with sauce. Don't overcook.

BEEF ANGUS KABOBS

Add 3 pounds lean beef round or chuck, cut in 1½-inch cubes, to California Marinade, turning to coat. Refrigerate 24 to 36 hours to give marinade time to tenderize beef; turn meat occasionally. Fill skewers, alternating meat with mushroom caps or other kabob tidbits. Broil over *hot* coals to rare or medium rare, brushing frequently with melted butter or margarine. (Use rotating skewers or turn often on grill.)

California Marinade: Combine 1 cup salad oil, ¾ cup soy sauce, ½ cup lemon juice, ¼ cup *each* Worcestershire sauce and prepared mustard, 1 tablespoon coarsely cracked pepper, and 2 cloves garlic, minced. Mix well to blend all ingredients.

ISLAND TERIYAKI

½ cup soy sauce
¼ cup brown sugar
2 tablespoons olive oil
1 tablespoon grated
   gingerroot *or*
   1 teaspoon dry
   ginger
½ teaspoon mono-
   sodium glutamate

¼ teaspoon cracked
   pepper
2 cloves garlic, minced
1½ pounds top sirloin
   steak, cut in strips
   ¼-inch thick and
   about 1-inch wide
Canned water chestnuts

Mix together first 7 ingredients. Add meat; stir to coat. Let stand 2 hours at room temperature. Lace meat accordion style on skewers; tip each end with water chestnut. Broil over *hot* coals 10 to 12 minutes; turn often and baste with marinade. Serves 4 or 5.

KAU KAU KABOBS

Beef and lobster kabobs, as served at the Hotel Royal Tahitian in Papeete, Tahiti, with a special sauce—

1½ pounds round
   steak, cut in
   1½-inch cubes
Instant meat tenderizer
   (seasoned)
6 7-ounce frozen rock-
   lobster tails,
   thawed and
   quartered

4 medium green
   peppers
Preserved kumquats

• • •

¼ cup sauterne
¼ cup lemon juice
¼ cup salad oil

Use meat tenderizer on meat cubes according to label directions. Cut sides from green peppers and trim to form ovals. Alternate beef, lobster, and green pepper ovals on 4 long or 8 medium skewers; finish off skewers with preserved kumquats, if desired.

Broil over *hot* coals about 20 minutes or till desired

doneness, turning often and basting with combined
sauterne, lemon juice, and salad oil. Serve kabobs with
Sauce Moorea. Makes 8 servings.

HAWAIIAN HAM ON A STICK

*Ham cubes lusciously glazed; pineapple hot and almost
caramelized—*

String 1½-inch squares of boneless fully cooked ham on
skewers along with quarters of pineapple. While broiling
over *slow* coals, brush cut sides of pineapple with melted
butter or margarine and daub ham with Honey-Orange
Glaze: Combine 1 cup brown sugar, ½ cup honey, and
½ cup orange juice. (Use rotating skewers or turn
kabobs often on grill.)

PICNIC PIGGIES

String skewer with brown-and-serve sausages, peach
halves with a cherry in center, and mushroom caps.
Brush generously with melted butter. Broil 4 to 5 inches
from heat for about 5 minutes on each side.

MILE-LONG SANDWICHES

Cut frankfurters in fourths. Thread one end of a
bacon slice on a skewer and weave over and under
chunks of frankfurters. Add large Bologna or salami
slices folded in fans, and dill-pickle chunks. (Another
time use pineapple chunks.) Repeat. Cook 4 to 5 inches
from heat for about 15 minutes, turning frequently.

Open a coney roll and scoot off as many pieces of
frankfurter, Bologna or salami, and pickle as you can
eat. Pass catsup and mustard. Long skewers hold enough
food for about three sandwiches. Use short skewers
for individual sandwich servings.

SAUCE MOOREA

3 tablespoons tarragon
    vinegar
1 teaspoon finely
    chopped onion
15 crushed peppercorns

• • •

1 tablespoon water
3 egg yolks, beaten

• • •

½ cup butter or
    margarine, melted

2 tablespoons tomato
    puree
1 tablespoon lemon
    juice
¼ teaspoon crushed
    tarragon leaves
Dash salt
Dash cayenne pepper

In a saucepan, combine vinegar, chopped onion, and crushed peppercorns. Boil gently till most of vinegar has evaporated. Cool; stir in water and strain.

Place beaten egg yolks in top of double boiler; add strained mixture. Place over hot, not boiling, water; cook, stirring constantly, till thick and creamy. Remove from water; stir till slightly cooled. *Gradually* stir in melted butter or margarine. Blend in tomato puree, lemon juice, crushed tarragon leaves, salt, and cayenne pepper. Makes 1 cup sauce. Serve with Kau Kau Kabobs.

HICKORY LAMB KABOBS

2 pounds boneless lamb
    shoulder, cut in
    1½-inch cubes
3 medium green
    peppers

• • •

1 can condensed onion
    soup

½ cup chili sauce
2 tablespoons salad oil
1 tablespoon vinegar
1 teaspoon salt
Dash bottled hot pepper
    sauce

Run skewers through piece of lamb fat. Alternate lamb and green pepper (cut in eighths to make squares) on skewers, leaving a little "elbowroom" between each piece so that meat will cook evenly.

Combine remaining ingredients for sauce; heat. Broil meat slowly over *hot* coals with hickory 20 to 30 minutes, brushing occasionally with sauce. (Use rotating skewers or turn kabobs often.) Pass sauce. Serves 4.

MARINATED BEEF CUBES

½ cup salad oil
¼ cup vinegar
¼ cup chopped onion
1 teaspoon salt
1 teaspoon coarsely
    ground or cracked
    pepper
2 teaspoons Worcester-
    shire sauce
    or steak sauce

2 pounds lean beef
    round or chuck,
    cut in 1½-inch
    cubes

• • •

In deep bowl, combine all ingredients except meat; mix well. Add meat to the marinade and stir to coat. Refrigerate overnight or let stand at room temperature 2 or 3 hours, turning meat occasionally. Serves 6.

MARINATED LAMB SQUARES

2 envelopes garlic
    salad-dressing mix
⅔ cup chopped onion
¾ cup chopped celery
    tips and leaves
⅓ cup vinegar
½ cup salad oil

½ cup cooking sherry
1 tablespoon Worces-
    tershire sauce
2 pounds boneless
    lamb, cut in
    1½-inch cubes

In deep bowl, combine all ingredients but meat; mix well. Add meat to the marinade and stir to coat. Refrigerate overnight or let stand at room temperature 2 or 3 hours, turning meat occasionally. Serves 6.

DAD'S DELIGHT

Combine ½ cup salad oil, ¼ cup vinegar, ¼ cup chopped onion, 1 teaspoon salt, dash pepper, and 2 teaspoons Worcestershire sauce; mix well. Add 2 pounds lean beef round, chuck, or sirloin, cut in 1- to 1½-inch cubes. Let meat marinate at least 2 hours, turning occasionally.

String on a long skewer a whole fresh mushroom, a cube of beef, and a ½-inch slice of cucumber. Repeat, saving room at end of skewer for tiny tomatoes.

Place skewers 4 to 5 inches from heat; cook about 25 minutes, turning frequently and basting often with marinade. The last 5 minutes of cooking, add tiny tomatoes to the end of skewer. Makes 6 servings.

COCKTAIL TOTEMS

There's a trick to making meat balls stay on the skewer: evaporated milk—

Kabob Meat Balls:
  2 tablespoons instant minced onion
  ¼ cup evaporated milk
  • • •
  ½ pound ground beef
  1 egg
  ½ cup fine cracker crumbs
  ½ teaspoon salt

  3 dashes bottled hot pepper sauce
  • • •
Canned or packaged cocktail franks
Large stuffed green olives
¼ cup butter or margarine, melted
Dash liquid smoke

Soak instant onion in evaporated milk a few minutes. Thoroughly combine meat and egg; add crumbs, milk, salt, and hot pepper sauce, mixing well. Shape in 1-inch balls—recipe makes about 16. For totem pole effect, fill skewers in this order: meat ball, 2 cocktail franks (threaded crosswise), stuffed olive. Combine butter and liquid smoke; brush on kabobs. Rotate over *hot* coals about 5 minutes or till meat balls are done, brushing frequently with smoke-butter.

BACON-CHEESE BITES

Wrap 1-inch cubes of sharp process American cheese in partially cooked slices of bacon. Rotate over coals, till bacon is done and cheese is melted—takes just a few minutes.

WESTERN STARTER

Can't beat this for a sophisticated appetizer—artichoke hearts, bacon-wrapped chicken livers, water chestnuts!—

Let canned artichoke hearts stand in Italian salad dressing for several hours. Slice canned water chestnuts in thirds. Cut chicken livers in slices slightly larger than the chestnut slices; dip in soy sauce. Sandwich a piece of chestnut between two slices of chicken liver; wrap with a half slice of bacon and fasten with toothpick. Alternate bacon-wrapped chicken livers and artichoke hearts on skewers. Rotate over *hot* coals about 7 minutes or till chicken livers are done and bacon is crisp.

BEST FRANKFURTERS KABOBS

1 pound (8 to 10)
   frankfurters, cut in
   1-inch slices
1 cup 1-inch slices celery
1 cup 1-inch slices onion

1 cup 1-inch squares
   green pepper
• • •
1 recipe Soy-sauce
   Marinade

Soak frankfurters and vegetables at room temperature for 3 hours in Soy-sauce Marinade: Combine ½ cup soy sauce, ⅓ cup catsup, ¼ cup salad oil, ¼ cup vinegar, 1 teaspoon thyme, and 1 teaspoon prepared mustard. Alternate the meat and vegetable slices on skewers. Broil kabobs 5 minutes on each side, brushing occasionally with Soy-sauce Marinade. Makes 6 servings.

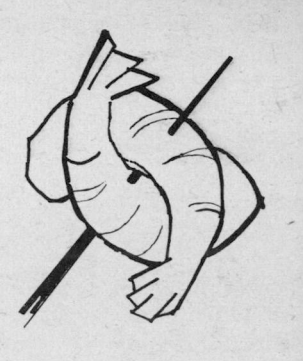

Skewer your shrimp in "shrimp-kin" style, as shown at right. Pair them—just turn the second upside down and reverse its direction.

SHRIMP-KIN

A piping-hot shrimp cocktail—

¾ cup chopped onion
½ cup salad oil
¾ cup catsup
¾ cup water
⅓ cup lemon juice
3 tablespoons sugar
3 tablespoons Worcestershire sauce

2 tablespoons prepared mustard
2 teaspoons salt
¼ teaspoon bottled hot pepper sauce

• • •

Fresh or frozen shrimp

For sauce cook onion in salad oil until tender but not brown; add next 8 ingredients, and simmer uncovered 15 minutes. Peel and devein shrimp, leaving last section of shell and tail intact. Brush with sauce. Rotate over *hot* coals until shrimp are done, about 5 to 8 minutes, brushing frequently with the sauce. Pass bowl of remaining sauce (recipe makes about 2½ cups).

APPETIZER HAM KABOBS

Spread thin boiled ham slices lightly with prepared mustard. Fold each slice in thirds, then cut in half or thirds to make bite-size pieces. String the ham fold-ups on skewers, alternating with stuffed green olives and cooked or canned small whole onions. Brush all generously with bottled Italian salad dressing. Broil over *hot* coals, about 5 minutes or till barbecue-y, turning and brushing frequently with Italian dressing.

GRILL FRILLS

Fun to do and fun to eat. The frills are Bologna "packages" of cheese or pickle—

For each appetizer: Spread a big Bologna slice with prepared mustard and center with ½-inch cube of sharp process American cheese. Enclose cheese by barely overlapping two opposite sides of meat; repeat with the two remaining sides to make "frill." Now push skewer through to hold together. Make another frill from Bologna slice centered with a slice of candied dill pickle. Intersperse frills on skewer with squares of green pepper, cooked tiny whole onions, and stuffed green olives. Broil over *hot* coals about 10 minutes or till lightly browned, brushing frequently with Italian dressing.

SUKIYAKI SKEWERS

⅓ cup soy sauce
¼ cup sugar
1 teaspoon fresh grated
    ginger *or* ¼ tea-
    spoon powdered
    ginger

1 pound sirloin tip, cut
    in thin strips
½ pound fresh whole
    green beans
4 large carrots, cut into
    3-inch sticks

For marinade combine soy sauce, sugar, and ginger. Add meat and let stand 1 to 2 hours. Meanwhile cook vegetables till barely tender. Wrap half the meat strips around bundles of 3 or 4 beans; repeat with remaining meat and carrot sticks.

Thread kabobs on 2 parallel skewers, ladder-fashion. Brush with melted butter. Broil about 5 minutes, turning once.

INDOOR-OUTDOOR KABOBS

1 envelope or can *dry*
    onion soup mix
¼ cup sugar
1 cup catsup
1 cup water
½ cup vinegar
½ cup salad oil
2 tablespoons prepared
    mustard
2 slices lemon
½ teaspoon salt

Bottled hot pepper
    sauce
1 pound round steak,
    cut in 1-inch cubes
4 medium potatoes,
    partially cooked
    and quartered
Instant nonseasoned
    meat tenderizer
2 green peppers, cut in
    large pieces

For sauce, combine first 9 ingredients with several dashes bottled hot pepper sauce. Bring to boiling; reduce heat, simmer 20 minutes. Cool completely. Then add meat

The ginger-soy sauce marinade gives thin strips of sirloin an Oriental tang. Cooked green beans and carrot sticks are the filling for these little bundles. Thread kabobs ladder-fashion.

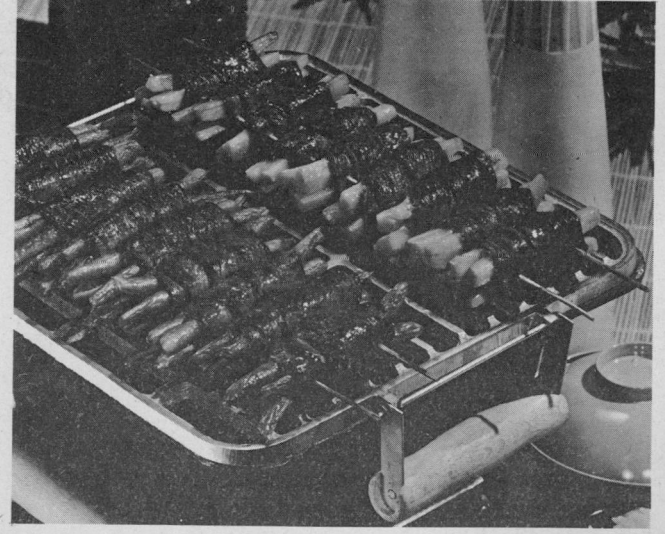

and potatoes; stir to coat. Marinate 2 to 3 hours. Remove meat; tenderize according to label directions.

Thread on skewers with vegetables. Broil 5 inches from heat about 15 minutes; brush with sauce occasionally, turning once. Heat extra sauce to pass. Makes 4 servings.

LAMB 'N HAM KABOBS

¼ cup salad oil	1 pound lamb, cut in
¼ cup dry red wine	1½-inch cubes
¼ cup soy sauce	½ pound ham, cut in
¼ cup tarragon vinegar	1-inch cubes
2 tablespoons chopped	1 medium onion, sliced
green pepper	and separated in
Dash pepper	rings
1 clove garlic, crushed	

Combine first 7 ingredients; add lamb, ham, and onions. Stir to coat. Let stand 2 to 3 hours, turning meat occasionally. Alternate lamb and ham on skewers. Broil about 5 inches from heat 15 minutes or till done. Heat marinade to pass. Makes 4 servings.

DEVILED MUSHROOM APPETIZERS

Guests won't mind waiting when you serve these savory starters—

Wash 12 large fresh mushrooms; trim off tips of stems. Remove stems, chop, and reserve. Melt 2 tablespoons butter in skillet; add mushroom caps and cook till tender. Remove caps from skillet and add stems and 2 tablespoons finely chopped onion; cook till tender. Stir in one 2¼-ounce can deviled ham, 1 tablespoon dry bread crumbs, and dash *each* pepper and *fines herbes*.

Place 1 tablespoon of mixture between 2 mushroom caps; thread on skewers. Repeat. Brush with melted butter. Broil over *hot* coals 2 to 3 minutes, turning often and brushing with melted butter. Serves 6.

RANCHER'S SHISH-KABOBS

Hefty squares of marinated lamb are wrapped in bacon and lined up with onions, olives, and green-pepper wedges on skewers—

Cut lamb in 1½- to 2-inch cubes. Let stand 1 hour in Tangy Marinade as directed below. Remove meat and wrap each cube with bacon. Thread skewer with meat cubes, small whole onions, pitted ripe olives, and green-pepper wedges. Cook 4 to 5 inches from heat 15 minutes; turn and cook about 15 minutes longer.

Brush with Marinade while cooking, if desired. Add tomato quarters to end of skewer for the last few minutes of cooking time. They need very little broiling.

Tangy Marinade: Combine ¾ cup hot water, ⅓ cup soy sauce, ¼ cup honey, 2 tablespoons salad oil, 2 tablespoons lemon juice, and 4 cloves garlic, crushed. Makes about 1½ cups. Use to marinate lamb.

SEA-FOOD KABOBS

Each green pepper side is carved in an oval—preventing burned corners on finished kabobs. Use leftover pepper in a tossed salad—

4 king crab legs (about 3½ pounds, unshelled)	4 medium green peppers
	• • •
5 medium onions	¼ cup lemon juice
4 medium tomatoes, quartered	¼ cup butter, melted

Remove crab meat from cracked shells and cut in 2-inch pieces. Peel and quarter onions; make each quarter into a "cup" by removing center. Slice off the 4 sides of each green pepper; trim each side to form an oval (no corners to char).

On 4 skewers (about 12 inches long), string pieces of

onion, crab, tomato, and green pepper. Combine lemon juice and butter; brush over crab and vegetables. Broil about 3 inches from heat for 7 minutes. Turn; brush with lemon juice and butter mixture, and broil 7 minutes longer. Makes 4 servings. Pass drawn butter and lemon wedges.

Another kabob tip: Set up a kabob assembly line! Instead of filling one skewer at a time, lay all skewers in a row. Thread the first ingredient on *each* skewer; repeat with each ingredient till skewers are filled.

SHORE DINNER

Partially cook frozen lobster tails by simmering in salted water 10 minutes. With scissors, snip each lobster shell open, remove meat, and cut in thirds. Peel and devein shrimp, leaving last section of shell and tail intact. String the following on rotating skewers: lobster chunks, shrimps, scallops, cherry tomatoes, and stuffed green olives.

Brush with lemon butter (1 part lemon juice to 2 parts melted butter). Sprinkle with salt. Place rotating skewers on grill. Broil till sea food is done, about 8 to 10 minutes, brushing frequently with lemon butter. Before serving, sprinkle with snipped parsley. Serve piping hot with Tartare Sauce (see index listing).

KEY WEST KABOBS

Shrimp and scallops on skewers: zesty soy sauce for stepped-up flavor—

¼ cup soy sauce
¼ cup salad oil
¼ cup lemon juice
¼ cup snipped parsley
½ teaspoon salt
Dash pepper
1 pound fresh or frozen
    (thawed) shrimp,
    cleaned

1 12-ounce package
    fresh or frozen
    (thawed) scallops
Stuffed green olives
Lemon wedges

Combine first 6 ingredients. Marinate shrimp and scallops in mixture for 1 hour. Alternate scallops, large stuffed green olives, lemon wedges, and shrimp on oiled skewers. Brush generously with soy mixture before broiling and frequently while broiling to keep shrimp and scallops moist. Broil 2 to 4 inches from heat 2 to 3 minutes on each side. Broil just long enough to brown scallops; overcooking toughens them. Serve with additional sauce. Makes 4 to 6 kabobs.

Cook Your Meal in Foil

Here's a real adventure in eating. The whole meal or each person's meal is packaged, cooked, and served in foil. The blend of flavors is absolutely delicious!

Cook these supper "kits" over the coals on an outdoor grill. Just arrange the foods in their wrappings (hours ahead, if you like) and stow in refrigerator till time to cook. Serve packages on paper plates (paper ones for no cleanup) and let each hungry diner open his own. Or you can open all and tuck a sprig of parsley in each for fresh color.

An added plus: If guests are late, dinner will keep warm in foil, not dry out.

To go with these easy meals, serve a simple salad or fresh relishes and pickles. Pass a basket of hard rolls (heated in foil). For dessert, how about fresh fruit? Mm-mmm.

FOILED VEGETABLES

Place one block of frozen vegetables on a large square of foil. Season; top with a butter pat. Wrap as shown, leaving space for expansion of steam. Place over *hot* coals 10 to 15 minutes. Turn occasionally.

Here's how to foil-wrap and to open your package

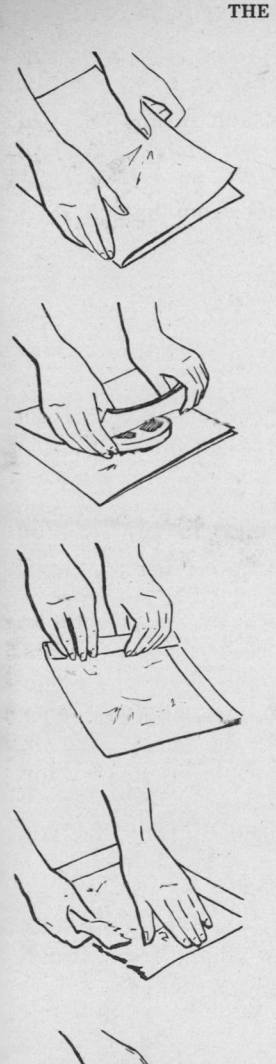

If using the regular 12-inch-wide aluminum foil, cut off twice length required to wrap food; fold double. Or use single thickness of 18-inch-wide heavy-duty foil.

Place food on top of foil just a bit off-center. Then bring the foil up over food, as shown, so edges meet on 3 open sides. Now you're ready to make a tight seal.

Take hold of one of the open sides (have the edges even) and fold toward food, 2 or more times, in ½ inch folds; press hard. Repeat on all sides for snug package.

Dinner's ready! Time to open your meal in a package. Foil cools in a hurry—just tear off the folded "zippers" by hand. Or snip 'em off with kitchen scissors.

Here's another easy way to get to a foil-wrapped dinner. Leave folded edges intact; cut a big crisscross in top of package. Fold the foil back and you're all set.

CAMPFIRE POT ROAST

4 pounds blade pot roast, 1½ inches thick

1 or 2 branches celery, sliced on bias

6 small whole carrots

1 medium green pepper, cut in rings

2 medium onions, quartered

2 firm medium tomatoes, in wedges

Brown roast on greased grill over *hot* coals with damp hickory added, about 15 minutes. Season well with salt and pepper. Tear off 5-foot length of aluminum foil; fold double. Place meat in center and cover with vegetables; generously salt and pepper. Fold foil over and seal securely; bake over *slow* coals 1½ to 2 hours or till tender. Pass bowl of 19th Hole Sauce (see index listing).

Campfire Pot Roast is the man's version of his wife's on-the-range pot roast. Snip open foil and whiff the mouth-watering aroma of beef browned over hickory, then wrapped up to cook vegetables.

PATIO FIESTA DINNER

Corn chips add crunch to a Mexican stew—

½ cup finely chopped
    onion
1 clove garlic, minced
3 tablespoons olive oil
1 10-ounce can (1¼
    cups) tomato puree
½ cup water
1 tablespoon all-purpose
    flour
1 to 2 tablespoons chili
    powder
1 teaspoon salt
¼ teaspoon oregano
¼ teaspoon cumin
1 pound boneless lean
    beef chuck, cut in
    1-inch cubes
1 12-ounce can (1½
    cups) whole kernel
    corn, drained

1 10-ounce package
    frozen baby Limas
1 medium onion, sliced
    and separated in
    rings
1 medium green
    pepper, sliced in
    rings
1 cup shredded sharp
    process American
    cheese
¼ cup finely chopped
    onion
1 6-ounce package
    corn chips

Cook ½ cup chopped onion and the garlic in hot oil till tender, add tomato, water, flour, and seasonings; simmer 10 minutes, stirring occasionally. Tear off four 12-inch lengths of 18-inch-wide foil. On each, place one-fourth of the meat, top with vegetables. Drizzle each serving with about ½ cup sauce. Bring edges of foil up, and leaving room for expansion of steam, seal well with double fold. Place packets on grill and cook over the coals till meat is tender about 1½ hours, turning once.

To serve: Cut a big crisscross in top of packets and fold foil back. Sprinkle each dinner with cheese, chopped onion, and corn chips. Makes 4 servings.

CINNAMON APPLES

Here's the perfect ending to your meal—

For each serving: Cut off a 24-inch length of aluminum foil and fold in half. Place one cored large tart baking apple in center of foil; fill hole with 1 tablespoon *each* of red cinnamon candies and seedless raisins. Dot with butter or margarine.

Bring foil up loosely over apple and twist ends together to seal well. Cook foil package over glowing coals till done. Serve warm with cream, if desired.

CHUCK-WAGON SPECIAL

Peek into your surprise package. Then pitch into that lusty fare. Wonderful, rich beef flavor; vegetables done just right—

Chili sauce
All-purpose flour *or*
   quick-cooking
   tapioca

• • •

Small onions
Large baking potatoes

Medium carrots
Celery
Beef sirloin tip, cut in
   1-inch cubes
Monosodium glutamate
Salt and pepper

For each serving: Cut off 36-inch length of aluminum foil and fold in half. Combine 2 tablespoons chili sauce and 2 teaspoons all-purpose flour (*or* 1 teaspoon quick-cooking tapioca); spread just off-center on foil. On sauce, arrange 3 peeled onions, 2 pieces pared and quartered potato, 1 pared and quartered carrot, and 1 medium branch celery cut in several pieces.

Top with about ⅓ pound beef cubes; sprinkle with ½ teaspoon monosodium glutamate, ¾ teaspoon salt, and dash pepper. Fold foil according to directions on page 145. Cook over glowing coals about 1 hour, or till all is tender and done. Serve from the grill in foil package.

PORK CHOP TREAT

Help yourself to a foil package of pork chops and acorn squash—

Acorn squashes, cut in half	**Pork chops, 1 inch thick**
Butter or margarine	**Salt and pepper**
Brown sugar	

. . .

For each serving: Cut off 50-inch length of aluminum foil and fold in half. Place ½ acorn squash, cut side up, just off-center of foil; dot with 1 tablespoon butter and sprinkle with 1 tablespoon brown sugar. Place one pork chop on squash; sprinkle with ¼ teaspoon salt and dash pepper.

Fold foil according to directions on opposite page. Cook over glowing coals, 1½ hours, or till the pork chop is tender and well done. Serve in foil package.

CHICKEN-IN-THE-GARDEN

Dark and light meat all beautifully browned and tender. Rice is hiding underneath—

Ready-to-cook broiler chicken, cut in pieces	**Packaged precooked rice**
Medium potatoes	**Worcestershire sauce**
Medium tomatoes	**Salt and pepper**
Medium onions	**Paprika**
Fresh mushrooms	**Butter or margarine**
Green peppers	

. . .

For each serving: Cut off 40-inch length of aluminum foil and fold in half. Just off-center on foil, place: 2 or 3 pieces chicken, 1 pared potato, 1 tomato, 1 peeled onion,

2 mushroom caps, and 2 green-pepper rings. Sprinkle with 2 tablespoons rice, 1 teaspoon Worcestershire sauce, ¾ teaspoon salt, dash pepper, paprika. Dot with butter.

Fold foil according to directions on page 145. Cook over glowing coals, about 1¼ hours, or till all is tender, turning package every 20 to 30 minutes.

NANI LUAU (BEAUTIFUL FEAST)

1 14-ounce can (1¾ cups) chicken broth
1½ cups fresh or bottled coconut milk*

• • •

2 fresh pineapples
3 ½-inch ham slices, halved (about 3 pounds)
5 pounds yams, cooked just tender, peeled, and halved lengthwise

2 oranges, sliced
1 lime, sliced
1½ pounds (6 cups) Chinese podded peas** or 3 7-ounce packages frozen Chinese pea pods

• • •

¾ cup orange marmalade
6 tablespoons butter or margarine
⅓ cup light corn syrup

Pour broth and coconut milk into a 24-inch coolie pan. Place a trivet or cake rack over liquid in center of coolie pan. Remove top from one of the pineapples and reserve. Pare whole pineapple and place on center of rack. Pare remaining pineapple and cut in wedges; remove core. Arrange pineapple wedges, ham slices, yams, orange and lime slices around whole pineapple. Cover with barbecue or coolie pan cover or with foil fitted closely around edge; steam 30 minutes.

Remove cover and arrange podded peas around other ingredients. Sprinkle peas and yams with salt; brush ham, yams, and fruits with *half* the Glaze. Replace cover and steam 30 minutes longer.

Brush all ingredients except peas with remaining Glaze.

Brush peas with a small amount of melted butter. Replace top of whole pineapple. Serves 10 to 12.

Glaze: Combine marmalade, butter, and corn syrup in saucepan. Heat and stir until mixture is well blended.

---

*If using fresh coconut milk, reserve coconut meat to grate and serve over fresh fruit for dessert.

**You eat these, pods and all. Cook like green beans. Edible podded peas, also called podded sugar peas in seed catalogs, are a favorite with home gardeners.

SUKIYAKI

2 to 4 ounces dry bean
    threads (optional)
Few small pieces beef
    suet
1 pound beef tender-
    loin, sliced paper-
    thin (across the
    grain)
2 tablespoons sugar
1 teaspoon mono-
    sodium glutamate
½ cup soy sauce
½ cup beef stock
2 cups 2-inch lengths
    bias-cut green
    onions
1 cup 2-inch bias-cut
    celery slices

½ cup thinly sliced
    fresh mushrooms
1 5-ounce can (⅔ cup)
    water chestnuts,
    drained and thinly
    sliced
1 5-ounce can (⅔ cup)
    bamboo shoots,
    slivered or diced,
    drained
5 cups small spinach
    leaves or 2-inch
    lengths (stems
    removed)
1 1-pound can (2 cups)
    bean sprouts,
    drained
Hot cooked rice

Prepare bean threads ahead by soaking 2 hours in cold water; drain.

Just before cooking time, arrange meat and vegetables attractively on large platter. Have small containers of sugar, monosodium glutamate, soy sauce, and beef stock handy. For "toss-stirring" you'll want to use two tools at once—big spoon and fork.

Preheat large (12-inch) skillet (or Oriental saucepan);

add suet and rub it over bottom and sides to grease; when you have about 2 tablespoons melted fat, remove suet. Add beef and cook briskly, turning it over and over, 1 or 2 minutes or just till browned. Now sprinkle meat with sugar and monosodium glutamate; pour soy sauce and beef stock over. Push meat to one side. Let soy mixture bubble over high heat.

Keeping in separate groups, add onions, celery, and mushrooms. Continue cooking and toss-stirring *each group* over high heat about 1 minute; push to one side. Keeping in separate groups, add bean threads and remaining vegetables. Cook and toss-stir each food just until heated through. Serve with rice. Pass soy sauce. Makes 4 servings.

BAKED SHOESTRING POTATOES

Baked to mellow perfection in a creamy cheese sauce; there's plenty for four—

4 medium baking
   potatoes, pared

• • •

3 tablespoons butter or
   margarine
1½ teaspoons salt
Dash pepper

½ cup grated sharp
   process American
   cheese
2 tablespoons snipped
   parsley
½ cup light cream

Cut a 48-inch length of aluminum foil and fold in half. Cut the potatoes into thin lengthwise strips as for French fries and place just off-center on the foil. Dot with butter or margarine; sprinkle with salt, pepper, cheese, and parsley. Pull edges of foil upward; pour cream over the potatoes.

Fold foil according to directions on page 145. Cook over glowing coals about 1 hour, or till done. Fold back edges of foil and sprinkle potatoes with extra snipped parsley. Makes 4 servings.

SAUCY POT ROAST

4 pounds pot roast, 1½ inches thick	**¾ cup catsup**
3 tablespoons all-purpose flour	**1 tablespoon Worcestershire sauce**
1 tablespoon brown sugar	**1 tablespoon vinegar**
1 teaspoon salt	**• • •**
Dash pepper	**1 or 2 branches celery, sliced on bias**
½ teaspoon dry mustard	**1 or 2 carrots, sliced**
	1 medium onion, sliced

Brown roast slowly over *hot* coals with hickory added, 20 to 30 minutes. Season. Combine next 8 ingredients for sauce. Fold 5-foot length of foil double. Spoon *half* of sauce in center of foil. Place meat atop; cover with vegetables and remaining sauce. Seal foil. Bake over *slow* coals (have a double thickness of extra foil on grill) 1½ to 2 hours or till tender. Serves 6.

DIXIE DINNER

Ham slice baked with orange marmalade and clove-studded pineapple ring atop. Come serving time, tuck in a pickled crab apple or two and some water cress for color—

Fully-cooked ham slice, 1-inch thick	**Whole cloves**
Orange marmalade *or* brown sugar and prepared mustard	**Canned pineapple slices, drained**
	Butter or margarine
• • •	**Large sweet potatoes**

For each serving: Cut off 32-inch length of aluminum foil and fold in half. Place serving-size piece of ham just off-center of foil; top with about 2 tablespoons orange marmalade *or* spread each serving of ham with a mixture of 2 tablespoons brown sugar and 1 teaspoon prepared mustard.

Stick a clove or two into drained pineapple slice and place on meat; dot with butter. Arrange 2 pieces pared and quartered sweet potato at side of ham.

Fold foil according to directions on page 145. Cook over glowing coals 1 hour, or till potato is done. For serving, open packages and tuck in a pickled crab apple and a sprig of water cress, if desired.

BEAN BAG

4 frankfurters
Liquid smoke

1 6-ounce roll process
sharp cheese food,
sliced

• • •

1 1-pound can or jar
(2 cups) pork and
beans in molasses
sauce

• • •

Tear off a 3-foot length of 18-inch-wide aluminum foil and fold in half to make a square. Arrange franks in a square in center of foil; brush lightly with liquid smoke. Empty beans in center. Bring up corners of foil and twist top as on a paper bag. Heat on grill over *slow* coals till hot, about 35 minutes.

Open foil and circle the cheese slices over beans and franks. Let heat a few minutes till cheese begins to melt. Crumple foil down to make a serving dish. Serves 4.

HOBO POPCORN

Foil takes this All-American favorite to the back-yard barbecue—

For 4 servings, cut an 18-inch square heavy-duty foil into 4 squares. In center of each, place 1 teaspoon salad oil and 1 tablespoon popcorn. Bring the 4 corners of foil to center, making pouch like hobo knapsack. Seal edges well. With string, tie corners of each pouch to long-handled barbecue tool or green stick. Place pouch directly on *hot* coals and shake often till corn is popped. Open pouch and season popcorn with melted butter and salt.

RIBS AND KRAUT

Tart apples, cut in rings	**Salt and pepper**
Sauerkraut	
Loin back ribs, cut in	
3-rib sections	

• • •

For each serving: Cut off a 36-inch length of aluminum foil and fold it in half. Just off-center of the foil, place 2 apple rings (½-inch thick); top with ½ cup sauerkraut, then with 2 sections (enough for a serving) of the loin back ribs.

Sprinkle with ½ teaspoon salt and dash pepper. Fold foil according to directions on page 145. Cook over glowing coals, about 1 hour, or till meat is well done.

CHEESED POTATOES IN FOIL

Easy potatoes all in one package feeds the family. And such flavor!—

3 large baking potatoes, pared	**1 large onion, sliced**
Salt	**½ pound sharp process American cheese,**
Cracked or coarsely ground pepper	**cubed (2 cups)**
	½ cup butter or margarine

• • •

4 or 5 slices bacon, crisp-cooked

• • •

Slice potatoes onto a big piece of aluminum foil and sprinkle with salt and pepper. Crumble bacon over. Add onion and cheese cubes. Slice butter over all. Mix on the foil; bring edges of foil up, and leaving a little space for expansion of steam, seal well with double fold. Place package on grill and cook over coals about 1 hour or till done, turning several times. (Or cook on grill with barbecue hood down, about 45 minutes.) Serve hot. Makes 6 servings.

BROWN-AND-SERVE ROLLS ON A SPIT

They get crusty on all sides, stay pillow-soft in the center—

Shortly before you give the come-and-get-it call, thread brown-and-serve rolls on a spit. Brush rolls with melted butter and let rotate over coals about 10 to 15 minutes.

Spin your complete dinner, each food on a separate sword. Brown-and-serve rolls need only a few minutes to get toasty all over when given a hot-coals finale. Brush generously with melted butter or margarine just before placing over coals. On the center spit is Stuffed Breast of Lamb (see index listing). The vegetable accompaniments are roasted yams and summer turnips. For dessert offer plump spit-baked apples. (This grill turns seven skewers at once.)

BROILED FRENCH BREAD

Slash bread on the bias in 1-inch slices, cutting to, *but not through*, the bottom crust. Blend 2 teaspoons garlic salad-dressing mix (from envelope) into ½ cup soft butter or margarine. Spread slices. Wrap in foil; heat on grill (turning often).

GRILLED SWEET ROLLS

Split sweet rolls crosswise. Spread with soft butter or margarine. Toast on griddle or skillet. To heat sweet rolls for your crowd, line up rolls, almost on edge in foil or pan; heat by the dozen. Serve warm.

OLIVE PIZZA BREAD

Perfect accompaniment for roast beef, roast chicken, or any meat cooked "plain"—

1 slightly beaten egg
1 cup pitted ripe olives,
    cut in large pieces
⅓ cup butter or
    margarine, melted
1 tablespoon instant
    minced onion
1 teaspoon Worcester-
    shire sauce
Dash bottled hot
    pepper sauce

2 cups shredded process
    American cheese

• • •

3 cups packaged biscuit
    mix
1 cup milk
1 teaspoon caraway
    seed

Mix egg, olives, butter, onion, Worcestershire sauce, hot pepper sauce, and cheese. Set aside while preparing dough. Combine biscuit mix and milk; stir to a soft dough. Spread dough in a greased 14-inch pizza pan. Spoon olive topping over dough; sprinkle with caraway seeds. Bake on grill (barbecue hood down to make an oven) over *medium* coals 20 to 25 minutes or till done. Cut in 12 wedges and serve *hot*.

EASY ONION BREAD

Fresh onion flavor without tears—

2 teaspoons instant
    minced onion
1 tablespoon water
½ cup soft butter or
    margarine

2 tablespoons snipped
    parsley
1 loaf French bread,
    about 18 inches
    long

Let onion stand in water 5 minutes, then combine with butter and parsley, mixing well. Slash bread on the bias in 1-inch slices, *cutting to but not through* bottom crust. Spread onion butter generously on one side of each slice. Wrap loaf in aluminum foil. Heat on grill 20 to 30 minutes or till hot, turning occasionally. Serve immediately.

BROILED REFRIGERATOR ROLLS

Hot rolls are ready in no time at all—

Fold a 36-inch length of heavy-duty aluminum foil in half; grease top side. Arrange packaged refrigerator rolls near one end of foil; fold other end over and pinch edges together—allow about ½ inch space in package, above rolls, for rising.

Place about 8 inches above coals and bake 7 minutes or so—peek now and then to see if bottoms of rolls are brown. Invert package and bake about 7 minutes longer.

ONION-CHEESE LOAF

1 loaf French bread
⅓ cup butter or
    margarine
3 tablespoons prepared
    mustard

½ pound sliced sharp
    process cheese
1 medium onion, *thinly*
    sliced

Slash French loaf diagonally into 1-inch slices, *cutting to but not through* bottom. Combine butter and mustard; spread over cut surfaces. Insert slices of cheese and onion in bread slashes. Wrap in foil and heat over *medium* coals about 15 minutes or till heated through and cheese melts.

LONG BOY LOAF

Toasty with warm undertones of garlic—

Slash long French loaf in even 1½-inch slices, making the cuts on the bias, *cutting to but not through* the bottom. Mash 1 clove garlic thoroughly (or use ¼ teaspoon garlic powder); cream into ½ cup butter.

Spread mixture generously between slices. Wrap loaf in aluminum foil. Place on edge of grill until hot, turning frequently.

RYE HERB LOAF

A blend of herbs plus the unexpected zingo of pepper and mustard!

½ cup butter or margarine	¼ teaspoon rosemary
1 large clove garlic, minced	¼ teaspoon thyme
½ teaspoon salt	¼ teaspoon dry mustard
¼ teaspoon coarsely ground pepper	¼ teaspoon tarragon
¼ teaspoon crushed sage	3 tablespoons finely snipped parsley
	1 1-pound loaf dark rye bread, sliced

Stir butter to soften. Add seasonings and mix well; spread generously on slices of rye. Reassemble loaf and wrap in foil. Heat at side of grill 15 to 20 minutes or till hot. Serve warm and fragrant.

BARBECUE BREAD

Cheese-mustard butter does exciting things for a pumpernickel loaf—

1 round loaf pumper-	2 tablespoons prepared
nickel	mustard
• • •	½ cup grated
½ cup soft butter or	Parmesan cheese
margarine	¼ cup snipped parsley

Cut bread in ½-inch slices. Mix butter, mustard, cheese, and parsley; spread slices. Put loaf together on large piece of foil; going *almost* to bottom crust, cut bread in half through center. Bring edges of foil over loaf to cover. Heat at side of grill 20 to 25 minutes or till hot, turning occasionally. Serve hot. Let folks break off their own servings.

SEASONED HARD ROLLS

Here's an outdoors way for "stuffing" to go with a roast chicken. Poultry seasoning is the secret. Next time try other herbs or spices and serve with beef or pork—

Split hard rolls lengthwise. Blend soft butter or margarine with a good dash of poultry seasoning (or with small dash of thyme and marjoram). Spread rolls, then wrap in foil. Heat on grill while you carve the chicken. Serve while warm.

Another time use loaves of French bread. Prepare same as hard rolls. Cut in slices. One loaf will make several servings.

GARLIC-BREAD SQUARES

Cut unsliced loaf of bread into 2-inch cubes. Mix thoroughly ¼ clove garlic, minced, and ¼ cup butter or margarine.

Spread the mixture on the outside of cubes and heat in foil over *hot* coals.

PARSLEY-LEMON LOAVES

Each little loaf will serve 2 to 3 people. Delicious flavor—

2 large brown-and-serve
    French rolls, each
    about 8 inches long

• • •

¼ cup soft butter or
    margarine
¼ cup snipped parsley
2 teaspoons lemon juice

Slice rolls diagonally in 1-inch slices. Combine butter and parsley; blend in lemon juice. Spread one side of each slice with parsley butter. Reassemble each roll on a long skewer, inserting skewer through center of slices. Broil 3 to 4 inches from *very hot* coals turning to brown evenly.

Note: Small wire whip is good tool for blending butter with lemon juice.

LITTLE LOAF SANDWICHES

The little loaves brown while the cheese filling melts to golden goodness—

½ pound Bologna
¼ pound sharp process
    American cheese
2 tablespoons prepared
    mustard
3 tablespoons salad
    dressing or
    mayonnaise
2 teaspoons minced
    onion

2 small loaves brown-
    and-serve French
    bread
Butter or margarine
Tomato slices
Sweet pickles, sliced
    lengthwise

Grind Bologna and cheese. Add mustard, salad dressing, and onion. Make a diagonal, lengthwise slit in loaves but do not cut through bottom crust. Carefully spread cut surface with softened butter.

Spread generously with cheese mixture. Place row of

tomato slices in each loaf. Put a slice of sweet pickle on each tomato slice. Wrap in foil and heat on edge of grill till heated through and cheese melts. Cut each loaf in thirds. Makes 6 servings.

TORPEDOES

Brown individual (miniature) brown-and-serve French loaves according to the package directions. Split loaves in half, but don't cut quite through. (If you like, scoop out some of centers to make room for plenty of filling.) Spread generously with mustard, garlic butter, and/or mayonnaise with curry powder. (Or sprinkle bread with clear French or Italian dressing and dash with oregano, basil, or other favorite herb.)

Line bottom halves with leaf lettuce. Pile on slices of corned beef, boiled ham, Bologna, salami, pickled tongue, chicken, tuna, herring—it's your choice of several or all. Add slices of American and Swiss cheese, onion rounds, green and ripe-olive slices, sweet pickles—you name it. More lettuce, too. Anchor with cocktail picks. Each loaf makes 1 supersize sandwich.

Note: Or how about one big sandwich with one long loaf of French or Italian bread? Then allow one-fourth to one-third loaf (cut on diagonal) per person.

FRIDAY-BURGER

1 cup (¼ pound) grated American cheese

3 hard-cooked eggs, chopped

1 6½- or 7-ounce can (1 cup) tuna, flaked

2 tablespoons chopped green pepper

2 tablespoons chopped onion

2 tablespoons chopped stuffed olives

2 tablespoons chopped sweet pickle

½ cup mayonnaise or salad dressing

• • •

8 hamburger buns

8 green-pepper rings

2 tablespoons grated American cheese

Combine ingredients, except last three. Cut thin slice from top of each bun. Remove center of buns, leaving sides ½ inch thick, and thin layer on bottom.

Fill with tuna salad. Put green-pepper ring around mound of salad; wrap in foil and heat till warmed. Sprinkle with 2 tablespoons cheese; heat a few minutes or till cheese melts. Makes 8 servings.

CHEESE-FRANKFURTER LOAF

¼ cup chopped onion
2 tablespoons butter or
    margarine
½ cup chili sauce
2 tablespoons vinegar
1 tablespoon Worcester-
    shire sauce
1 tablespoon prepared
    mustard
2 teaspoons brown
    sugar

½ teaspoon celery salt
1 loaf French bread
    (about 16 to 18
    inches long)
1¼ cups shredded
    sharp process
    American cheese
10 frankfurters, cut in
    half crosswise

Cook onion in butter till tender but not brown. Add chili sauce and seasonings. Simmer about 10 minutes or till sauce is thick. Here's the idea for cutting the bread: Slices will be ¾ inch wide and cut crosswise off the loaf. Cut first slice, going *almost to bottom crust*; cut second slice *all the way through*. Continue in same manner the length of loaf. Between the attached slices, spread the sauce, sprinkle in *half* of cheese, and insert 2 frank halves, letting uncut ends poke out and up at jaunty angle. Hide cut ends of franks with remaining cheese.

With long skewer, fasten sandwiches together in a loaf and wrap in aluminum foil. Heat on grill over charcoal till piping. Open the foil and sprinkle sandwiches with additional shredded cheese, if desired. Remove skewer. Serve hot. Makes 10 servings.

HOT HAM BUNS

¼ cup soft butter or
   margarine
2 tablespoons prepared
   horseradish-
   mustard
2 teaspoons poppy seed

2 tablespoons finely
   chopped onion
4 hamburger buns, split
4 thin slices boiled ham
4 slices process Swiss
   cheese

Mix butter, mustard, poppy seed, and onion; spread on cut surfaces of buns. Tuck a slice of ham and cheese in each bun. Place the sandwiches on aluminum foil and heat on grill till hot through. Makes 4 sandwiches.

HOBOLOGNA BUNWICHES

Bologna gets a new twist. With long-handled fork, you can cook over fire just as you would for frankfurters—

For each sandwich: Alternate 2 half-slices sharp process American cheese and 2 slices big Bologna, centering cheese on meat each time. Roll up tightly and wrap with slice of bacon; anchor with toothpick.

Push 2 skewers through roll-up of cheese and meat— you can slip several roll-ups on a pair of skewers. Broil over coals till bacon is cooked and roll-ups hot through (7 to 10 minutes), turning once. Remove toothpicks and skewers and slip roll-ups into buns. Pass catsup and prepared mustard.

HOT CORNED-BEEF SANDWICHES

The flavors blend when heated—

12 slices pumpernickel
½ cup Thousand Island
   dressing
6 slices Swiss cheese
6 tablespoons drained
   sauerkraut

¼ pound cooked or
   canned corned
   beef, sliced
Butter or margarine,
   softened

Spread 6 slices of bread with dressing. Top each with cheese, 1 tablespoon sauerkraut, corned beef, and bread slice. Butter top and bottom of sandwiches. Grill both sides on griddle, sandwich grill, or in a skillet until hot and cheese melts. Makes 6.

PIZZA SANDWICHES

A quickie to please those pizza fans in your family. You'll like this sandwich for lunches or casual Sunday-night suppers—

⅔ cup canned pizza
    sauce
8 slices bread
4 large or 8 small slices
    salami

4 slices sharp process
    American cheese
Garlic salt or salt
Soft butter or
    margarine

Spread pizza sauce on one side of each bread slice. Top 4 with salami slices, then with cheese; sprinkle with garlic salt. Add remaining bread slices, sauce side down. Generously butter top and bottom of sandwiches. Grill both sides on griddle, sandwich grill, or in a skillet until sandwiches are toasted and cheese melts. Makes 4.

CHOO-CHOO SANDWICH

1 loaf French bread
¼ cup butter or
    margarine
1 clove garlic, minced
Tomato slices

Cheese slices
Thin slices corned-beef
    loaf
Green-pepper rings

Cut bread diagonally in 1½-inch slices, *cutting to, but not through,* the bottom crust. Cream butter with minced garlic. Spread on bread slices. Place tomato slice, cheese slice, corned-beef slice, and green-pepper ring between bread slices.

Stick skewer through loaf lengthwise; wrap in aluminum foil and place on grill. Turn frequently, heating till cheese melts. Remove foil. Cut through bottom crust just before serving. Makes 7 to 10 servings.

POW-WOW SANDWICHES

Bring to the table wrapped in foil—

½ pound sliced bacon	⅓ cup sweet-pickle
2½ ounces (¾ cup)	relish
shredded dried	6 buttered round buns
beef	6 slices American
¾ cup chili sauce	cheese

Fry bacon crisp; drain on absorbent paper. Crush into small pieces. Add dried beef, chili sauce, and pickle relish. Spread on half of split buns. Top each with a cheese slice. Place top on buns. Wrap sandwiches in foil. Heat on grill till hot through.

BOLOGNA-CHEESE BUNWICHES

Recipe makes 6 Bunwiches, but number of servings depends on appetites!—

½ pound unsliced	2 tablespoons prepared
Bologna, diced	mustard
(1½ cups)	2 tablespoons
½ cup diced sharp	mayonnaise or
process American	salad dressing
cheese	• • •
¼ cup pickle relish	6 frankfurter buns,
2 tablespoons finely	split and toasted
chopped onion	

Mix diced Bologna, cheese, pickle relish, chopped onion, mustard, and mayonnaise; divide mixture evenly among buns. Wrap each bun in aluminum foil. Chill if to be taken some distance before eating. (A picnic cooler is helpful in keeping wrapped Bunwiches cool till needed.)

Half hour before time to eat, heat foil-wrapped Bunwiches over coals on grill until piping hot, about 25 minutes. Serve hot.

BEANWICHES

6 slices bacon
1 1-pound can (2 cups)
    baked beans,
    drained and chilled
½ cup catsup
⅓ cup diced celery
¼ cup chopped green
    onions

1½ teaspoons prepared
    horseradish
6 hamburger buns
Melted butter or
    margarine
Dill-pickle slices

Cook the bacon till crisp; drain; crumble. Combine the bacon, beans, catsup, celery, onions, and horseradish. Brush inside of buns with butter; toast lightly till warm throughout. Fill buns with the bean mixture. Tuck 2 pickle slices in each. Serves 6.

HAM LINE-UP LOAF

One loaf will serve several guests. Heat and serve in the same foil—cleanup is easy—

3 2¼-ounce cans
    (¾ cup) deviled
    ham
¼ cup pickle relish
1 loaf French bread
    (about 12 inches
    long)

Soft butter or
    margarine
Tomato slices

Combine ham and pickle relish. Cut loaf in ½-inch slices, *cutting to, but not through,* the bottom crust. Spread with soft butter or margarine and ham mixture between every other slice. Wrap in aluminum foil; heat on edge of grill till warm through.

Fold foil back; tuck tomato slices in with the ham filling. (Or, put the tomato slices between the unfilled bread slices—then each sandwich will have a tomato topper.) Let guests break off their own servings. Makes about 10 sandwiches.

LUNCHEON MEAT BOAT

Cut slice off top of a loaf of Italian or French bread and hollow out, leaving a 1-inch wall. Measure 1 cup bread crumbs (from center); combine with one 12-ounce can luncheon meat, diced or chopped, 4 hard-cooked eggs, diced, 1 cup diced celery, 2 tablespoons chopped dill pickles, 1 tablespoon minced green onions, 2 tablespoons chopped stuffed olives, ½ cup mayonnaise, and 1 teaspoon Worcestershire sauce.

Spoon mixture lightly onto loaf, replace top. Brush entire loaf with butter or margarine; wrap in foil. Bake over coals about 30 minutes or till heated through.

CRAB SANDWICHES

Crab salad is sandwiched and heated till golden. Serve with broiled pineapple rings—

1 6½- or 7½-ounce can (about 1 cup) crab meat, drained and flaked	1 hard-cooked egg, chopped
½ cup shredded sharp process American cheese	3 tablespoons salad dressing or mayonnaise
¼ cup chopped celery	½ teaspoon lemon juice
2 tablespoons drained sweet-pickle relish	½ teaspoon prepared horseradish
2 tablespoons chopped green onions and tops	• • • 10 slices bread, buttered generously 5 tomato slices

Combine crab meat, cheese, celery, pickle relish, onion, egg, salad dressing, lemon juice, and horseradish; spread on *unbuttered* side of 5 bread slices. Add tomato slices; season with salt and pepper. Top with bread slices, buttered side up. Grill on griddle, sandwich grill, or in skillet till sandwiches are golden brown. Makes 5.

CHEESE-MEAT SANDWICH

Cut a loaf of French or Vienna bread at 1-inch intervals, almost through the bottom crust. In the cuts spread butter or margarine and mustard. Place in the cuts slices of canned luncheon meat, American cheese, and large slices of pickle. Wrap loaf in aluminum foil, leaving top partially open and heat on grill over coals about 20 minutes. Serve piping hot.

Note: Brown-and-serve breads can be used in place of French or Vienna loaves; wrap completely but loosely and turn 2 or 3 times on grill to heat all sides.

CHAPTER 4

VEGETABLES

Corn on the cob and off takes top billing as a summer-time barbecue special. Kernels take on a caramel flavor.

Beans cook in smoky-sweet sauces flavored with pork, brown sugar, molasses, or even pineapple.

Tomatoes, plump and red, team with a variety of herb seasonings for spectacular color and flavor.

Potatoes start many a flavor creation. Baked in the skin, sliced with onion, or topped with cheese or butter, they're great!

Squash and eggplant offer variety to any barbecue. Serve them large or miniature, butter broiled or seasoned to your taste.

Peas blend popularly with mushrooms or delightfully change mealtime pace with oriental treatment.

Rice comes fluffy and white. Just right to serve under those delicious barbecue sauces.

HICKORY-SMOKED EARS

Smoky barbecue flavor penetrates each kernel—

Turn back husks of fresh corn and strip off silk. Lay corn husks back in position. Place the ears (in husks) on grill over *hot* coals. Add damp hickory to coals; lower hood and cook about 1 hour.

ANISE CORN

In a foilware pan, melt 2 or 3 tablespoons butter or margarine. Drain one 12-ounce or one 1-pound can whole kernel corn, and add to butter with ¼ teaspoon anise seed. Add a dash each of salt and pepper to taste. Heat, stirring often till corn is piping hot.

GOLDEN CORN FRY

A wonderful way for leftover corn on the cob—

2 tablespoons butter or
    margarine
3 cups (4 to 6 medium
    ears) fresh or
    frozen cut corn
½ cup light cream
2 tablespoons chopped
    chives

1 clove garlic, minced
Dash salt
Dash pepper
¼ cup shredded
    Parmesan cheese

Tear off a 3-foot length of 18-inch-wide aluminum foil and fold in half to make a square. With your fist, form in a pouch. Add butter or margarine, corn, light cream, chives, garlic, salt, and pepper.

Fold edges of foil to seal pouch tightly. Place pouch on grill and heat about 10 to 15 minutes. Before serving, remove from heat, and open foil package; sprinkle corn with Parmesan cheese. Let set at side of grill till cheese melts. Makes 4 to 6 servings.

GOURMET GRILLED CORN

A few easy steps lead to a very elegant corn-on-the-cob dish—

8 ears sweet corn
½ cup cashew nut
   spread or creamy
   peanut butter

8 slices bacon

Turn back husks of corn and strip off silk. Spread each ear of corn with a tablespoon of nut spread. Spiral a slice of bacon, barber-pole style, around each ear. Lay husks back in position. Place on grill over hot coals; turn frequently until done, about 20 minutes. Makes 8 servings.

BROCCOLI IN FOIL

Next time try frozen asparagus spears—

Place two 10-ounce packages frozen broccoli spears on large square of double-thickness aluminum foil. Season with salt and pepper. Tuck in thin slices of lemon *or* sprinkle with 1 tablespoon lemon juice. Top with 2 or 3 generous pats of butter or margarine. Bring edges of foil up, and, leaving a little space for expansion of steam, seal tightly with double fold.

Heat over *hot* coals about 40 minutes, turning frequently. Makes 6 to 8 servings.

PEAS AND MUSHROOMS

1 10-ounce package
   frozen peas
Salt and pepper
3 tablespoons butter or
   margarine

1 3-ounce can (⅔ cup)
   broiled sliced
   mushrooms,
   drained

Place block of frozen peas on large square of aluminum foil. Season with salt and pepper, and top with butter and drained mushrooms. Bring edges of foil up and, leaving a little space for expansion of steam, seal tightly with double fold. Place package over *hot* coals about 10 to 15 minutes. Turn occasionally. Makes 4 servings.

INDIAN-STYLE CORN ON THE COB

Turn back husks and strip off silk. Lay husks back in position. Place ears on grill over *hot* coals; roast, turning frequently, 15 to 20 minutes or till husks are dry and browned. (A longer roasting time will give sweeter, more caramelized corn.)

FROZEN CORN

Place one block of frozen whole kernel corn on a big square of aluminum foil. Season with salt and pepper. Top with 2 or 3 generous pats of butter. Bring edges of foil up and, leaving a little space for expansion of steam, seal tightly with double fold. Place package on the grill about 15 to 20 minutes, turning occasionally.

HORSERADISH BUTTER

Puts corn on the cob in the gourmet class. It's gently flavored with horseradish and mustard. Try it with other vegetables too—

½ cup soft butter or
    margarine
1 tablespoon prepared
    mustard
1 teaspoon prepared
    horseradish

½ teaspoon salt
Dash freshly ground
    pepper
Snipped parsley

Combine butter, mustard, horseradish, salt, and pepper; cream till light and fluffy. If desired, garnish butter with snipped parsley and pass with corn on the cob.

What could be better with a barbecue than fresh succulent corn on the cob? Wrapped in aluminum foil, all the sweet moistness stays inside to make each kernel plump and juicy.

FRESH CORN ON THE COB

Remove husks from fresh corn. Remove silk with a stiff brush. Place each ear on a piece of aluminum foil. Spread corn liberally with soft butter or margarine and sprinkle with salt and pepper.

Wrap aluminum foil securely around each ear of corn—don't seal seam, but fold or twist foil around ends (that way corn will roast instead of steam). Place on grill and roast over *hot* coals 15 to 20 minutes or till corn is tender, turning ears frequently. Offer extra butter, salt, and freshly ground pepper.

Or pass a variety of whipped butters flavored with horseradish, anise, or herbs.

HERB BUTTER

Rosemary and marjoram add subtle flavor—

Cream ½ cup slightly soft butter or margarine, using electric mixer or wooden spoon, till fluffy. Stir in 1 teaspoon dried rosemary, crushed (*or* 4 teaspoons fresh rosemary chopped), and ½ teaspoon dried marjoram, crushed (*or* 2 teaspoons fresh marjoram, chopped).

CREAMY CORN

Tender corn kernels in a satin-smooth sauce—the preparation is only a matter of minutes, a package of cream cheese, and a can of corn—

1 3-ounce package
    cream cheese,
    softened
¼ cup milk
1 tablespoon butter or
    margarine

½ teaspoon onion salt
   . . .
1 1-pound can (2 cups)
    whole kernel corn,
    drained

In a skillet, combine cream cheese, milk, butter or margarine, and onion salt. Stir mixture over *low* coals till cheese melts. Add corn; heat through and serve, garnishing with parsley or a sprinkle of paprika.

ANISE BUTTER

Soften 1 teaspoon anise seed in 1 teaspoon boiling water for 30 minutes. Add both anise seed and water to ½ cup slightly soft butter or margarine. Beat with electric mixer or wooden spoon till fluffy.

ONIONED POTATOES

Open the foil jacket and you're greeted with a wonderful aroma! These potatoes go well with burgers or steaks—

6 medium baking
    potatoes
½ cup soft butter or
    margarine

1 envelope dry onion-
    soup mix

Scrub potatoes but do not pare. Cut each in 3 or 4 lengthwise slices. Blend butter and soup mix; spread on slices; reassemble the potatoes. Wrap each potato in square of foil, overlapping ends. Bake till tender, turning once—45 to 60 minutes on the grill or right on top of coals. Pass additional butter.

SILVER-PLATED POTATOES

Choose firm, medium-size baking potatoes (or yams or sweet potatoes). Scrub and brush with salad oil. Wrap each in a square of foil, overlapping the ends.

Bake 45 to 60 minutes on the grill (about twice as long if hood is down) or right on top of the coals. Turn potatoes occasionally (unless hood is down).

When potatoes are tender, open with a fork and push ends to fluff. (Protect hands with paper towels or pot-holder when potatoes are hot-off-the-coals.) Season with salt and pepper, and serve. Pass butter and favorite toppers.

CHEESED SPUDS

Scrub medium baking potatoes (1 per serving); pare or not. Cut each into ¼-inch lengthwise slices, then into ¼-inch sticks. Pile each "potato's worth" on a piece of foil. Sprinkle each pile of potato sticks liberally with onion salt, celery salt, freshly ground pepper, and 2 tablespoons grated Parmesan cheese, making sure all surfaces are seasoned; then dot each serving with 2 table-spoons butter or margarine. Bring edges of foil together, and allowing plenty of room for expansion of steam in each package, seal securely with double fold. Cook po-tatoes on grill top over coals about 30 minutes or till tender, turning packages several times. Serve piping hot in foil.

INSTANT FRENCH FRIES

With beverage-can opener, punch hole in top of can of French fries or shoestring potatoes. Place can on grill and roll occasionally as it heats. Open and serve. Try the same with French-fried onion rings.

SIZZLING FRENCH FRIES

Place thawed, frozen French fries in corn popper. Shake over heat until piping hot. Sprinkle hot fries to taste with salt.

APPLE-BUTTERED SWEETS

For each serving, place several lengthwise slices of cooked or canned sweet potatoes on a 6-inch square of foil. Season potatoes with salt and pepper. Spread a tablespoon of apple butter over potato slices and sprinkle with 1 teaspoon of brown sugar. Dash lightly with cinnamon and dot each serving of potatoes with 2 teaspoons butter or margarine. Seal foil; heat on grill, apple-butter side up, 25 to 30 minutes.

PLUGGED POTATOES

With an apple corer, cut a lengthwise plug in a baking potato—remove plug and cut off end, leaving ½ inch. Pour a spoonful or two evaporated milk into hole in potato; replace the ½-inch plug. Brush each potato with salad oil and wrap in aluminum foil.

Bake potatoes over coals till tender.

QUICKIE CHEESED SKILLET POTATOES

1 1-pound package
   frozen French fried
   potatoes
⅓ cup Italian salad
   dressing
1 teaspoon instant
   minced onion

1 teaspoon parsley
   flakes
1 cup shredded sharp
   process cheese

Place French fries in shallow skillet; pour dressing over, tossing to coat the potatoes evenly. Sprinkle with onion and parsley flakes. Heat, turning as needed, till browned slightly. When potatoes are heated through, place in bowl; top with cheese; toss lightly and serve at once. Makes 6 servings.

HERBED SKILLET FRENCH FRIES

1 1-pound package
    frozen French fried
    potatoes
2 tablespoons butter or
    margarine
1 6-ounce can (⅔ cup)
    evaporated milk

Salt and pepper to taste
1 teaspoon dried dill
    weed
1 tablespoon chopped
    pimiento
½ cup shredded sharp
    process cheese

Brown French fries in butter over *slow* coals, turning potatoes with pancake turner; pour evaporated milk over and sprinkle with remaining ingredients. Heat just till cheese melts, turning occasionally with pancake turner. Makes 6 servings.

POTATOES ON TOTEM POLES

String scrubbed small potatoes on skewers. Stand them upright in a tall can (from fruit juice or coffee) of boiling salted water. Cook till tender. Remove from can. Brush with oil, melted butter, or margarine. Sprinkle with salt and pepper. Serve pronto.

CHEESE-TOPPED TOMATOES

5 large ripe tomatoes
Salt
Pepper
¼ cup soft bread
    crumbs
¼ cup shredded sharp
    process American
    cheese

1 tablespoon butter or
    margarine, melted
Snipped parsley

Slice off tops of tomatoes. Cut zigzag edges; season with salt and pepper. Combine bread crumbs, cheese, and butter; sprinkle over tomatoes. Garnish with snipped parsley. Heat tomatoes on foil over coals till warm through. Serve immediately. Makes 5 servings.

SKILLET POTATOES

6 medium potatoes, cooked and diced	2 tablespoons chopped pimiento
2 cups sliced onions	½ teaspoon salt
2 tablespoons snipped parsley	¼ teaspoon pepper
	¼ cup fat

Combine first 4 ingredients. Add seasonings. Brown in hot fat in large skillet until golden brown and crisp—keep turning potatoes carefully. Makes 6 servings.

FOIL-BAKED TOMATOES

Select medium, firm tomatoes (one to a person). Cut each tomato in half crosswise, sprinkle cut surfaces with salt and pepper, then put together again with a thin slice of onion between. Use a toothpick to hold the reassembled tomato intact.

Wrap each tomato in a 6-inch square of heavy aluminum foil, and heat at edge of grill over *hot* coals 15 to 20 minutes. Just right to serve with broiled ham slices.

HERBED TOMATOES

6 ripe tomatoes	¼ cup finely snipped parsley
1 teaspoon salt	
¼ teaspoon coarse black pepper	¼ cup snipped chives
Few leaves fresh thyme *or* marjoram *or* ½ teaspoon of dried	⅔ cup salad oil
	¼ cup tarragon vinegar

Peel the tomatoes. Place in bowl; sprinkle with seasonings and herbs. Combine oil and vinegar and pour over.

Cover and chill an hour or so, occasionally spooning the dressing over tomatoes. At serving time, drain off dressing to pass in bowl.

Serve tomatoes chilled, or wrap in aluminum foil and heat over coals. Garnish with additional parsley or chives. Serves 6.

BROILED TOMATOES IN BACON COATS

Tangy and juicy inside; crisp jacket—

12 bacon slices	Dash salt
1 tablespoon brown sugar	6 medium tomatoes, peeled
1 tablespoon prepared mustard	

Fry bacon on pan made of aluminum foil or on griddle over *hot* coals till partially done but *not crisp*.

Blend brown sugar, mustard, and salt. Make a vertical cut down center of tomatoes, about ⅔ of the way through. Spread cut edges with mustard mixture. Crisscross 2 bacon slices. Place tomato on bacon where slices cross; bring strips to top of tomato and secure with toothpicks. Place tomatoes on aluminum foil. Cook covered over coals till tomatoes are hot. Makes 6 servings.

TOMATO-EGGPLANT STACKUPS

Melting cheese for extra-delicious flavor—

12 ½-inch pared eggplant slices	6 slices process American cheese
Salt	6 thick slices peeled tomato
Butter or margarine	

Sprinkle eggplant slices with salt. In a skillet, fry eggplant in butter or margarine till nearly tender. Cut cheese slices in half. Arrange half of the eggplant slices on aluminum foil. Top each slice with a slice of tomato and cover with a half slice of cheese; toothpick together to hold.

Add another slice eggplant to each and cover with half slices of cheese. Cook, hood down, till cheese melts and stackups are hot through. Makes 6 servings.

GRILL-TOP TOMATOES

Cut tomatoes in half. Brush cut surfaces with Italian salad dressing; sprinkle with salt, fresh-ground coarse pepper, and basil. Place cut side up on aluminum foil or greased grill over *hot* coals about 10 minutes or till hot through—don't turn.

MESA ONIONS

Tender golden slices of buttery goodness—

Peel and slice large onions in ⅓-inch slices. Place onion slices in a large skillet and cook in butter or margarine slowly over *hot* coals until they are golden, turning frequently. Season to taste with salt and pepper and serve immediately.

HOBO RICE

Here's a fun trick that gives a carefree air to your campfire cooking—and good eating with lamb, steaks, or burgers. Cook it right on the grill—the fluffiest rice you've ever seen—

1½ cups water	1⅓ cups packaged
½ teaspoon salt	precooked rice

• • •

Combine water and salt in a 1-pound-size coffee can. Heat to boiling on grill over *hot* coals. *Remove from heat* and add precooked rice; stir just to moisten.

Cover coffee can tightly with metal lid or a piece of aluminum foil and set at grill side, *away from heat;* let rice stand at least 13 minutes to get fluffy. Makes 3 cups rice.

BARBECUED RICE IN FOIL KETTLE

This time fluffy rice boasts mushroom flavor. So good with broiled steak, lamb chops, or hamburgers—

1⅓ cups packaged precooked rice

1 3-ounce can (⅔ cup) broiled sliced mushrooms

1 cup cold water

¼ cup finely chopped onion

1 teaspoon Worcestershire sauce

½ teaspoon salt

• • •

2 tablespoons butter or margarine

Tear off a 3-foot length of 18-inch wide aluminum foil and fold in half to make a square. With your fist, form foil into a pouch. Add rice, mushrooms (with liquid), water, onion, and seasonings. Stir carefully to mix; dot top with butter. Fold edges of foil to seal pouch tightly.

Place on grill over *hot* coals and heat about 15 to 18 minutes. Before serving, open foil and add an extra pat of butter; fluff rice with fork. Makes 4 servings.

BARBECUED VEGETABLES

Vegetables never tasted so good before! Have butter waiting—

Scrub baking potatoes, red yams, white turnips, and tomatoes—leave all whole in jackets. String each kind of vegetable on its own skewer. Let rotate with *hot* coals lined up in rows between skewers.

Start the baking potatoes and yams first—they'll take 45 minutes to an hour. Allow about 30 minutes for the turnips to get done. Tomatoes cook lickety-split, so put them on last. If vegetables are done before meat (they'll stand still on rotating spit) wrap them in aluminum foil and lay them in the firebox away from the coals so they stay warm.

ORIENTAL SNOW PEAS

Almost no cooking is the secret of the crisp goodness of these specialty peas—

2 tablespoons salad oil or peanut oil	1 teaspoon sugar
¼ cup chopped green onions	1 teaspoon mono-sodium glutamate
1 5-ounce can (⅔ cup) water chestnuts, drained and sliced very thin	• • •
	½ cup chicken broth
	2 teaspoons cornstarch
½ pound (2 cups) Chinese podded peas* or 1 7-ounce package frozen Chinese pea pods	

Heat oil in skillet, or in Chinese wok. (A wok has a round bottom, fits on cooking ring that holds it level. Or wok can go directly over an hibachi.) Cook onion in hot oil till tender but not brown. Add chestnuts, peas, and seasonings. *Reserve 2 tablespoons* broth; add remainder to skillet. Bring to boiling, separating frozen pods with fork. Cover with aluminum foil and cook about 2 minutes over high heat. Combine cornstarch and the reserved broth. Push vegetables to one side and stir cornstarch mixture into broth; cook and stir till mixture thickens and comes to boiling, about 1 minute. Salt to taste. Makes 3 or 4 servings.

----

*You eat these, pods and all. Instead of shelling them, cook like green beans. Edible podded peas, also called podded sugar peas in seed catalogs, are a tender vegetable favorite with home gardeners.

Skewered squash cooks right along with the rest of the meal. Above, tiny crookneck, patty-pan, and zucchini squashes team with brown-and-serve rolls, and Pineapple-glazed Pork. Basted with plenty of melted butter, these small vegetables cook easily and offer a delightful change.

SPITTED SQUASH

String small crookneck, patty-pan, and zucchini squash on spits, securing with long holding forks. Brush with melted butter and spin over *hot* coals about 45 minutes or till done, basting with butter occasionally.

CHINESE FRIED RICE

Perfect for teriyaki or a barbecued roast—

1⅓ cups packaged
    precooked rice

• • •

¼ cup salad oil

1 onion, minced
2 eggs
Soy sauce

Cook rice in heavy pan according to package directions. In a skillet, heat oil and cook onion till tender but not brown. Add eggs, and scramble with onions. Then add hot rice before eggs set. Mix well; add soy sauce to taste. Makes about 5 or 6 servings.

ZUCCHINI PARMESAN

4 cups thinly sliced zucchini
1 small onion, sliced
1 tablespoon water
2 tablespoons butter or margarine

1 teaspoon salt
Dash pepper
3 tablespoons grated Parmesan cheese

Put all ingredients except cheese in skillet. Cover and cook 1 minute. Uncover and continue to cook, turning with a wide spatula, till barely tender, about 5 minutes longer. Sprinkle with cheese; toss. Serves 8.

CHUCK-WAGON BEANS—LONG-COOK

Real pioneer cooking—

2 cups dry navy beans
1½ quarts cold water
1 teaspoon salt
¼ pound salt pork, diced
• • •
1½ teaspoons salt

½ teaspoon dry mustard
¼ cup granulated or brown sugar
2 tablespoons molasses
1 small onion, quartered

Rinse beans; cover with the cold water. Bring to boiling and simmer 2 minutes. Remove from heat. Cover; let stand 1 hour (or overnight). Add 1 teaspoon salt to beans and *soaking water;* cover and simmer just till tender, 45 minutes to 1 hour.

Drain, reserving liquid. Place half the beans in Dutch

oven. Bury part of pork in beans; combine remaining ingredients and add half. Add remaining beans and seasonings. Place remaining salt pork over top. Cover with bean liquid. Cover Dutch oven and bury in campfire coals 6 to 8 hours. (If necessary, add more liquid as beans bake.) For smoky beans: If you have hood, you can cook last 2 or 3 hours on grill—uncover beans, toss damp hickory on coals. Makes 6 to 8 servings.

SKEWERED EGGPLANT

Pare eggplant; cut in 2-inch chunks and string on a spit. Spin over *hot* coals about 30 minutes or till done, basting occasionally with melted butter or margarine.

If necessary to keep eggplant hot after cooking, leave on spit, wrap loosely in aluminum foil, and move to side of grill.

PINK BEANS SUPREME

If you like, soak beans the night before, then finish on the grill—

1 pound (2½ cups) large dry Limas	½ cup sliced mushrooms
• • •	2 tablespoons paprika
2 cups chopped onions	2 cups dairy sour cream
¼ cup butter or margarine	1 teaspoon salt

Rinse Limas; cover with 6 cups cold water and bring to boiling. Simmer 2 minutes; remove from heat. Cover and let stand 1 hour. Add 2 teaspoons salt to beans (don't drain); bring to boiling, reduce heat, cover and simmer 45 to 60 minutes. Drain.

Cook onions in butter till tender. Add mushrooms and paprika; cook 5 minutes longer. Stir in beans, sour cream, and salt; heat through, stirring now and then. Garnish with parsley. Makes 12 servings.

BARBECUE BEANS

Vienna sausage bakes in middle. Crusty topping of brown sugar is extra reward for bean lovers who like 'em sweet—

3 branches celery
    (½ cup), chopped
2 No. 2½ cans (7 cups)
    pork and beans
2 4-ounce cans Vienna
    sausage, drained,
    or 1 12-ounce can
    luncheon meat,
    cut in strips

1 cup brown sugar

Lay celery in bottom of 2½-quart casserole. Pour in *one can* beans. Arrange sausage links on top and cover with second can of beans. Sprinkle with brown sugar. Bake on grill, hood down, 2 to 3 hours. Makes 8 servings.

SKILLET BEANS 'N FRANKS

Sure to win kid approval—can be ready in 5 to 10 minutes—

1 cup diced tomato
½ teaspoon crushed
    oregano
¼ teaspoon garlic
    powder
2 tablespoons butter or
    margarine

2 1-pound cans (4
    cups) beans and
    franks in tomato
    sauce

In skillet, cook tomato, oregano, and garlic powder in butter briefly to blend flavors; add beans and franks. Heat over *slow* coals, stirring often, till piping hot. Garnish with parsley if desired. Makes 6 servings.

CHUCK-WAGON BEANS—QUICK-COOK

Canned pork and beans give you a head start. The woodsy aroma of hickory smoke will permeate the beans—

2 1-pound cans (4 cups)
    pork and beans
½ cup catsup

¼ cup brown sugar
1 teaspoon dry mustard
8 slices Canadian bacon

In 2-quart bean pot, combine beans, catsup, sugar, and mustard. Bury Canadian bacon in beans. Bake uncovered on grill of hickory-smoker, hood down, 1½ hours or longer. (If necessary, add more catsup as beans bake.) Toward end of cooking time, lift bacon to top with fork; center with drained canned onions. Makes 8 servings.

LUAU BEANS

½ pound sliced bacon
2 onions, sliced
4 1-pound cans (8 cups)
    pork and beans
1 9-ounce can (1 cup)
    crushed pineapple

¼ cup chili sauce
2 tablespoons molasses
1½ teaspoons dry
    mustard
½ teaspoon salt

Fry bacon till crisp; remove from skillet, reserving bacon drippings. Cook onions in bacon drippings. Crumble bacon and combine in Dutch oven with onions and remaining ingredients.

Cover and bake on grill over *medium hot* coals 1½ hours. Then remove cover and cook about 25 minutes longer. Stir occasionally. Makes 10 to 12 servings.

QUICK SMOKED BEANS

4 ounces salt pork, cut
    in 1-inch cubes
2 1-pound cans (4 cups)
    pork and beans

½ cup catsup
¼ cup brown sugar
1 teaspoon dry mustard

Brown salt pork in skillet; drain. In 2-quart bean pot, combine remaining ingredients. Top with salt pork. Bake uncovered on grill of hickory-smoker with hood down, 1 hour or longer. Makes 8 servings.

EL PASO BEANS

Fix ahead and warm on the grill—

1 pound dry pinto beans
• • •
1 pound lean beef stew
    meat, cut in
    1/2-inch cubes
1 teaspoon salt
1/2 teaspoon mono-
    sodium glutamate
1/2 teaspoon crushed
    oregano

4 ounces salt pork,
    diced
1 cup chopped onion
2 8-ounce cans tomato
    sauce
3 cloves garlic, minced
1 to 3 teaspoons finely
    minced hot pickled
    peppers

Rinse beans; drain. Add 6 cups cold water; cover and bring to boiling. Reduce heat and simmer 1 1/2 hours. Add meat and remaining ingredients. Cover and simmer about 1 1/2 hours, stirring occasionally—beans should have burst, giving soup a nice consistency. Salt to taste. Serve in soup bowls. Serves 8.

HERB-STUFFED MUSHROOMS

1 6-ounce can broiled
    whole mushroom
    crowns *or* 12 large
    fresh mushrooms
• • •
1/3 cup sauterne
1 beef bouillon cube
1/2 teaspoon mono-
    sodium glutamate
• • •

2 tablespoons finely
    chopped onion
2 tablespoons butter or
    margarine
1/4 cup packaged herb-
    seasoned stuffing

Remove stems from canned or fresh mushrooms and reserve. In a saucepan, combine sauterne, beef bouillon cube, and monosodium glutamate; heat till cube dissolves. Add mushroom caps; cover and simmer, tops down, 2 to 3 minutes.

Chop mushroom stems and cook with finely chopped onion in butter or margarine till tender. Stir in herb-seasoned stuffing and 2 tablespoons of the wine mixture.

Fit 2 mushroom caps together with about 1 tablespoon of the filling between. String on skewers. Turn skewers over *hot* coals 2 or 3 minutes, brushing occasionally with melted butter or margarine. Recipe makes 6 double mushrooms. Double filling recipe for very large mushroom caps.

EGGPLANT HEROES

Pair up your vegetables and bread in one savory Italian-style dish—

6 ½-inch slices unpared eggplant
½ cup olive oil
• • •
6 French or hero rolls, split
Mozzarella cheese, sliced *thin*

1 8-ounce can (1 cup) spaghetti sauce with mushrooms
Shredded Parmesan cheese
Butter or margarine

Dip eggplant slices in olive oil. Broil on foil close to *hot* coals till brown and tender. Sandwich each slice in split roll.*

Top eggplant with Mozzarella slices and drizzle with spaghetti sauce. Sprinkle shredded Parmesan over. Top with other half of roll. Butter roll on the outside; wrap in aluminum foil and heat on grill.

---

*For a jumbo sandwich, place unpared eggplant slices between halves of a long loaf of Italian or French bread and slice to serve.

CHAPTER 5

SALADS AND RELISHES

Exciting salad imports from across the seas and south of the border are yours in addition to all-time potato salad and coleslaw favorites. Light crisp greens present monochromatic harmony, spicy marinades produce appetizing relishes. What complements to barbecued meat!

The Art of Making a Tossed Salad

Rinse greens in cold water; whirl in a lettuce basket or pat dry with paper towels. Pop into refrigerator crisper to keep fresh, crunchy, bright. Wet greens get limp, and salad dressing won't cling to them.

Variety's the spice. Why limit your salad tossing to one kind of greens? Try water cress, Bibb lettuce, romaine, endive, escarole, or tender leaves of fresh spinach.

To remove core from head lettuce, cut out with pointed knife or hit core on hard surface. Run water into opening for easy separation of leaves. For salad cups from flat leaves, split halfway; lap one side over other.

Tear or break the greens instead of cutting. Keep the pieces small enough so that they're easy to eat but large enough to be distinctive.

Save time by cutting several onion slices or branches of celery at once. For attractive sliced celery, cut on the bias.

For eye appeal and flavor contrast: Add tomato wedges, onion rings, green pepper, radishes, grated cheese, pimiento, egg slices, olives, small fruits, or nuts.

Bonus tidbits for nibbling: radish roses, carrot sticks, celery curls, green onions, crisp rye wafers, and Melba toast.

Make the dressing ahead of time or at the table. Add dressing (either your own or one from a bottle) the last minute to chilled vegetables so salad will be crisp.

Sprinkle crisp croutons on top to give crunch and flavor to your salad.

For drama, place your salad bowl in a larger bowl of crushed ice—set on your outdoor buffet table. Frame it with your best salad plate or platter and arrange it with a flair. You'll have an eyestopper!

ITALIAN SALAD BOWL

½ medium head lettuce,
    torn into bite-size
    pieces
½ medium head
    romaine, torn into
    bite-size pieces
2 cups thinly sliced raw
    zucchini
½ cup sliced radishes

½ cup sliced fresh
    mushrooms
    (optional)
3 green onions, sliced
Salt and pepper
Italian or wine-vinegar
    dressing
½ cup crumbled blue
    cheese

In large bowl, combine lettuce, romaine, zucchini, radishes, mushrooms, and sliced green onions. Season to taste. Toss lightly with dressing; sprinkle crumbled blue cheese over top. Makes 6 servings.

GARDEN PLATTER SALAD WITH DUTCH ONION RINGS

Surprise texture of onions makes this a favorite for summer barbecues—

Dutch Onion Rings
2 or 3 large tomatoes,
    sliced
1 small cucumber,
    sliced
Italian salad dressing

¼ teaspoon salt
¼ teaspoon coarsely
    ground pepper
½ teaspoon dill seed
1 teaspoon snipped
    parsley

Prepare Dutch Onion Rings ahead. At serving time, pile onions in center of platter; border with overlapping tomato and cucumber slices. Drizzle tomatoes and cucumbers with Italian salad dressing, then sprinkle with salt, pepper, dill seed, and parsley. Trim platter with ripe olives and leaf lettuce. Makes 4 to 6 servings.

Dutch Onion Rings: Slice 2 medium onions ¼ inch thick; separate in rings. Place in bowl and cover with boiling water; let stand 2 minutes; drain. Chill. Before serving, combine ¼ cup dairy sour cream, ¼ teaspoon salt, ½ teaspoon celery seed, and 1 teaspoon lemon juice; toss with onions.

WILTED SPINACH SALAD

Simply delicious!—

1 pound fresh spinach	1 tablespoon lemon
4 green onions and	juice
tops, sliced	1 teaspoon sugar
Coarsely ground black	½ teaspoon salt
pepper	1 coarsely chopped
• • •	hard-cooked egg
5 slices bacon, diced	
2 tablespoons wine	
vinegar	

Wash spinach, discarding stems. Pat dry on paper towels, then tear in bite-size pieces in bowl. Add onions and sprinkle with pepper. Refrigerate till chilled through.

At serving time, slowly fry bacon bits in a deep skillet. Add wine vinegar, lemon juice, sugar, and salt. Add spinach and onion mixture; toss just till leaves are coated and wilted slightly. Sprinkle with coarsely chopped hard-cooked egg. Makes 4 to 6 servings.

WESTERN SALAD BOWL

A salad idea that's become almost classic in California—

½ head lettuce	3 green onions,
¼ bunch curly endive	chopped
½ bunch water cress	½ green pepper, sliced
2 tomatoes, cut in	• • •
wedges	¼ cup Blue-cheese
2 branches celery, cut	French Dressing
in sticks	*or* bottled blue
6 radishes, sliced	cheese dressing

Break the lettuce in large bowl; tear endive and water cress in small pieces. For a crisp salad, be sure that greens are chilled, that no water clings to leaves. Arrange the remaining vegetables on top. Pour dressing over salad and toss lightly. Serves 6.

Blue-cheese French Dressing: Crumble 3 ounces blue cheese with a fork. Add ½ cup olive or salad oil, 2 tablespoons vinegar, 1 tablespoon lemon juice, 1 teaspoon anchovy paste, dash steak sauce, ½ clove garlic, minced, and salt and pepper; mix thoroughly. Makes about ¾ cup dressing.

CAESAR SALAD

1 clove garlic
½ cup salad oil
2 to 3 slices enriched
　　white bread
Grated Parmesan cheese

• • •

½ head lettuce
½ bunch curly endive
1 2-ounce can anchovy
　　fillets

3 or 4 tomatoes, diced
1 beaten egg
½ cup grated
　　Parmesan cheese
¼ cup lemon juice
1 teaspoon Worcester-
　　shire sauce
½ teaspoon pepper
½ teaspoon salt

Mash the garlic clove and add to the salad oil; let stand. Prepare croutons by cutting oil; let stand. Prepare croutons by cutting each slice of bread in 5 strips one way, then across 5 times to make squares. Spread out on baking sheet; pour a little garlic salad oil over. Heat in extremely slow oven (225°) for 2 hours. Sprinkle with grated Parmesan.

Break lettuce in salad bowl; tear endive. Add the croutons, anchovies, and tomatoes.

Strain salad oil to remove garlic. Pour over vegetables. Combine the remaining ingredients; beat well.

Pour dressing over the salad and toss lightly. Garnish with sliced tomatoes, if desired. Makes about 6 servings.

Note: You can serve this hearty salad as a main dish for outdoor luncheons.

SPRING SALAD BOWL

Time short? Rub the salad bowl with a garlic clove then toss salad with bottled French or Italian dressing—

1⅓ cups salad oil
½ cup vinegar
1½ teaspoons salt
1 teaspoon sugar
½ teaspoon dry
    mustard
4 cloves garlic, halved
• • •
½ head lettuce

1 cup sliced celery
1 cup sliced radishes
½ small head
    cauliflower, sliced
½ teaspoon salt
⅓ cup (2 ounces)
    crumbled blue
    cheese

Combine first 6 ingredients in a bottle or jar for dressing; cover and shake well. Store mixture in refrigerator. (The flavor is better if you let dressing stand several hours before using.) Shake well at serving time. Makes about 2 cups dressing.

For salad, break lettuce in bite-size pieces. Add celery, radishes, cauliflower, and salt. Sprinkle with crumbled blue cheese. Toss at the table, or just before eating with enough dressing to coat leaves. Serve immediately. Makes about 6 to 8 servings.

CHEF'S BOWL

1 small head romaine
    lettuce*
½ medium head lettuce
¼ bunch curly endive
½ unpared cucumber,
    sliced
3 ripe tomatoes,
    quartered

½ cup julienne strips
    sharp natural
    Cheddar or Swiss
    cheese
6 thin square slices
    boiled ham

Chill all ingredients. Line salad bowl with romaine leaves; break remaining greens in bite-size pieces into bowl. Arrange cucumber, tomato, and cheese. Roll up each ham slice; place seam side down, atop salad. Serve with favorite dressing. Serves 6.

---

*Fix some romaine French-style to line individual salad bowls. Cut out the rib in each leaf with two knife strokes.

BACON, LETTUCE, AND TOMATO SALAD

Line salad bowl with romaine lettuce; break ½ medium head lettuce into bowl. Cut 3 ripe tomatoes into wedges; add to lettuce with 1 cup croutons,* 8 slices bacon, crisp-cooked and coarsely crumbled, and ½ cup mayonnaise or salad dressing. Toss ingredients lightly. Season to taste with salt and pepper. Makes about 4 to 5 servings.

---

*To make your own croutons, toast ½-inch cubes of bread in extremely slow oven (225°) till dry, about 2 hours.

Radish Roses

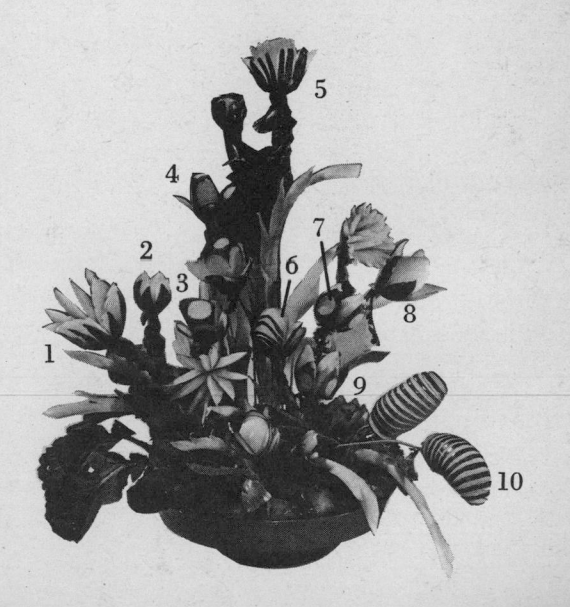

A radish rose by any other name tastes just as crisp and good! Here's a bouquet of ideas for your relish garden. To bring radish roses into bloom, chill in ice water after cutting. For radish bouquet, above, use florists' wire, split bamboo, or skewers as stems. Make arrangement in a flower holder, tucking in celery sticks and radish leaves. Fill bowl with crushed ice.

1. *Chrysanthemum.* Barely cut off root end of a radish. Make 6 to 8 crisscross cuts at the root end, cutting almost to the stem, making pointed petals on radish.

2. *Tulip.* Slice off root end of ball-shaped radish. Make deep notches around cut edge.

3. *Topsy-turvy.* Cut small slice from stem end. Starting at stem end, cut 4 or 5 petals.

4. *Rosebud.* With hook blade on end of vegetable parer, cut 4 or 5 petals. If radish is large, stagger second row of petals below.

5. *Daisy.* Cut off ¼ of radish at root end. Make 5 to 8 deep, parallel slices one way, almost to stem; then repeat, cutting across.

6. *American Beauty rose.* On three sides of radish, cut a row of slits at angle toward stem. Remove peel at the root end.

7. *Domino.* Cut deep X at root end; cut thin circle of peel off center of each fourth.

8. *Daffodil.* With tip of knife, mark 5 or 6 petals on radish, starting at root end; pare back thin petals. Use a sharp blade!

9. *Gadget rose.* Quick with a radish-rose cutter; just press radish on plastic blades.

10. *Accordion.* Cut a slim-jim radish crosswise in narrow slices, not quite through.

ICY NIBBLES

Fill an outdoorsy bowl or ice keeper with crushed ice. Poke in green onions, celery, and carrot strips in porcupine style. Add radishes, pickles, and olives to the snowbank. Set out a variety of cheese dips.

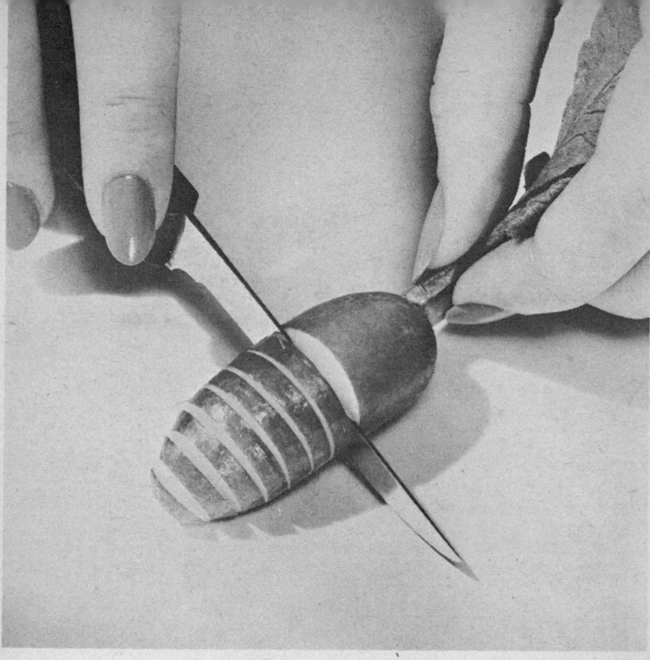

Accordion cut needs very thin slices of radish.

Plastic gadget for radish roses makes them fast.

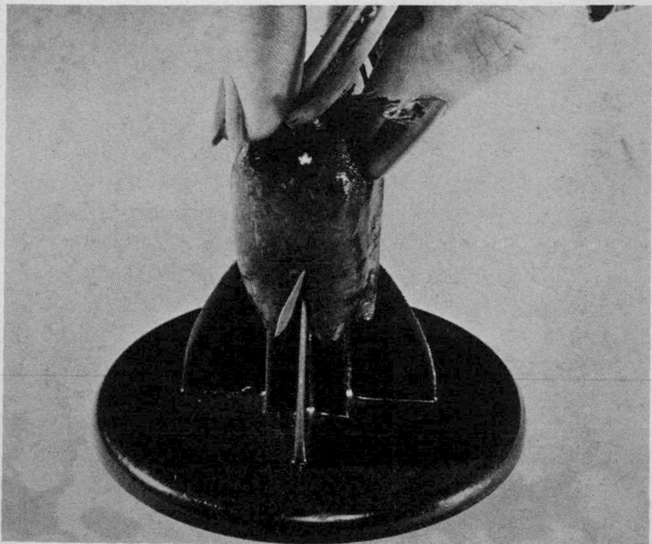

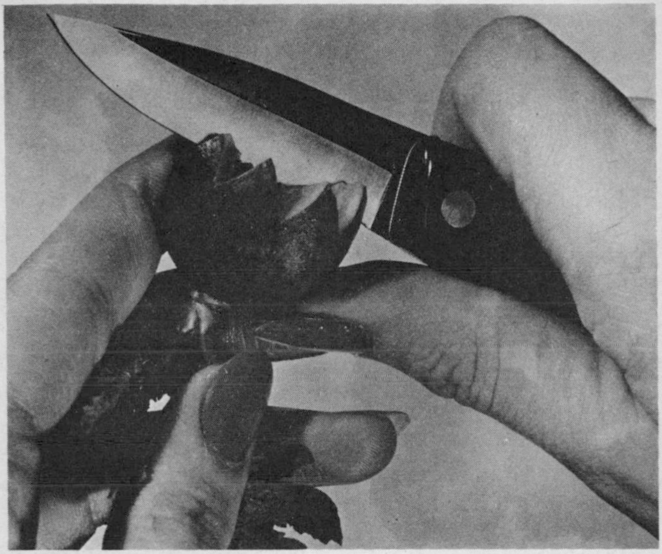

Tulip trim requires even notches all around radish.

Rosebuds are easy with the hook blade of parer.

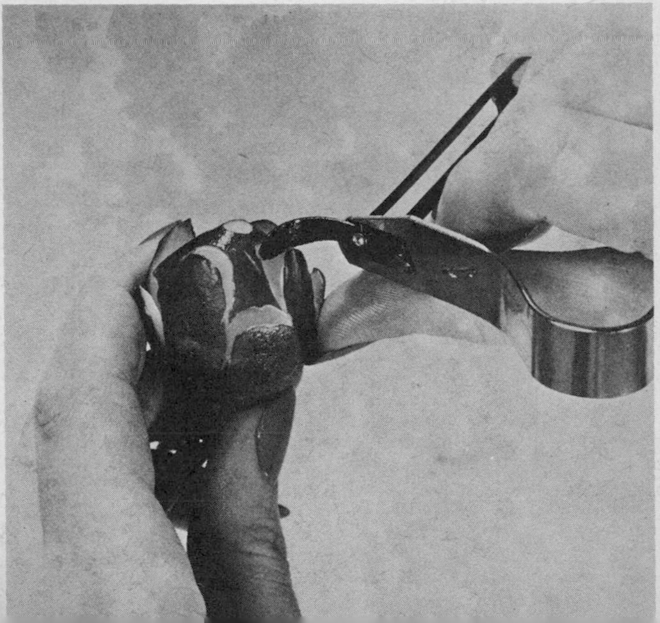

These individual antipasto salads smack of Italy. Choose a variety of colorful relishes to tuck into crisp green-pepper Roman Cups. Helps you out of the relish-tray rut.

ROMAN CUPS

To prepare cups, slice tops off fresh green peppers; scoop out. (Cut sliver off bottoms of tipsy ones.) Stuff with Marinated Artichoke Hearts, stuffed green olives and ripe olives, pickles, tomato wedges, and hot peppers. Add green onions, celery, and carrot sticks. Serve with cornucopias of salami slices twisted around cheese sticks and tacked with whole cloves.

MARINATED ARTICHOKE HEARTS

1 9-ounce package
    frozen artichoke
    hearts *or* 1 1-pound
    can artichoke
    hearts
2½ tablespoons lemon
    juice

3 tablespoons olive oil
    or salad oil
1 envelope Italian salad-
    dressing mix

Cook frozen artichoke hearts according to package directions (or drain and halve canned artichokes). Combine lemon juice, olive or salad oil, and salad-dressing mix; pour over artichoke hearts. Chill thoroughly, spooning marinade over artichokes a few times. Drain well before using.

COTTAGE-CHEESE POTATO SALAD

3 hard-cooked eggs
4 cups cooled, sliced, cooked potatoes
1 cup diced celery
1 cup large-curd cream-style cottage cheese
¾ cup mayonnaise or salad dressing
½ cup sliced radishes
½ cup diced green pepper
½ cup sliced green onions
2 teaspoons salt
¼ teaspoon pepper
Ripe olives

Set aside 1 egg for garnishing. Chop 2 eggs; mix with remaining ingredients except olives. Chill. Garnish with egg slices and olives. Makes 6 to 8 servings.

POTATO SALAD SPECIAL

Something new! Add cauliflower slices and bacon dressing—it's terrific—

3 cups diced cooked potatoes
1½ cups sliced raw cauliflower
1 cup diced celery
2 hard-cooked eggs, chopped
¼ cup chopped onion
6 slices crisp bacon, crumbled
1 cup mayonnaise or salad dressing
1 tablespoon bacon fat
2 teaspoons caraway seed (optional)

Combine first 6 ingredients. Mix remaining ingredients. Pour over salad; toss lightly; salt to taste. Chill. Makes 5 or 6 servings.

DEVILED EGGS

For extra flavor and color, add chopped pimiento, olives, or green onions to the yolk mixture—

6 hard-cooked eggs,
    halved lengthwise
          • • •
¼ cup mayonnaise or
    salad dressing

1 teaspoon vinegar
1 teaspoon prepared
    mustard
⅛ teaspoon salt
Dash pepper

Remove egg yolk; mash and combine with remaining ingredients. Refill egg whites, using pastry tube if desired. (For plump stuffed eggs, refill only 8 of the whites, chop extras for salad.) Chill thoroughly.

SOUR-CREAM POTATO SALAD

Salad dressing poured over warm potatoes gives them extra special flavor—

7 medium potatoes,
    cooked in jacket,
    peeled and sliced
    (6 cups)
⅓ cup clear French or
    Italian dressing
          • • •
¾ cup sliced celery
⅓ cup sliced green
    onions and tops

4 hard-cooked eggs
1 cup mayonnaise
½ cup dairy sour cream
1½ teaspoons prepared
    horseradish
    mustard
Salt and celery seed to
    taste
⅓ cup diced pared
    cucumber

While potatoes are warm, pour dressing over; chill 2 hours. Add celery and onion. Chop egg white; add. Sieve yolks; reserve some for garnish. Combine remaining sieved yolk with mayonnaise, sour cream, and horseradish mustard. Fold into salad. Add salt and celery seed to taste. Chill 2 hours. Add diced cucumber. Sprinkle reserved yolk over top. Makes 8 servings.

TOTE-'EM RELISHES

String all those extras that go on hamburgers or frank-furters on small individual skewers. Then each person picks up his own portable relish tray. Some folks will slip the onion slice or cheese triangle into a bun and nibble on the remaining relishes. Others will build a vegetable burger.

PATIO RICE SALAD

3 cups cooked rice	¼ cup chopped dill
6 hard-cooked eggs, coarsely chopped	pickle
	1 teaspoon salt
½ cup chopped onion	Dash pepper
¼ cup chopped pimiento	¼ cup French dressing
	⅓ cup mayonnaise or salad dressing
¼ cup chopped green pepper	2 tablespoons prepared mustard
¼ cup chopped celery	

Mix first 9 ingredients. Blend next 3 ingredients; add to rice mixture and toss. Chill well. For individual servings, lightly pack rice mixture into a custard cup; turn out on crisp lettuce. Repeat. Serves 5.

HOT GERMAN POTATO SALAD

To make this sweet-sour salad a little more hearty, slice 2 hard-cooked eggs and add to skillet with bacon and potatoes—

½ pound bacon	Dash pepper
½ cup chopped onion	½ cup vinegar
• • •	1 cup water
2 tablespoons all-purpose flour	6 cups sliced cooked potatoes
2 tablespoons sugar	• • •
1½ teaspoons salt	2 tablespoons snipped parsley
1 teaspoon celery seed	

Cook bacon till crisp; drain and crumble, reserving ¼ cup fat. Cook onion in reserved fat till tender but not brown. Blend in flour, sugar, salt, celery seed, and pepper. Add vinegar and water. Cook and stir till mixture thickens and bubbles. Add crisp crumbled bacon and sliced potatoes. Heat thoroughly, tossing lightly. Sprinkle with snipped parsley. Makes 8 or 9 servings.

CONTINENTAL POTATO SALAD

A delicious salad combination coated with a zippy horseradish dressing—

5 medium potatoes, cooked and sliced (about 5 cups)	½ cup sliced radishes
	• • •
2 cups drained cooked cut green beans	1 teaspoon salt
1 8-ounce can (1 cup) tiny whole beets, drained	½ teaspoon freshly ground black pepper
½ cup sliced celery	• • •
½ cup sliced green onions	1 cup chilled Horseradish Dressing

Chill vegetables thoroughly (cut larger beets in half). Combine, and season with salt and pepper. Just before serving, toss with 1 cup Horseradish Dressing. Serves 8.

Horseradish Dressing: Blend ½ cup mayonnaise or salad dressing, ¼ cup dairy sour cream, and 3 tablespoons horseradish. Add 1 cup clear French dressing, stirring till smooth. Chill. Makes 1¾ cups dressing.

MACARONI-AND-CHEESE SALAD

Cook one 7-ounce package elbow macaroni according to package directions. Drain and rinse with cold water. Add 2 tablespoons vinegar and mix lightly; let stand 10 minutes. Add 1 cup diced American cheese, ½ cup chopped green pepper, ¼ cup diced celery, 2 tablespoons chopped pimiento, 2 to 3 tablespoons minced onion, and ⅔ cup mayonnaise or salad dressing. Garnish with green pepper rings. Serves 6 to 8.

DUBLIN POTATO SALAD

1 teaspoon celery seed
1 teaspoon mustard seed
2 tablespoons vinegar
3 cups *warm* diced
    cooked potatoes
2 teaspoons sugar
½ teaspoon salt
1 12-ounce can corned
    beef, chilled and
    diced
2 cups finely shredded
    crisp cabbage

¼ cup finely chopped
    dill pickle
¼ cup chopped green
    onions
¾ cup mayonnaise or
    salad dressing
2 tablespoons milk
1 tablespoon vinegar
½ teaspoon salt

Soak celery and mustard seeds in 2 tablespoons vinegar; drizzle over potatoes. Sprinkle with sugar and ½ teaspoon salt. Chill. Add next 4 ingredients. Mix remaining ingredients; pour over potato mixture; toss lightly. Makes 7 or 8 servings.

RICE AND OLIVE SALAD

¾ cup uncooked rice
¼ cup chopped
    pimiento
¼ cup chopped green
    onions
½ cup chopped celery
⅓ cup chopped stuffed
    green olives

½ cup mayonnaise or
    salad dressing
½ cup dairy sour
    cream
½ teaspoon salt
½ to 1 tablespoon
    vinegar
Dash cayenne

Cook rice according to package directions; cool to lukewarm, tossing lightly several times. Combine chopped vegetables and olives with rice. Mix the remaining ingredients for dressing; pour over rice mixture and toss together. Chill thoroughly or serve at once at room temperature. Makes 6 servings.

CURRIED PICNIC SALAD

Sour cream and a subtle curry flavor turn potato salad into a gourmet dish—

6 cups diced cooked
   potatoes
2 tablespoons chopped
   green onions and
   tops
4 hard-cooked eggs,
   chopped
1 teaspoon celery seed
1½ teaspoons salt
¼ teaspoon pepper

½ to 1 teaspoon curry
   powder
1 cup dairy sour cream
½ cup mayonnaise or
   salad dressing
2 tablespoons vinegar
1 6-ounce jar marinated
   artichoke hearts,*
   drained

• • •

Combine diced cooked potatoes, green onions, eggs, celery seed, salt, and pepper. Toss lightly and chill thoroughly.

Combine the curry powder, sour cream, mayonnaise, and vinegar. Pour dressing over chilled potato mixture; toss lightly to mix. Garnish with border of marinated artichoke hearts. Keep chilled. Makes 6 to 8 servings.

---

*Or cook one package frozen artichoke hearts; drain. Chill in Italian dressing.

Cabbage Slaw

CABBAGE-PEPPER SLAW

4 cups shredded crisp
   cabbage

½ cup chopped green
   pepper

2 tablespoons sugar
1 teaspoon salt
1 teaspoon celery seed
Dash white pepper

2 tablespoons tarragon
    vinegar
1 teaspoon prepared
    mustard
½ cup salad dressing

Combine vegetables, sugar, salt, celery seed, and pepper.
Combine vinegar, mustard, and salad dressing; add to
vegetables and mix thoroughly. Makes 6 servings.

HOT RED CABBAGE

2 tablespoons salad oil
1 medium head red
    cabbage (4 cups
    shredded)
2 medium apples,
    chopped

2 cups hot water
⅔ cup vinegar
3 tablespoons sugar
½ teaspoon salt

Heat oil; add remaining ingredients; cook till apples are
tender. Makes 6 servings.

BLUE CHEESE SLAW

6 cups shredded
    cabbage
2 tablespoons chopped
    pimiento
2 tablespoons chopped
    green onion tops
      •   •   •
½ cup dairy sour
    cream

2 tablespoons
    mayonnaise
1 tablespoon lemon
    juice
½ teaspoon sugar
Dash salt
1 4-ounce package blue
    cheese,
    crumbled (1 cup)

Combine cabbage, pimiento, and onion tops; chill thoroughly. Mix together remaining ingredients; chill. Pour
over cabbage and toss lightly. If desired, garnish with
slices of hard-cooked egg and Bologna ruffles. Makes
4 to 6 servings.

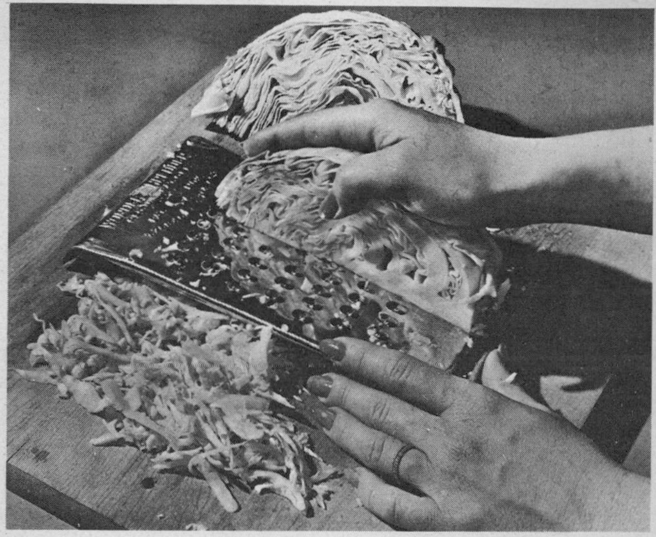

A grater makes fine, short shreds. Hold grater on board; push quarter heads across as shown.

Sharp knife will cut even shreds. Quarter head; hold firmly and slice crisp, even shreds.

Use a three-edged chopper for fine, juicy slaw. First shred the cabbage with a sharp knife.

For extra-crisp cabbage: Toss shreds with ice cubes; hold in refrigerator 1 hour. Remove ice.

SPRING COLESLAW

4 cups shredded
    cabbage
½ cup diced cucumber
½ cup diced celery
¼ cup chopped green
    pepper
   • • •

½ cup mayonnaise or
    salad dressing
2 tablespoons vinegar
2 teaspoons prepared
    mustard
¼ teaspoon paprika
¼ teaspoon salt

Combine all vegetables and chill well. Combine remaining
ingredients and pour over vegetables. Toss lightly. Serves
6.

COTTAGE-CHEESE COLESLAW

½ cup cream-style
    cottage cheese
½ cup mayonnaise
2 tablespoons vinegar
½ teaspoon caraway
    seed

½ teaspoon onion juice
¼ teaspoon Worcester-
    shire sauce
8 cups finely shredded
    chilled cabbage

Combine the cottage cheese and mayonnaise; add vinegar, caraway seed, onion juice, and Worcestershire
sauce. For stronger caraway flavor, chill dressing several
hours. Mix dressing lightly with cabbage just before
serving. Place slaw in large bowl lined with cabbage
leaves. If desired, garnish with cottage cheese and
green-pepper rings. Makes 8 to 10 servings.

OLD-FASHIONED COLESLAW

A dandy complement to barbecued meat—

1 6-ounce can (⅔ cup)
    evaporated milk
2 to 4 tablespoons sugar
½ teaspoon salt
¼ teaspoon pepper

2 to 3 tablespoons
    vinegar
3 cups finely shredded
    cabbage

Combine milk, sugar, salt, and pepper; stir briskly. Add vinegar slowly, to suit taste. Chill. (Mixture will thicken upon standing.) Rinse shredded cabbage in tepid or slightly warm water and drain well.

Place in bowl; cover tightly and chill 1 hour or more. Toss cabbage with the dressing. Makes 3 to 4 servings.

CALICO COLESLAW

Traditional slaw sparked with corn—

4 cups finely shredded
    crisp green cabbage
1 12-ounce can (1½
    cups) whole kernel
    corn, drained*
½ cup finely chopped
    onion
¼ cup chopped green
    pepper

¼ cup chopped
    pimiento
½ teaspoon salt
½ to ¾ cup mayon-
    naise or salad
    dressing

In a salad bowl, combine shredded cabbage, corn, onion, green pepper, and pimiento. Chill thoroughly. Just before serving, add salt and mayonnaise or salad dressing; toss lightly. Makes 6 to 8 servings.

*Or use one 10-ounce package frozen whole kernel corn, cooked and drained.

CABBAGE-PINEAPPLE SLAW

3 cups shredded crisp
    cabbage
1 9-ounce can (1 cup)
    pineapple tidbits,
    drained
1 cup diced apples

1 cup marshmallows
    (10), cut in
    eighths
½ cup chopped celery
½ cup mayonnaise

Combine, tossing till mayonnaise coats all ingredients. Line salad bowl with garden lettuce; fill with salad. Garnish with red apple wedges. Makes 4 to 6 servings.

GREEN AND GOLD BEAN SALAD

1 1-pound can (2 cups)
  cut green beans,
  drained
1 1-pound can (2 cups)
  cut wax beans,
  drained
¼ cup finely chopped
  onion
1 tablespoon snipped
  parsley

½ cup garlic dressing
1 teaspoon dill seed
  (optional)
½ teaspoon salt
¼ to ½ teaspoon
  cracked or
  coarsely ground
  pepper

Combine first 4 ingredients, tossing lightly to mix. Pour dressing over. Sprinkle with dill seed, salt, and pepper; toss lightly. Chill several hours. Before serving, toss again to coat beans with dressing; drain. Serves 6.

ASPARAGUS TOSS

1 pound fresh aspara-
  gus, cut in 2-inch
  pieces (2 cups)
1 small head lettuce,
  torn in bite-size
  pieces (4 cups)
1 cup sliced celery
¼ cup sliced green
  onions and tops
½ cup salad oil
2 tablespoons white
  wine vinegar
2 tablespoons lemon
  juice

¼ cup finely chopped
  cooked beets
1 hard-cooked egg,
  finely chopped
1 tablespoon snipped
  parsley
1 teaspoon paprika
1 teaspoon *each* sugar
  and salt
½ teaspoon dry
  mustard
4 drops bottled hot
  pepper sauce

Cook asparagus till just tender; drain. Chill. Combine with lettuce, celery, and onion. For dressing, combine remaining ingredients in jar; cover and shake well. Pour over salad; toss lightly. Serves 6 to 8.

MIXED EMOTIONS SALAD

Bet it's the most Italian-tasting salad you'll ever eat—

1 tablespoon olive oil
Dash garlic powder
2 tablespoons sesame
 seed
 • • •
1 large head lettuce,
 torn in bite-size
 pieces
1 6½- or 7-ounce can
 tuna, flaked

1 4-ounce jar antipasto
1 cup pitted ripe olives
1 2-ounce can
 anchovies, cut in
 ½-inch pieces
2 medium tomatoes,
 cut up
¼ cup olive oil
2 tablespoons wine
 vinegar

Combine 1 tablespoon olive oil with garlic powder in small skillet; add sesame seed. Heat and stir till lightly brown. Place next 6 ingredients in large bowl and toss with ¼ cup olive oil and the vinegar. Sprinkle with sesame seed. Makes 6 to 8 servings.

GUACAMOLE SALAD BOWL

½ medium head lettuce
2 tomatoes, cut in
 wedges
½ cup sliced pitted
 ripe olives
¼ cup chopped green
 onions
1 cup corn chips

1 6½-, or 7-, or 9¼-
 ounce can tuna,
 drained
 • • •
1 recipe Avocado
 Dressing
½ cup shredded
 Cheddar cheese

Break lettuce into salad bowl. Add tomato wedges, olives, onions, corn chips, and drained tuna. Toss lightly with Avocado Dressing. Top with shredded cheese and additional ripe olives. Makes 4 servings.

Avocado Dressing: Combine ½ cup mashed ripe avocado, 1 tablespoon lemon juice, ½ cup dairy sour cream, 1/3 cup salad oil, 1 clove garlic, crushed, 1/2 teaspoon sugar, 1/2 teaspoon chili powder, 1/4 teaspoon salt, and 1/4 teaspoon bottled hot pepper sauce; beat with electric beater or blender.

FOUR BEAN SALAD

An adaptable specialty you can concoct the night ahead of your barbecue—or just a few hours beforehand—

1 1-pound can (2 cups) green beans, drained

1 1-pound can (2 cups) cut yellow wax beans, drained

1 1-pound can (2 cups) red kidney beans, drained

1 1-pound can (2 cups) black-eyed peas or Limas, drained

1 medium green pepper, thinly sliced in rings

1 medium onion, thinly sliced and separated in rings

Dressing:

1/2 cup sugar
1/2 cup wine vinegar
1/2 cup salad oil
1 teaspoon salt
1/2 teaspoon dry mustard
1/2 teaspoon crumbled dried tarragon leaves *or* 2 teaspoons finely snipped fresh tarragon

1/2 teaspoon basil leaves *or* 2 teaspoons finely snipped fresh basil
2 tablespoons snipped parsley

Mix all vegetables in a bowl. Combine ingredients for Dressing, mixing well; drizzle over vegetables. Cover; marinate several hours or overnight, stirring several times. Before serving, stir to coat vegetables, then drain. Makes 12 servings.

SHOESTRING TOSS

Combine 1 cup julienne carrot strips, cooked and drained, 1 cup drained cooked or canned French-style green beans, and 1 cup celery strips. Pour ½ cup clear French dressing over. Chill 3 hours. Drain off excess dressing; reserve. Break ½ medium head lettuce, 1 small head romaine, and 1 head Bibb lettuce into bite-size pieces in large salad bowl. Arrange vegetables and 2 sliced hard-cooked eggs over greens. Dash with salt and freshly ground pepper. Toss lightly; add enough dressing to coat leaves. Serves 6.

CHEESE MARINATED ONIONS

**3 ounces blue cheese,
crumbled (about
¾ cup)**
½ cup salad oil
**2 tablespoons lemon
juice**
1 teaspoon salt

½ teaspoon sugar
Dash pepper
Dash paprika
**4 medium onions,
thinly sliced
(about 4 cups
onion rings)**

Mix all ingredients except onions. Pour over onion rings and chill thoroughly. Serve as a meat relish or add to a green salad.

MEXICAN BEAN SALAD

Here's a happy new twist for the traditional three-bean combo—

**1 1-pound can (2 cups)
cut green beans**
**1 1-pound can (2 cups)
red kidney beans**
**1 1-pound can (2 cups)
chick peas or
garbanzos**

**1 cup garlic French
dressing**
Crisp salad greens

Drain beans and peas. Toss with dressing. Chill several hours or overnight, stirring a few times. Just before serving, stir again; drain off excess dressing. Spoon salad onto lettuce-lined plates. Sprinkle with sweet pickle relish, if desired. Makes 10 servings.

MUSTARD BEANS

A sensation to serve—

1 cup sugar
½ cup cider vinegar
3 tablespoons prepared
    mustard
½ teaspoon instant
    minced onion
¼ teaspoon salt

1 1-pound can yellow
    wax beans, drained
    or 1 9-ounce
    package frozen
    yellow wax beans,
    thawed

Combine all ingredients except beans; bring to boiling point, stirring till sugar is dissolved. Add beans; simmer uncovered 5 minutes; cool. Cover; refrigerate overnight. Serve as relish or salad ingredient.

PICKLED CARROTS

Sweet 'n sour spiced carrot sticks—

6 medium carrots
    (about 1 pound),
    scraped and cut in
    3-inch lengths
¾ cup sugar
¾ cup vinegar

¾ cup water
1 tablespoon mustard
    seed
2½-inches stick
    cinnamon, broken
3 whole cloves

Precook carrots 5 minutes. Drain; cut in thin sticks. Combine next 4 ingredients. Tie cinnamon and cloves in cloth bag; add to sugar-water mixture. Simmer 10 minutes; pour over carrots. Cool; refrigerate 8 hours or overnight. Drain well before serving.

ZIPPY MUSHROOM APPETIZERS

Tasty pickles with just the right bite—

⅔ cup tarragon vinegar
½ cup salad oil
1 medium clove garlic,
    minced
1 tablespoon sugar
1½ teaspoons salt
Dash freshly ground
    pepper
2 tablespoons water
Dash bottled hot
    pepper sauce

1 medium onion, sliced
    and separated in
    rings
2 6-ounce cans broiled
    mushroom crowns,
    drained, *or* 2 pints
    fresh mushrooms,
    washed and
    trimmed

• • •

Combine first 8 ingredients. Add onions and mushrooms.
Cover and refrigerate mixture for at least 8 hours, stirring several times. Drain and serve as an appetizer.

ONIONS FIRST

3 large red onions,
    sliced paper-thin
1 lemon, sliced paper-
    thin

• • •

½ cup salad or olive oil

¼ cup vinegar
2 tablespoons lemon
    juice
1 teaspoon savory
½ teaspoon salt

Layer onion and lemon slices in bowl, ending with a
few lemon slices. Combine remaining ingredients; pour
over. Chill 8 hours or overnight, basting occasionally
with dressing. Drain; serve as a relish—or a before-
dinner appetizer with thin slices of tiny "ice-box" rye
for make-your-own sandwiches. Makes about 2 cups.

ORANGE-GLAZED BEETS

No cooking required for this delicacy—

¼ cup honey
½ to 1 teaspoon
    shredded orange
    peel
¼ cup orange juice

¼ cup lemon juice
½ teaspoon salt
1 1-pound can (2 cups)
    julienne-style
    beets, well-drained

In a small mixing bowl, combine honey, orange peel and juice, lemon juice, and salt. Add drained beets; mix gently. Refrigerate several hours or overnight, turning occasionally. Drain and serve as a relish.

CHAPTER 6

BEVERAGES

These summertime coolers tinkle a welcome to thirsty barbecuers. Tall frosty glasses hold lemonade, limeade, or exotic fruit blends. Fresh green mint, citrus fruit slices, or maraschino cherry garnishes make each glassful a gay sensation. Or, consider the refreshing flavor of iced tea. With sugar and lemon, or simply chilled with ice, its deep amber tones are the promise of cooling enjoyment. Satisfy coffee lovers with a large steaming potful from the grill, or serve chilled over cracked ice.

CAMPFIRE COFFEE

Heat 2 quarts cold water to boiling. Mix 1 cup regular-grind coffee, 3 tablespoons water, and 1 egg. Pour boiling water over coffee in coffeepot. Heat just to boiling; cover and let stand 12 minutes at edge of grill.

ICED COFFEE

Refrigerator method: Make coffee regular strength (for 1 cup use 2 tablespoons coffee to ¾ standard measuring cup water).

Cool in tightly covered glass, earthenware, or enameled-ware container not more than 3 hours, or chill in refrigerator before icing. Pour over ice cubes made with coffee.

Quick Method: Make coffee double strength. Use half the amount of water to the usual amount of coffee. To make 2 glasses, use 8 tablespoons coffee to 1½ standard measuring cups water. Pour hot, freshly made coffee into tall ice-filled tumblers.

KONA ICED COFFEE

This refreshing cream-rich beverage can double for dessert. Not too sweet—the sugar just accents the flavor—

3 tablespoons instant coffee	2 cups cold water
¼ cup sugar	1 cup light cream
• • •	• • •
1 quart milk, scalded	½ cup whipping cream, whipped

Dissolve instant coffee and sugar in hot milk; add cold water; let cool to room temperature. Add light cream; chill thoroughly.

Pour mixture into tall glasses with an ice cube in each. Sail spoonfuls of whipped cream on top. Makes 8 to 10 servings.

PATIO PUNCH

1 envelope cherry-
    flavored soft drink
    powder
1 envelope strawberry-
    flavored soft drink
    powder
2 cups sugar
2 quarts cold water
1 6-ounce can frozen
    orange-juice
    concentrate

1 6-ounce can frozen
    lemonade
    concentrate
1 quart ice cubes
1 1-pint 12-ounce bottle
    ginger ale (about
    3½ cups), chilled

Combine first 3 ingredients. Add water; stir to dissolve.
Add concentrates. Chill. Pour over ice cubes. Pour
ginger ale slowly down *side* of container. Makes 4 quarts.

HOT MULLED CIDER

Have this for a snappy October barbecue—

½ cup brown sugar
¼ teaspoon salt
2 quarts cider
1 teaspoon whole
    allspice

1 teaspoon whole cloves
3 inches stick cinnamon
Dash nutmeg

Combine first 3 ingredients. Tie spices in small piece of
cheesecloth; add. Slowly bring to a boil; simmer, covered, 20 minutes. Serve hot with orange peel twist. Use
cinnamon sticks as muddlers. Serves 10.

PINEAPPLE MALLOWADE

24 marshmallows
1 cup water
1 No. 2 can (2¼ cups)
    unsweetened
    pineapple juice

¼ cup lemon juice
Dash salt
1 1-pint 12-ounce bottle
    (3½ cups) ginger
    ale, chilled

Place marshmallows and water in top of double boiler. Heat over boiling water till marshmallows are melted; stir occasionally. Blend in fruit juices and salt. Mix well; chill. Add ginger ale just before serving. Pour into ice-filled glasses. Serves 6 to 8.

RASPBERRY-MINT CRUSH

A dazzler for fresh color and flavor!

¼ cup sugar
½ cup lightly packed
    fresh mint leaves
1 cup *boiling* water
1 10-ounce package
    frozen red
    raspberries

1 6-ounce can frozen
    lemonade
    concentrate
2 cups cold water

Combine sugar, mint leaves, and boiling water; let stand 5 minutes. Add raspberries and concentrate; stir until thawed. Strain into chilled pitcher half full of ice; add cold water, stir. If desired, float a few fresh raspberries in punch and garnish glasses with fresh mint leaves. Makes about 8 servings.

CITRUS SUNSHINE PUNCH

1 6-ounce can frozen
    orange-juice
    concentrate
1 6-ounce can frozen
    lemonade
    concentrate
1 6-ounce can frozen
    limeade
    concentrate

4 cups cold water
1 1-pint 12-ounce bottle
    (3½ cups) ginger
    ale, chilled

Combine all ingredients except ginger ale. Pour over ice block in bowl. Add ginger ale just before serving.

Garnish with mint leaves, if desired. Makes 12 to 15 servings.

For fruited muddlers: Slip a lemon slice on each long muddler just above rim of glass. Then alternate a few maraschino cherries and pineapple chunks almost to top.

For sugar-frosted glass rims: Dip rims in fruit juice, then in sugar. Let dry.

TEA SPARKLE

1 cup *boiling* water
4 teaspoons tea leaves
   or 4 tea bags
1 cup light corn syrup
4 cups cold water
1 cup lime juice

1 1-pint 12-ounce bottle
   (3½ cups) ginger
   ale, chilled
Lime slices
Maraschino cherries

Pour boiling water over tea; steep 3 minutes; strain. Add corn syrup, cold water, and lime juice; mix thoroughly. Chill.

Pour into pitcher over ice. Add ginger ale when ready to serve. Garnish with lime slices and maraschino cherries. Serves 12.

FROSTY MINT TEA

3 cups *boiling* water
6 teaspoons tea leaves
   or 6 tea bags
1 tablespoon mint jelly
Lime juice

Confectioners' *or*
   granulated sugar
1 1-pint 12-ounce bottle
   (3½ cups) ginger
   ale, chilled

Pour boiling water over the tea. Let steep 5 minutes. Strain and pour hot tea over jelly; stir to dissolve. Chill. To front rims of chilled glasses, dip into lime juice, then into sugar. Fill glasses half full of tea; add crushed ice; fill to frost line with ginger ale. Garnish with lime slices and mint sprigs. Serves 6.

SPICED-TEA SPECIAL

2½ cups *boiling* water
2 tablespoons tea leaves
   or 6 tea bags
¼ teaspoon allspice
¼ teaspoon cinnamon
¼ teaspoon nutmeg

   • • •

¾ cup sugar
1 1-pint bottle (2 cups)
   cranberry-juice
   cocktail
1½ cups water
½ cup orange juice
⅓ cup lemon juice

Pour boiling water over the tea and spices. Cover; let steep 5 minutes. Strain; add sugar; cool. Add remaining ingredients; chill. Garnish with lemon slices. Serves 6 to 8.

MULLED GRAPE FROST

¾ cup sugar
1¼ cups water
¼ teaspoon nutmeg
1 tablespoon grated
   orange peel
4 teaspoons grated
   lemon peel
1 teaspoon snipped
   crystallized ginger

4-inch stick cinnamon
6 whole cloves
4 cups bottled grape
   juice
⅓ cup orange juice
¼ cup lemon juice

Combine first 8 ingredients; simmer 10 minutes. Cool. Strain. Stir in juices. Chill. Pour into ice-filled glasses. Makes 10 servings.

PERFECT ICED TEA

Measure 2 tablespoons tea leaves (or 6 bags) into teapot. Pour 2 cups fresh, *boiling* water over leaves. Cover and let stand 5 minutes. Stir a second or two. Then pour brew through a tea strainer. Immediately add 2 cups cold water; let tea cool at room temperature till ready to serve. Serves 4.

Note: If you happen to make tea too strong, it's likely to cloud. To make it sparkle again, pour tea into glass or enamelware pan and reheat (don't boil) till clear. Remove from heat immediately and add about ½ cup *boiling* water for each quart tea.

COLD WATER ICED TEA

So clear and amber it sparkles. And as easy as filling a water pitcher—

4 cups cold water   **6 tea bags**

Fill a one-quart jar with cold water. Add tea bags and cover. Chill in the refrigerator 12 to 18 hours or overnight.

Remove tea bags and pour tea into tall glasses filled with ice cubes or crushed ice. Offer juicy lemon or lime wedges and sugar to taste. Trim glasses with fresh mint sprigs if desired. Makes about 4 to 6 servings.

APRICOT SWIZZLE

Here's a refreshing fruit punch you can fix at the drop of an ice cube—

4 teaspoons instant tea
½ cup sugar
2 cups cold water
1 12-ounce can (1½ cups) apricot nectar
½ teaspoon aromatic bitters (optional)

1 6-ounce can (¾ cup) frozen lemonade concentrate
1 1-pint 12-ounce bottle (3½ cups) ginger ale, chilled

• • •

In large pitcher, mix instant tea, sugar, cold water, apricot nectar, and aromatic bitters; stir mixture till sugar dissolves.

Just before serving, add frozen lemonade concentrate and several ice cubes; stir. Place 3 or 4 additional ice cubes in each of 8 tall glasses and pour in fruit mixture to fill glasses about ⅔ full. Pour chilled ginger ale down the *side* of each glass to fill and stir gently with an up and down motion.

LIMEADE

As cool as its fresh green color—

½ teaspoon grated
    lime peel
Juice of 10 limes
    (¾ cup)

¾ cup sugar
2 cups water

Combine all ingredients and stir to dissolve sugar. Chill thoroughly. Half-fill each glass with ice cubes or crushed ice; fill with lime mixture. Garnish glasses with lime slices, if desired. Makes about 6 servings.

FAVORITE PATIO REFRESHER

1 envelope strawberry-
    flavored soft drink
    powder
1 envelope cherry-
    flavored soft drink
    powder
1 cup sugar
8 cups cold water
2 12-ounce cans
    (3 cups) apricot
    nectar, chilled

1 6-ounce can (¾ cup)
    frozen limeade
    concentrate
1 6-ounce can (¾ cup)
    frozen lemonade
    concentrate
    • • •
1 1-pint 12-ounce bottle
    (3½ cups) lemon-
    lime carbonated
    beverage, chilled

Combine first 7 ingredients; chill thoroughly. Place ice cubes in tall chilled glasses; fill ¾ full with fruit mixture. Tip each glass and pour carbonated beverage down *side* to fill. Makes 12 to 16 servings.

RIO CHOCOLATE

A spicy chocolate-coffee drink—it'll be one of your favorites—

2 1-ounce squares unsweetened chocolate	Dash salt
	1 cup water
¼ cup sugar	• • •
4 teaspoons instant coffee	3 cups milk
¾ teaspoon cinnamon	• • •
¼ teaspoon nutmeg	Whipping cream, whipped
	Stick cinnamon

In top of double boiler, combine chocolate, sugar, coffee, spices, salt, and water.

Cook mixture over low heat, stirring till chocolate is melted and blended. Bring to boiling and cook 4 minutes, stirring constantly. Then place over boiling water and stir in milk; heat thoroughly.

To serve, beat with rotary beater till foamy. Pour into cups. Top with fluff of whipped cream. If desired, use cinnamon sticks as stirrers. Makes about 6 servings.

OLD-TIME LEMONADE

For a quickie, keep this syrup on hand—

1 cup sugar	6 tablespoons lemon juice
1 cup water	
• • •	4 cups water

Combine sugar and water in a saucepan. Heat, stirring constantly, until sugar dissolves, then bring to a full rolling boil. Cool; add lemon juice and water. Pour into ice-filled glasses. Trim each glass with mint sprigs and lemon slices.

For individual servings, combine 3 to 4 tablespoons of the syrup with 1½ tablespoons lemon juice and 1 cup water.

ROSE-COLORED GLASSES

Place a small block of ice or ice cubes in a large pitcher. Add a few sliced strawberries, then pour in chilled cranberry-juice cocktail (a pint or quart bottle). Carefully pour an equal quantity of chilled lemon-lime carbonated beverage (two 7-ounce bottles or one 1-pint 12-ounce bottle) carefully down the *side* of the pitcher. Makes 4 or 8 servings.

HONOLULU PUNCH

½ cup sugar
1 cup water

• • •

1 cup strong tea
1 cup unsweetened
    pineapple juice
¾ cup lemon juice

⅓ cup orange juice
2 7-ounce bottles (about
    2 cups) ginger ale,
    chilled
Orange slices
Mint sprigs

Make simple syrup by boiling sugar and water 5 minutes; set aside. Combine tea and fruit juices; chill. Just before serving, add ginger ale and syrup to taste. Garnish with orange slices and mint sprigs. Serves 6.

MINTY GRAPE COOLER

1 cup sugar
1½ cups water
1 cup mint leaves
1 cup lemon juice

• • •

2 cups grape juice
1 1-pint 12-ounce bottle
    (3½ cups) ginger
    ale, chilled

Combine sugar and water; cook for 5 minutes. Cool slightly. Pour over mint leaves. Add lemon juice. Cover and let steep 1 hour.

Strain mixture. Add grape juice. Just before serving add ginger ale. Garnish glasses with sprigs of mint. Makes 2 quarts.

CRANBERRY PUNCH

Plenty of sparkle and tang—

¼ cup sugar
½ cup boiling water
1 1-pint bottle (2 cups)
    cranberry-juice
    cocktail
1 cup orange juice

¼ cup lemon juice
• • •
2 7-ounce bottles
    (about 2 cups)
    ginger ale, chilled

Add sugar to water, stirring to dissolve. Add fruit juices. Chill. Just before serving, pour over crushed ice or cubes and add ginger ale. If you like, garnish with an orange slice slipped over the rim of each glass and tuck in a sprig of mint. Makes about 6 to 8 servings, or 1½ quarts of punch.

PINK LADY PUNCH

1½ to 2 pounds fresh
    rhubarb, cut up
2½ cups water
1 cup sugar
2 cups unsweetened
    pineapple juice

¼ cup lemon juice
1 1-pint 12-ounce bottle
    (3½ cups) ginger
    ale, chilled

Rinse rhubarb and drain. Cook uncovered in water till soft, about 10 minutes. Sieve mixture, reserving 3¾ cups juice; chill. Stir in sugar, pineapple and lemon juices; add ginger ale. Makes about 2½ quarts.

MINT SPARKLE

1 10-ounce jar (about
    1 cup) mint jelly
1 cup water
2 12-ounce cans (3 cups)
    unsweetened
    pineapple juice

1 cup water
½ cup lemon juice
1 1-pint 12-ounce bottle
    (3½ cups) ginger
    ale, chilled

Combine mint jelly and 1 *cup* water in saucepan. Place over low heat and stir till jelly is melted. Cool. Add pineapple juice, remaining 1 *cup* water, and lemon juice. Chill mixture thoroughly.

Place ice cubes in tall chilled glasses; fill half full with fruit mixture. Tip each glass and pour ginger ale down *side* to fill. Garnish with lemon slices and sprigs of fresh mint. Makes 10 to 12 servings.

SPICED PINEAPPLE COOLER

⅔ cup sugar
1½ cups water
12 inches stick
    cinnamon
12 whole cloves
1 46-ounce can (6 cups)
    unsweetened
    pineapple juice

1½ cups orange juice
½ cup lemon juice
1 1-quart tray ice cubes
1 1-pint 12-ounce bottle
    (3½ cups) ginger
    ale, chilled
Cinnamon sticks

Combine first 4 ingredients. Cover and simmer 15 minutes; strain. Cool. Add fruit juices. Chill. Just before serving, add ice cubes; carefully pour ginger ale down *side* of bowl. Serve with cinnamon-stick stirrers. Makes about 12 servings.

CHAPTER 7

DESSERTS

Create and re-create memories with generous scoops of home-made ice cream. Of course everyone samples first right from the dasher. Strawberry, chocolate, peach, or good old vanilla—whatever the flavor of the day, it'll be a hit. Don't forget those warm coals at the grill. They'll do delightful things to fresh fruit. Toasted cake and doughnuts will disappear before your eyes, and ice cream sauces are at their best when warm. Dessert cheeses are worth knowing too. Get acquainted with new ones along with your standard favorites.

HOT BANANA SHORTCAKE

A dandy cookout dessert—

¼ cup butter or
   margarine

• • •

2 or 3 green-tipped
   bananas, peeled
   and quartered
2 tablespoons lemon
   juice

⅔ cup brown sugar
¼ teaspoon cinnamon

• • •

4 1-inch slices pound
   cake

• • •

Vanilla ice cream *or*
   dairy sour cream

Melt butter or margarine in foilware pan over *hot* coals. Add quartered bananas, drizzle with lemon juice, and sprinkle with brown sugar and cinnamon. Cook until bananas are just soft, spooning the syrup over now and then. Meanwhile toast slices of pound cake on both sides on grill.

To serve, place the warm cake slices on plates, spoon bananas and syrup over. Top with scoops of ice cream or dollops of sour cream. Makes 4 servings.

ROLL-'N-FRUIT DESSERT BOBS

Snippets of sweet rolls and multi-fruits string along together to put a toasty finish on your outdoor supper—

Open and bake 1 tube refrigerated cinnamon rolls on barbecue grill.*

Cut or snip each baked roll in thirds. Fill skewers, alternating pieces of roll with marshmallows, canned pineapple chunks, maraschino cherries, canned apricot halves, cooked pitted prunes, and spiced crab apples. Mix icing that comes in cinnamon-roll package with 1 tablespoon pineapple or apricot syrup; set aside. Roast kabobs over *hot* coals, turning often, till rolls and marshmallows are toasted. With fork, scoot foods off skewers;

drizzle with icing mixture. Eat them at once while they're hot!

---

*To bake refrigerated rolls on grill, fold 1 yard heavy-duty aluminum foil in half; grease top. Arrange rolls near one end of foil; fold other end over and pinch edges together allowing about ½ inch in package, above rolls, for rising. Place foil package about 8 inches above coals and bake about 7 minutes (peek now and then to see if bottoms of rolls are brown). Invert package and bake about 7 minutes longer.

HEAVENLY HAWAIIAN CREAM

You'll like it for its luscious flavor, for saving you time—

1 No. 2 can (2½ cups) pineapple tidbits
¼ pound (16) marshmallows, cut in eighths
¼ cup well-drained maraschino cherries, cut in fourths

• • •

1 cup whipping cream, whipped

• • •

¼ cup slivered blanched almonds, toasted
Shredded coconut

Drain the pineapple tidbits, reserving ¼ cup of the syrup. Combine pineapple, cut marshmallows, cherries, and reserved ¼ cup pineapple syrup.

Let mixture stand 1 hour. Fold in whipped cream. Spoon into dessert dishes and chill. To serve, sprinkle with nuts and top with coconut. Makes about 6 to 8 servings.

CANDY-COOKY POLES

Skewer large marshmallows between commercial chocolate drop cookies. Toast over coals until marshmallows are gooey-soft.

FRUIT-BOBS

Place a maraschino cherry in the center of a canned peach half; thread on skewer. Repeat, beginning and ending skewer with halved canned pineapple rings.

Brush kabobs with melted butter and broil.

GRILL-BAKED PUDDING CAKE

Let this convenient dessert bake on covered grill while you eat dinner—

Prepare 1 package pudding-cake mix (chocolate, lemon, or orange flavor) according to package directions, but using an ungreased 8x1½-inch round foilware pan. Place on grill top over *slow* coals and lower hood to make oven. Bake about 25 to 30 minutes or till done. Spoon out servings while warm, turning each serving pudding-side up. If desired, top each serving with a scoop of vanilla ice cream.

Note: Wait till you are ready to bake before preparing the mix.

BASIC ICE CREAM

Make simple variations of this recipe for five delicious flavors—

¾ cup sugar	4 cups light cream
½ envelope (1½ tea-	1 egg slightly beaten
spoons) unflavored	1 teaspoon vanilla
gelatin	Dash salt

• • •

Thoroughly combine sugar and gelatin. Add *half* the cream. Stir over low heat till gelatin dissolves. Slowly stir a small amount of hot mixture into egg; mix well. Return to hot mixture; cook and stir till mixture thickens slightly (about 1 minute). Chill. Add remaining cream, vanilla, and salt. Include one of the following flavor variations. Makes about 1½ quarts of ice cream.

Vanilla: Increase vanilla in basic recipe to 2 teaspoons. Freeze till firm.

Strawberry: Decrease sugar in recipe to ½ cup. Crush 1 quart fresh, ripe strawberries with ¾ cup sugar; add to mix. Freeze.

Peach: Decrease sugar in recipe to ½ cup. Combine 2 cups mashed peaches, ¾ cup sugar, and ¼ teaspoon almond extract; add to chilled mix. Freeze till firm.

Maraschino Cherry: To the chilled mix, add ⅓ cup maraschino cherries, chopped, and 1 tablespoon maraschino juice. Freeze.

Chocolate-Almond: Increase sugar in basic recipe to 1 cup. To sugar-gelatin mixture, add three 1-ounce squares unsweetened chocolate *or* one 6-ounce package (about 1 cup) semisweet chocolate pieces. Proceed as directed. To the chilled mix, add ¾ cup slivered almonds, toasted. Freeze.

To freeze ice cream, pour chilled mixture into freezer can. (Fill can only ⅔ full to allow for expansion of mix during freezing.) Fit can into freezer. Adjust dasher and cover. Pack crushed ice and coarse ice-cream salt (rock salt) around can, using 6 parts ice to 1 part salt. (Pack ice and salt up to—*but not over*—lid of can.)

*Turn handle slowly till ice partially melts and forms brine; add more ice and salt as needed to maintain ice level. Turn handle rapidly and constantly till brank becomes difficult to turn. Remove ice to well below lid of freezer can; thoroughly wipe cover and top of freezer can; take off lid; remove and scrape dasher.

To ripen ice cream, plug opening in lid. For a tight fitting lid, cover the freezer can with several thicknesses of waxed paper or foil. Replace lid. Pack more ice and salt (using proportions of 4 parts ice to 1 part salt) around freezer can to fill the freezer. Cover freezer with heavy cloth or newspapers. Let ice cream ripen about 4 hours to improve and mellow the flavor.

*If using an electric freezer, follow the manufacturer's directions.

Cheese Guide to

Cheese	How it looks and tastes
Blue Gorgonzola (gor-gun-zo'-luh) Roquefort (rok-for') Stilton	Compact, creamy cheeses veined with blue o blue-green mold. Sometimes crumbly. Mild t sharp, salty flavor.
Brick	About brick size; texture ranging from soft t firm with many tiny round holes. Creamy yel low color; mild to moderately sharp flavor.
Brie (bree)	Soft-ripening, similar to Camembert, bu slightly firmer. Creamy yellow with thin brow and white crust. Mild to pungent flavor; pro nounced odor.
Camembert (kam-'em-bear)	Creamy yellow inside with a thin gray-whit crust. When ripe it softens to the consistenc of thick cream. Full, rich, mildly pungen flavor.
Chantelle (shahn-tell')	Pale yellow interior with a red coat. Mello flavor; semisoft texture.
Cheddar or American	Favorite all-round firm cheese. Flavor varie from mild to sharp. Color ranges from natura to yellow-orange; texture from firm to crumbl May come in wedges, sticks, rectangular cut called "blunts," slices, or cubes. Also availabl in process form.
Cream	Soft buttery texture; very mild flavor; ric and smooth. Comes plain, whipped, or flavore with pineapple, dates and nuts, etc.
Edam, Gouda (ee'-dum, goo'-da)	Round, red-coated; creamy yellow to yellow orange inside; firm, smooth texture. Mil sweet nutlike flavor. "Baby Gouda" weigh less than a pound, Edam weighs 2 to 4 pounds

Good Dessert Eating

How to serve

At room temperature with fresh apples and pears, crackers, or crusty French or Italian bread.

Especially good with fresh peaches, apricots, cherries, or melon. Or, string cubes on toothpicks with chunks of fresh apple and pear.

With fresh peaches or pears. Be sure to eat the crust. Good with a variety of dark, whole-grain breads.

One of the world's classic dessert cheeses. Leave at room temperature before serving for best eating quality—the consistency of thick cream is ideal. Team with fresh peaches, apples, and pears, or with fresh tart plums and cracked roasted walnuts. The crust is good eating, too.

Best with red or yellow apples.

Excellent with fruit pie, crisp crackers, fresh cherries, or pears.

Thin with cream and serve with crackers and your favorite jellies. Also good with preserved kumquats, fresh apricots, grapes, peaches, and pears, sectioned oranges, and salted nuts.

Bright hub for dessert tray. Serve in wedges, or cut off top; hollow out center; dice and refill. Or, let each person scoop out his own. Best fruits are fresh grapes, peeled oranges.

Cheese Guide to

Cheese	How it looks and tastes
Liederkranz *(lee'-dir-krahnz)*	Soft-ripening; robust flavor and odor resembling Limburger. Golden yellow color.
Muenster *(mun'-stir)*	Similar to Brick cheese. Mild and mellow flavor; white creamy. Medium hard with tiny holes. Now made in the United States, but longer European curing time makes a sharper flavor.
Process cheeses American Brick Gruyere *(gree-air')* Swiss Others	Smooth, creamy texture. Spreads easily at room temperature; sliced when chilled. Melts smoothly and quickly. Selected lots of fresh and aged natural cheeses are blended and pasteurized so that no further ripening takes place. May be flavored with bacon, pineapple, etc.
Swiss	Firm, pale yellow cheese, with large round holes. Mild sweet, nutlike flavor. Comes in chunks or already sliced.
Cheese Spreads	Glassed and packaged ready-to-spread blends; mild to very sharp. Plain or flavored with smoke, relish, olive, pineapple, garlic, or pepper. Like process cheese but with higher moisture and lower milk fat content. Added stabilizer prevents separation.

HOT CAKES

Not the usual kind, but a hot dessert—

Cut a pound cake or angel cake in 1½-inch cubes. Spear each on fork and dip in melted currant jelly, sweetened condensed milk, or in a mixture of ½ cup honey and 1 tablespoon lemon juice. Then roll in flaked coconut to cover. String on skewers and toast over *very hot* coals, turning often.

Good Dessert Eating (continued)

How to serve

Spread on toast and crackers, rye and pumpernickel breads. Especially good with fresh apples, pears, and Tokay grapes.

Serve with fresh dark cherries and wedges of canteloupe or honeydew melon.

Serve at room temperature to spread on crusty French or Italian bread. Chill to cut in thin slices or cubes. Goes well with many fruits.

With fresh apricots, grapes, melon wedges, peaches, or sectioned oranges, and tangerines. Or, serve with dark breads and fruit juice.

With crackers or your favorite bread. Good with most fruits.

BARBECUED BANANAS

Choose 4 yellow bananas, tipped with green. Peel the bananas, but *save* the peels. Coat with mixture of ½ cup maple syrup, a pinch of brown sugar, dash salt, and about 2 tablespoons lemon juice. Let stand a little while, then place them back in their skins (save the syrup mixture to pour over later). Wrap each in foil and place on the coals for a few minutes. Serve with syrup mixture. If desired, top with ice cream. Serves 4.

Serve a cheese-tray sampler with fresh fruit for the finale
of your barbecue. Look over varieties on the cheese counter
in your market—mild and sharp, hard and soft. Include
old stand-bys; add new ones for adventure.

POWWOW SUNDAE

Fun to do and fun to eat—a luscious mingling of cho-
colate sauce and bits of marshmallow, part soft and melty,
part crunchy from toasting over the coals—

¼ pound (about 16) large marsh- mallows	**1 cup canned chocolate syrup Vanilla ice cream**

String marshmallows on skewers. Toast over coals till
melty inside and well-browned outside (best of all if
marshmallows blaze a little to get crackly edges!) Scoot

hot, gooey marshmallows off skewers into a serving bowl of chocolate sauce. Stir just to marble, then ladle over big scoops of ice cream. Makes 1½ cups sauce.

DONUT HOLES

If you're looking for a spectacular on a small scale, this is it—

Cut refrigerated biscuits (from a tube) in thirds, and roll each piece into a ball. String on skewers, leaving about ½ inch between balls. "Bake" over *hot* coals, *turning constantly* until browned and completely done, about 7 minutes. At once, push off skewers into melted butter or margarine; roll in cinnamon-sugar mixture. Eat right away. One tube of refrigerated biscuits makes 30.

PINEAPPLE-ON-A-SPIT

Pare a medium pineapple, leaving leafy crown intact. Remove pineapple eyes and replace with 15 to 20 whole cloves. Center pineapple on spit (pull out a few spikes from center and pierce with a small skewer first); secure with holding fork. Wrap leafy end in foil. Let rotate over *hot* coals 45 minutes to 1 hour, basting frequently with mixture of ½ cup maple-flavored syrup and ½ teaspoon cinnamon. Slice and serve hot.

CART-WHEEL BANANAS

Leave peel on firm bananas; cut in diagonal slices, about ¾ inch thick. Dip cut ends in lemon juice, then dunk in mixture of brown sugar and cinnamon.

Thread on skewers (going through skin), alternating with quartered orange slices (thick and unpeeled). Broil fruits until hot through and banana peel turns brown.

OUTDOOR APPLE DUMPLINGS

Combine two No. 2½ cans (7 cups) apple-pie filling and ⅔ cup water in a large skillet that has a *tight* cover. When apples come to boiling, cut refrigerated biscuits from one tube in quarters and let the pieces drop on the bubbling apples. Sprinkle biscuits with a cinnamon-sugar mixture. *Cover* and simmer 20 minutes. Serve with cream.

CHAPTER 8

FIRE BUILDING

Barbecue information—instruction and suggestions on fire building and control. Arrangement of the hot coals are pictured for various types of cooking situations. Smoke cooking helps are included.

Equipment—grills and accessories to make your barbecue cooking more convenient, and the food more flavorful.

Over the Coals Information

Whatever the meat you choose for your barbecue—from steaks to burgers to tender ribs—follow directions for cooking carefully. Have the best for your dollars spent!

For broiling, all meats call for glowing coals. *No flame*. Let the fire burn down till a gray-ash film covers the charcoal. If fire's too hot, you dry the meat, lose good juices.

Try our ideas from the preceding pages as a take-off, then experiment on your own. Have a practice run with the family—then invite friends in and collect the compliments.

YOU'RE ALL SET TO COOK

Be smart—use a meat thermometer when roasting (ham, turkey, leg of lamb, or beef). Insert thermometer so tip is in center of meat. Tip must not touch bone, fat, or the metal spit. Don't guess when roast is done—use this dependable helper!

Try rubbing steaks or chops with a cut clove of garlic, or rubbing poultry seasoning or sage lightly over chicken or ribs about an hour or so before broiling.

Spear fat trimmings—or use a bacon strip—to rub over grill or wire broiler basket. Keeps meats from sticking to grill.

Score edges of meat—ham slices, steaks, chops—so they won't cup up. Or cook in a wire broiler basket to keep them flat.

Trim outer edge of fat from steaks, pork chops, and ham slices so drippings won't blaze up too much. If drippings flare up during the cooking, sprinkle lightly with water to quench the blaze.

Select meats that fit together well on the grill. Club steaks will arrange to good advantage; so will loin lamb chops.

Use a narrow paintbrush to brush butter or margarine on meats or vegetables before broiling on the grill and for basting. Give barbecue sauce its own special brush— saves time in brushing it on.

Step up seasoning for meats with a preliminary rub of dried herbs, blended spices, or your favorite seasoning salts.

GRILL SAVERS

Before you begin to build the fire, read the directions that came with the barbecue unit. You may need to line the base of the firebox with pea gravel, coarse grit, or special insulating pellets. A bed of gravel about 1 inch deep will help to prevent the burning out of the firebox. The gravel also lets air in so the heat will be more evenly distributed. After you have used the grill about a dozen times with the gravel in the firebox, wash the gravel in hot water and spread it out to dry *thoroughly*. (If your firebox is perforated on the bottom, there will be no need for gravel.)

SILVER LINING

Here's a trick to save fuel and keep your barbecue unit new looking. Line the firebox with heavy-duty aluminum foil. (Or line the ash pit if there is a grate to hold the coals.) Place gravel or insulating pellets on top of the foil and cover with the amount of charcoal needed for the fire. The foil reflects the heat back on the food and speeds up the cooking time. It also keeps your equipment cleaner—it catches the melted fat and drippings. Smoke chefs like to line the hood of their smoker with aluminum foil, too.

HOW MUCH CHARCOAL?

The amount of charcoal needed differs with your equipment and the food you plan to cook. Large roasts require more charcoal than foods for broiling, as steaks or burgers. Estimate your needs for the fire and then start with all the charcoal that will be needed in your firebox.

Beginner chefs are often too ambitious, build too big a fire. After you've built several barbecue fires, you'll be able to gauge the amount easily. Shallow fire is simple to control, fine for broiling. No need to make a large fire over the whole grill area for one steak or a few chops.

TERMS USED IN MEAT COOKERY

Barbecue—To roast meat slowly on a spit over coals, in a rotisserie basket, basting occasionally with a highly seasoned sauce. Often refers to foods cooked or served with a barbecue sauce.

Baste—To moisten foods during cooking with the pan drippings, water, oil, or a special sauce to prevent drying, or to add flavor.

Braise—To brown in a small amount of hot fat, then add a small amount of liquid and to cook slowly in a tightly covered utensil.

Broil—To cook by direct heat, in a broiler or over hot coals.

Dredge—To sprinkle or coat meat or fish with flour or corn meal.

Fry—To cook in hot fat. To cook in a small amount of fat is called pan-frying or sauteing; to cook in a 1- to 2-inch layer of hot fat is called shallow-fat frying, and to cook in a deep layer of hot fat is called deep-fat frying.

Garnish—To trim with small pieces of colorful food, *i.e.* pepper, pimiento.

Lard—To insert strips of fat in gashes made in meat; or to place slices of fat on top of uncooked lean meat or fish for flavor, or to prevent dryness.

Marinate—To allow a food to stand in a liquid—usually a French dressing or a mixture of oil and vinegar—to tenderize or add to the flavor.

Pan-broil—To cook uncovered in a hot frying pan, pouring off fat as it accumulates.

Score—To cut narrow grooves or gashes part way through the outer surface of food.

Sear—To brown meat very quickly by intense heat. This method increases the shrinkage, but develops the flavor and improves the appearance of the meat.

Truss—To tie chicken, turkey, or other meat with cord laced around metal or wooden pins (skewers) to hold its shape during cooking.

JUST RIGHT COALS FOR COOKING

A well-made fire is the essential first step in outdoor cooking. The right fire makes barbecuing smooth and simple.

Coals are ready for cooking when they look ash-gray by day, and have a red glow after dark. No flames! Don't start cooking too soon. The fastest way to get a bed of cooking coals (about 15 minutes) is with an electric fire starter. Most other methods of fire starting take approximately 45 minutes.

TEST OF FIRE

The temperature of the fire needed depends on the type of meat you are going to cook. For cuts of meat such as steaks, burgers, and kabobs which you intend to cook rapidly, use a relatively hot fire. A moderate fire is fine for roasts and larger pieces of meat. For slower cooking cuts of meat such as pork chops and spareribs, use a slow fire.

An easy way to tell the heat of the fire is to hold your hand over the coals at the height the food will be for cooking. Begin counting "one thousand one, one thousand two," and so on. The number of seconds you can comfortably hold your hand over the fire will tell you how hot the fire is. If you can count to "one thousand two," you have a relatively hot fire; "one thousand three" or "one thousand four" is about a moderate fire, and "one thousand five" or "one thousand six" is a slow fire.

FIRE NEEDS MOTHERING

You're not cooking by thermo control as on a range or in an oven, so take a look every now and then. No profit in finding the fire dwindling at cooking time—or in losing the food to the flames!

TO REDUCE HEAT

With practice, you will work out the best method for your needs and your barbecue equipment. You may use any one or all of these ways:

Lower the firebox if it is adjustable.

Raise the grill height from the fire.

If you are rotisserie cooking and using the gypsy method of a ring of coals, move the coals out from the food to make a larger oval. The heat will decrease.

TO INCREASE HEAT

Reverse the procedures under "to reduce heat," or do the following:

For short-time cooking, tap the ashes off the burning coals with tongs instead of adding new briquets. Ashes on the briquets insulate and retard the heat.

Open drafts to let more air through.

To add more coals: For a reserve supply of hot coals, warm extras around the edges of your fire after it is ready for cooking. Don't top your cooking fire with cold coals—they will lower the temperature more than you think. To increase heat, add warm coals from the reserve around the fire's edge.

SMOKE PREVENTION

Everyone votes "yes" to hickory smoke but "no" to smoke from fat. A charcoal fire will smoke till it has died down to cooking coals. Fat from steaks and chops on grill will drip, then smoke. You can lessen this by trimming fat off edges before broiling. When cooking large roasts, use an aluminum foil drip pan underneath.

TO AVOID FLARE-UPS

Keep handy a clothes sprinkler filled with water to put out flare-ups caused by fat drippings. Use only enough water to do the trick—don't soak the coals. It will take some time for very wet coals to dry out and begin to burn again. It will also reduce the intensity of the heat of the fire.

SAVE THOSE COALS

When you're finished cooking, don't let the charcoal just burn away. If your barbecue unit has a hood, lower it and close the dampers; the fire will be snuffed out. The same procedure will work for a kettle-type grill that has a lid. If you have an open-type unit, use tongs to transfer the hot coals from the firebox to a bucket. Smother the fire by covering bucket tightly.

SAVE YOUR GRILL TOP

You will add to the life of the grill top if you wait to place it over the fire until cooking time. Also save it by removing it (with asbestos gloves) right after use.

BARBECUE CLEANUP

When cooking is completed remove hot grill and swathe it with wet paper towels or newspapers while you eat. Later a few swipes will clean the grill. For stubborn spots on the grill, smoky coffeepots, or greasy skillets, use scouring or abrasive-type pads for quick and easier cleaning.

FOILWARE FIGURES

Foilware is available in many sizes and shapes. There are cake pans and pie pans, bake trays, casserole dishes, and divided serving plates. Make use of them in outdoor cooking. Handy to have a variety on deck for outdoor cooking and serving.

Hot appetizers are a snap when heated first in a foilware pan—pass in it too.

To broil appetizers that are small such as shrimp or chicken livers, prick the bottom of a foilware pan here and there with a two-tined fork or an ice pick. Have these bite-size foods well brushed with a flavored butter to keep them moist and to add flavor.

Turn to brown all sides. Spear each tidbit with a toothpick for easy pickup and let the guests help themselves.

HOW TO MAKE A FOIL DRIP PAN

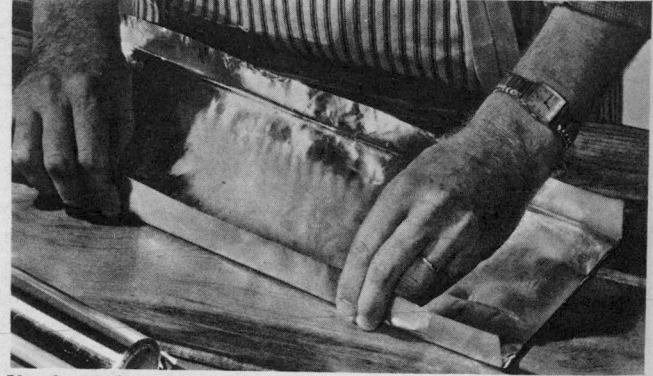

Use heavy-duty aluminum foil (18 inches wide). Tear off a piece large enough for a double thickness the length of the grill. (If your grill is round, make drip pan in half circle.)

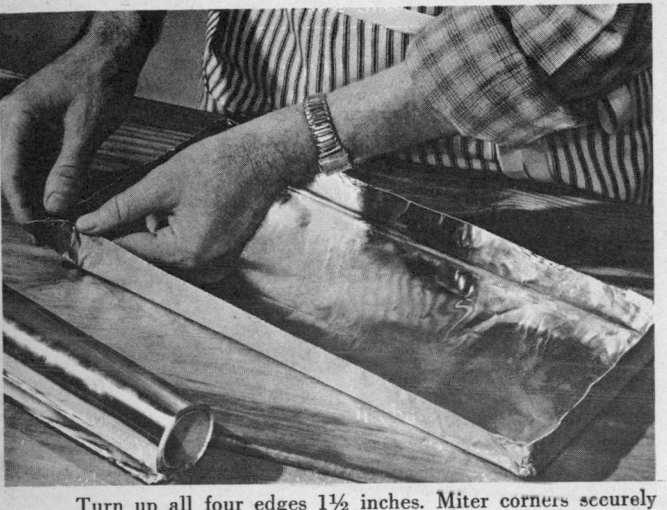

Turn up all four edges 1½ inches. Miter corners securely and fold the tips to the inside for reinforcement. With care, your drip pan will last all summer. Empty pan after each use.

Drip pan can be set in place before or after you build the fire. It goes in front of coals directly under meat on spit. (In foreground are holding forks that slip on the spit.)

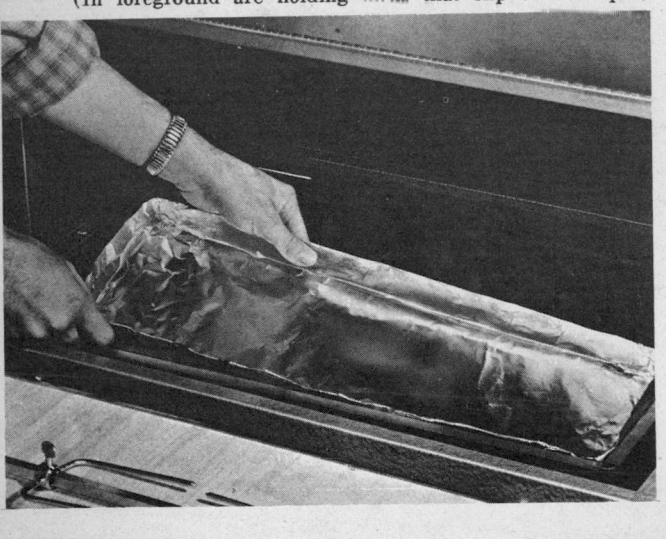

FOIL HELPERS

Broil on foil. It is the best cooking trick yet. No grill losses. If you're planning to have burgers for a crowd, tear off a strip of foil the size of your grill top. With a two-tined fork, puncture the foil here and there at about 2-inch intervals—you can steady the foil on the grill. Be careful—don't tear, just poke little holes in the aluminum foil. Turn up a half-inch edge on your "pan" all around. Lay the burger patties on the hot foil. They will brown to a turn and stay moist and juicy. (The holes let the heat up and fat drippings out so meat broils instead of sizzling.) Another plus: you can throw your pan away. Instant cleanup!

Use this same idea for broiling bacon, but *do not puncture* the foil. For a pan, use a piece of aluminum foil just large enough to hold the bacon strips; turn up slight edge. Allows perfect browning and crisping! Nary a slip through the grill bars and no fat fires. You can even fry thin-sliced bacon this way. It is also a good way to broil Canadian-style bacon for a large group.

CHOOSE FOODS THAT TRAVEL

If you are planning a barbecue picnic at a park or other area which is some distance from your home, it is important to plan meals with the keeping qualities of food in mind. Check the list below.

These foods all travel safely without special handling: canned meats, fruit, fruit juices, and vegetables; process cheese; bread and rolls; cookies, cakes (but *no* cream fillings), doughnuts; powdered instant products (coffee, tea, cocoa, dry milk, cream); dehydrated soups and potatoes; jelly, jam, and peanut butter; potato chips and crackers in moisture-proof containers; ready-to-eat cereals; tomatoes and fresh fruit.

To avoid spoilage, you'll be wise to fix the hot foods on the spot. They will taste better, too. Since egg-milk mixtures are particularly sensitive to spoilage, avoid cakes or pastries with custard and cream fillings and any salad or sandwich mixtures heavy with mayonnaise. Be careful, too, of such perishable items as potato salad, deviled eggs, raw hamburger, and salad fillings made of egg or fish. They should be kept well refrigerated and taken on short excursions only to prevent spoilage.

OUT OF THE FREEZER— ONTO THE HIGHWAY

Utilize foods from your home freezer. Basic sandwiches, from peanut butter to salami, can be made in advance, frozen, then thawed safely as you travel along. Trimmings like lettuce, mustard, and mayonnaise can be added just before eating.

Some prepared frozen dinners carry cooking instructions for grill or campfire; and frozen vegetables dotted with butter, then wrapped loosely (but sealed tightly) in aluminum foil, can be steamed in their own moisture over the coals of the campfire. The same trick works well for roasting corn on the cob, for baking potatoes, and for freshening bread and rolls.

Frozen foods should be solidly frozen when you start out. In packing picnic hamper or thermal bag, you can use frozen foods (each in plastic bag or foil to prevent dripping) to help keep other foods cold. Place individual cans of fruit juices or soft drink (super-chilled in the freezer) next to relishes packed in a plastic bag to keep them crisp.

Fire Building Tips

You want a fire that will come to the temperature you need quickly so you can get on with the cooking. Charcoal takes about 20 minutes to burn to a gray-ash after you light it. Charcoal comes in two forms—lump charcoal and briquets. Lump charcoal is in odd-sized pieces just as they come from the charcoal kiln. It is less uniform in burning quality and more difficult to handle. Briquets are ground, lump charcoal pressed into uniform blocks. They are easier to use, burn evenly, and produce uniform heat. They are easier to control and burn longer than lump charcoal.

HOW TO BUILD A CHARCOAL FIRE

Pile the charcoal in a pyramid on the firebox of the grill. You don't need much charcoal. Add liquid lighter

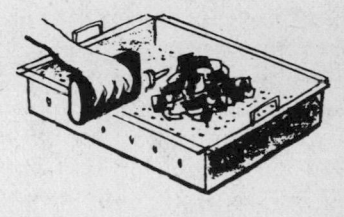

to charcoal; wait a minute, then light. *Do not use gasoline or kerosene*. Let charcoal burn for 15 to 20 minutes until the briquets are about two-thirds covered with gray-ash. A blower or fireplace bellows will speed it up. Spread the briquets evenly throughout the grill. Now you are ready to begin the cooking.

Other aids: Candle stubs; jelly fire starter; electric starters (have fire going in 5 minutes), or put 3 or 4 tablespoons canned heat in a cup fashioned of aluminum foil, place in the firebox, and heap the charcoal over it.

CHARCOAL FAST-START

Place 6 or 7 briquets in a 2-pound coffee can. Add about 1 pint charcoal liquid lighter. Cover can tightly and let stand 15 to 20 minutes. With tongs, mound soaked charcoal in firebox. Place metal chimney (see

directions for making below) over charcoal. Add 6 to 8 untreated briquets. For safety, cover can and set it away from heat.

Ignite at base of chimney. When these briquets are burning, add a few more untreated ones at the top—or the amount you'll need to do the cooking job. Allow to burn about 15 minutes. Lift off chimney, rake coals where you want them.

HOW TO MAKE CHIMNEY

A chimney is the secret of the fast take-off. Make your own from a tall juice can or a 2-pound coffee can. Remove ends from can. Using tin snips, cut out triangles or circles around bottom, 1 inch apart, to allow draft. Or punch triangular holes with a beverage opener; bend down for legs.

To make a sturdier chimney, you need: 1 piece 24-gauge black sheet metal, 11½x24¾ inches (you can have this rolled in cylinder at metal shop).

One 9-inch length of 1-inch scrap iron (cut to make 3 legs), or have holes punched in the bottom at the metal shop.

9 No. 6 ½-inch sheet-metal screws.

Use 3 of the screws to secure the side seam of the

cylinder—the remainder to fasten legs (leave clearance of 1½ inches under cylinder to allow good bottom draft).

Bed of coals—no flame! To use the full grill surface for broiling, rake coals over entire firebox. Wait! Don't start to cook till the fire dies down to glowing coals.

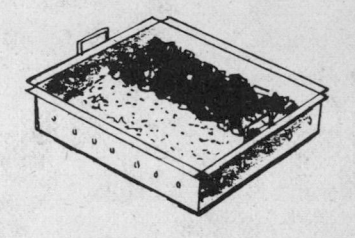

Use only part of firebox to broil on half grill or for spit roasting on unit with a reflector hood. Arrange the coals a little deeper than usual and slightly to rear of spit extending beyond the ends of the meat on spit. Place a drip pan under meat; check the position once juices start.

If you are cooking a large piece of meat that requires a long cooking time, plan to replenish the coals from time to time. Allow briquets to warm up at side of the fire.

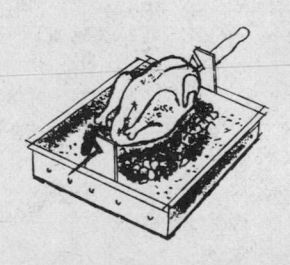

Use ring-of-fire roasting (gypsy way) for rotisserie roasting on unit with open top. Form an oval of live coals around and slightly larger than the roast or bird on spit—the meat should not be placed directly over the hot coals.

To slow down the fire, move hot coals out to make a larger oval; to increase heat, move hot coals in to make narrower oval. This technique helps maintain the even cooking. Fire is ready only when flames die down. In daytime the coals will look ash-gray and after dark, they'll have a red glow (they burn from outside in).

To add more charcoal: For a reserve of hot coals, add a little extra charcoal around the edges after your barbecue fire is ready for cooking. The bed of coals for broiling should be shallow (easy to control) and just a little larger than the area of food you are cooking. Why waste fuel?

PARALLEL ROWS FOR KABOBS

String burning hot coals along the firebox so they are spaced in between the rows of kabobs above; also have coals around the sides of the firebox.

The same arrangement is efficient if you have a line-up of skewers, one with meat, one with baking potatoes, and so on.

POLKA DOTS FOR STEAKS

Use this arrangement of coals for steaks, chops, and foods that are broiled flat on the grill. Once coals are hot enough for broiling, place them about half an inch apart under the grill area you'll use. This will give even heat and reduce flare-ups when meat fat drips down.

HOW TO BUILD A WOOD FIRE

A wood fire takes longer to build and to burn down to a bed of coals. Start your fire well ahead of time. Expect to spend about 2 hours building the fire and letting it burn into a satisfactory bed of coals.

Choose dry, slow-burning woods that give long-lasting coals such as hickory, oak, hard maple, walnut, and pecan. Fruit woods and vines give a wonderful flavor to food cooked over them.

Start with some easily lighted material such as dry paper. Follow this with some small, dry twigs. When you have a good fire base started, keep adding larger pieces of wood. Remember, larger pieces burn slower and take longer to produce a bed of coals. Follow this method for starting a wood fire for campfire or smoke cooking.

SMOKE CONTROL

If your oven is designed to burn wood, you can get a consistent, natural smoke by using green, freshly cut wood or by soaking dry wood in a bucket of water before placing it on a hot bed of coals. If you are limited to charcoal as a fuel, or want to increase the quantity of smoke, add chips of specially prepared aromatic wood, or hardwood shavings soaked in water.

You can best judge timing by experience, and in the beginning, by using a good thermometer. For smaller pieces of meat, you'll have to develop a practiced eye—and slice off an occasional sample.

Use kindling and charcoal to start your smoke cooking fire, add hardwood chips and allow the fire to burn to glowing embers. Then smother fire with slightly dampened hardwood chips or sawdust—the idea is for it to smoke, not burn. Soak hickory hunks, crosscuts, or bark at least an hour in water. Use slow coals. The slower the cooking, the more piquant the flavor. You're using hickory for its taste merits, not as fuel. If it flares, haul it out with tongs and soak again in water. Hardwoods give off a smoke which gives a distinctive flavor to food. Soft or resinous woods should be avoided, as the burning resin will discolor the food and give an unpleasant odor.

SMOKE COOKING

Smoke cooking imparts a delicious woodsy flavor to food. Cooking times and methods of preparing foods for smoke cooking will vary according to the type of unit that you use, the heat of the fire, and the distance of the smoking rack or hooks from the firebox. The racks and hooks should be placed toward the front of the firebox to avoid having flames reach the food.

In most "smokers" the cooking food hangs in a chamber away from the direct heat of the fire. Drippings fall away from the coals. Draft is controlled at the top and at the firebox opening. Hot smoke (from green wood or wet chips) fills the cooking chamber.

Some units allow smoke cooking directly over the fire, with their covers closed. Other equipment permits direct, indirect, and rotisserie smoke cooking. For adjustments of firebox and draft, and for cooking times, see the manufacturer's directions.

EASY TO USE FOOD WARMERS

Keep foods hot with candles, alcohol, or canned heat. Make use of the warming shelf or oven space above your rotisserie or below the firebox. Some charcoal-broiler hoods double as warming shelves. Most useful for warming coffee or breads.

CARRY CHAFING DISH OUTDOORS

Keeps your food hot to last bite—gives service with glamour. Good for warming foods as heated appetizers, baked beans—or for cooking. For actual cooking, most people vote for heat you can adjust—as the electric unit with heat control, alcohol burner, or canned heat. Chafing dishes come in all styles and sizes, from individual size to jumbos to serve 20 or more.

PUSH COALS TO SIDE OF THE GRILL

Set the coffeepot, casserole, or pie on the edge of the grill. Or use a double boiler as a warmer. The hot water below keeps foods piping but not too hot. Warm buns, heat appetizers, and melt butter for corn on the cob this way. Bean pots also hold heat well.

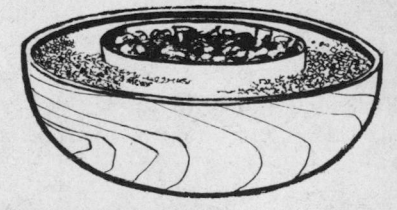

HEAT ROCK SALT

Keep foods warm with rock salt the same way you use crushed ice to chill. Heat salt in pan on grill or in the oven; then put appetizers, hot potato salad, barbecue sauce in a small bowl nestled in a larger pan or bowl filled with the heated salt. This method keeps food warm 1 to 2 hours.

WRAP FOODS IN FOIL

Wrap buns in foil; keep hot or heat on edge of grill. Breads don't dry out—stay fresh and moist with no danger of burning. Keep foods cooked in foil wrapped; they will stay warm and moist till time to eat.

Barbecue Equipment — Your Choice

Whether for simple cooking or grand-style, there's good-looking gear to please the expert or first-timer. You can have delicious charcoal-broiled meats with a small, inexpensive grill or supermodel barbecue (some have up to seven revolving spits). A firebox that is adjustable by a lever or a crank can make a great deal of difference in your cooking. Heat control is flexible.

The cost of equipment for outdoor cooking ranges from as low as a few dollars for small units to several hundred dollars for the very elaborate outfits. If you

have not yet had any firsthand experience with open fire cooking, resist that temptation to build a barbecue pit or to invest in a large mobile unit. Only by some happy trials and a few errors can you possibly decide which unit or combination of units will give you and your family the most satisfaction.

Start your career as a barbecue chef with a small unit. Find out by becoming familiar with the techniques of outdoor cooking how much of it you really want to do and how you plan to use your outdoor cooking area. Your first small grill will not be wasted. After it has served its valuable experimental purpose it will continue to be useful as a supplementary unit for broiling appetizers. Or use it when the children want to toast marshmallows. A collapsible unit can easily be moved to the beach or to a picnic area.

Any back-yard chef will appreciate the tools pictured above and on the following pages. As your interest in barbecue cooking grows you may want to add to your equipment—a huge coffeepot, a Dutch oven, a meat thermometer for roasts, a clothes sprinkler to douse blazes from meat drippings, an adjustable wire broiler basket, a sturdy carving board, and a razor-sharp carving knife. For extra large pieces of equipment for outdoor cooking needs, check with the restaurant supply houses.

Barbecue Grills — All Kinds

When you have mastered the art of barbecue cooking you may want to purchase a cooking wagon or table. Some of the more elaborate units have warming ovens, self lighters, electric motor-driven rotisseries, storage drawers, attached working surfaces, and rubber tires for easier mobility. The grills can be raised or lowered to obtain the degree of heat desired. A few units have thermometers in the hoods which are useful if the unit is to be used as a smoke oven or covered cooker.

Cooking kettles are similar to very large Dutch ovens on legs. They have adjustable dampers in both the lid and bowl.

265

Smoke ovens are an adaptation of the Chinese way of cooking. The food is placed on a rack or hung from a hook and is cooked by the hot smoke from a smoldering wood fire.

Braziers are one of the most popular units used today. They are round or square fire bowls set on legs. Some units have no windshield; others have a partial hood. Many braziers have a draft control at the bottom of the fire bowl, most helpful in heat control.

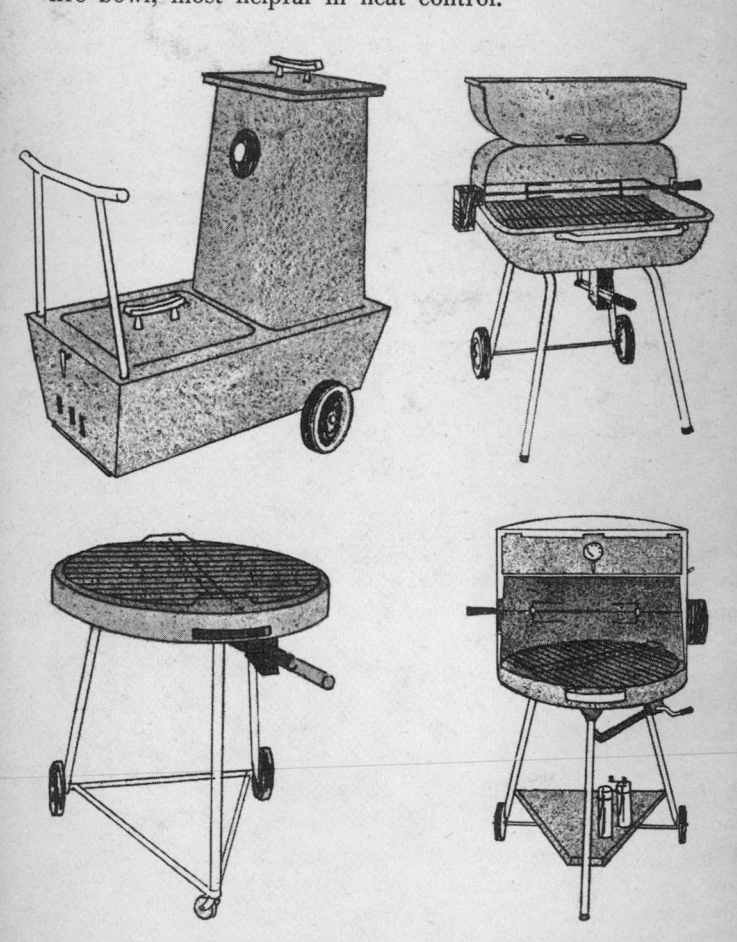

Covered cooker grill provides constant, controlled heat with gas-fired ceramic coals. Circular design of cast aluminum reflects heat evenly without flare-ups. For extra cooking surface, you can attach the second split-level grill. Knob below controls gas.

With this unit you can charcoal broil foods in your living room or game room fireplace as well as out of doors. The crank handle allows adjustment of the grid top.

This versatile little grill can broil a few burgers for the family or offer piping hot appetizers for a crowd. The chrome grid can be moved to two positions.

Perfect for camping trips as well as picnics this unit can be used three different ways: Fully open (as shown) it provides two cooking surfaces; half open it gives you one cooking surface; closed it can be used for covered cooking.

SMALL BARBECUE UNITS ARE IDEAL FOR BEGINNERS, ARE GRAND AS SUPPLEMENTARY UNITS FOR CHEFS

You can make a whole group of multi-size grills from clay flowerpots and saucers. Line pots to brim with foil; fill ⅔ full of mica-like insulating pellets—or use sand or gravel topped with a square of foil. Add 6 to 8 charcoal briquets, lighter fluid, and set aflame. Cover top with wire mesh or cake rack.

This portable barbecue grill is self-contained and folds to make a carrying case. It has a two-position firebox. This unit is a good size for eager children and adults to prepare toasted marshmallows over.

Make your cast-iron skillet do double duty. Line the skillet with heavy-duty aluminum foil and set on bricks for a base. Place the food in a wire broiler basket or on skewers. Add charcoal briquets to the skillet-hibachi and get set to cook.

A small meal could be broiled on this 18-inch round chrome plated grill. The screw-type adjustment permits several levels of height. Handles on sides make for easier portability. The three plastic tipped legs help keep it stable even on a picnic table.

FAST FIRE STARTER

You can have an average-size charcoal fire blazing in short order with an electric fire starter. The heating element is placed on the charcoal and a fan provides the necessary draft to start the fire in a hurry.

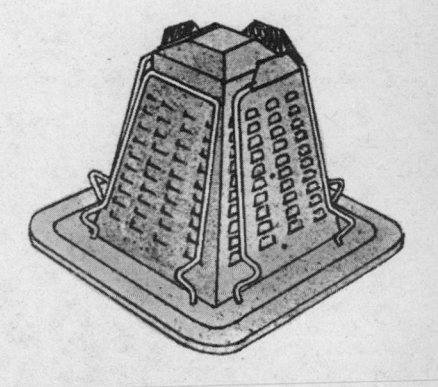

MAKE TOAST ANYWHERE

Toaster sits right over the barbecue or camp fire embers. Perforated metal stand toasts four slices of bread to golden brown. It's sturdy and ideal for camping trips, summer cottages, or back-yard cookouts.

LIGHT CHARCOAL QUICKLY

A tapered shape and grate provide the draft to get a
fire going. Put newspaper under the grate, add charcoal
in top; light the paper. In a few minutes lift lighter—
hinged grate drops down and charcoal falls into place.

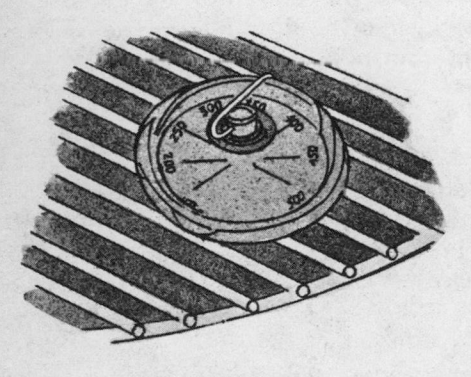

CHECK THE TEMPERATURE

This instrument will give an indication of the radiant
heat. Prepare fire as usual and place thermometer on
grill after coals have grayed. Watch for desired temperature indication and adjust grill or fire to maintain
temperature.

GEAR TO GET UP AND GO

The camping and cooking aids available today make "roughing it" as archaic as traveling by covered wagon. Today's nomad can safely carry with him as elaborate a feast as he could wish. There are portable ice chests ranging in size from a small ice bucket to the large chest type holding 85 pounds of ice, and a whole range of coolers from lightweight, efficient plastic foam boxes, to flexible fiberglass insulated bags. Vacuum jugs of every size incorporate such refinements as spigots for easy pouring and wide mouths for ladling. There is even neatly canned artificial ice.

Cooking on the spot never need be a problem. There are inexpensive canned heat stoves that tuck away; one-burner folding units, as compact as a camera, that maintain a three-hour hot flame on a few ounces of specially prepared fuel; and one-, two-, or three-burner stoves that operate on a disposable cartridge of liquid petroleum gas.

The ultimate in simplicity is a portable grill which uses nothing more than crushed newspapers as fuel. Four or five sheets of newspaper will cook a steak in minutes!

KEEP TAB ON TIMES AND TEMPERATURES

Attention to a few simple rules about foodstuffs, their proper handling and storage, will pay off handsomely.

Food may look and taste all right but still be hazardous. The only safe way is to keep hot foods really hot and cold foods icy cold—or else not to keep them long. Bacteria thrive in temperatures between 40° and 140°. Know and respect the limits of the equipment you use. Keep ice chests well-packed, and replenish with new ice if their temperatures get above 40°. (Small freezer thermometers are useful here.) Always preheat or prechill vacuum jugs and bottles for maximum efficiency.

Beyond the safety features, an ice chest or cooler maintains textures and temperatures for pleasant eating. Salad ingredients, washed at home and packed in plastic sack, stay crisp and firm for a day or more with chilling. Iced fruits are wonderfully refreshing, especially fresh melons cut in slices, just as they are needed. Part of the fun of a trip can be shopping stops at roadside stands.

GET SET TO RELAX!

Be sure to get all the equipment you need for easy barbecuing and then relax. Check your menu and see that you have all the tools needed. Assemble everything before you begin to pack for a picnic or before you start the fire for your back-yard barbecue party. It can be an unhappy occasion if someone has to keep running back for the forgotten items.

Check this list:
  Sturdy pepper mill and salt shaker
  Barbecue seasonings and spices
  Tongs; one for coals, one for food
  Long skewers with a protective hand shield
  Long handled fork, spoon, and turner
  Small brush or glass-tube baster
  Wire broiler basket which is adjustable to the thickness of the meat
  Heavy frying pan with long handle
  Durable hot pads and asbestos mitts
  Sharp knives including a roast slicer, carving knife, steak knives, paring knife, and a two-tined fork to keep the roast from skittering
  Little cutting boards
  Large carving boards
  Wooden spoons
  Meat thermometer
  Pliers for adjusting holding forks on a rotisserie spit
  Foil—serves many purposes
  A work surface near the grill
  Large serving spoons
  Bun warmer with cover

Ovenproof casserole dish
Clothes sprinkler to douse flames
Can and bottle openers
Ice bucket or cooler
Coffeepot
Straw bread basket
Griddle for flapjacks
Salad serving fork and spoon
Salad and vegetable bowls

And don't forget the "staples" for outdoor eating
enjoyment. Paper and plastic cups and dishes, paper
napkins and place mats, and paper toweling all make
for easy cleanup. Before you place the pots and pans
over the fire rub the outside with soap. It saves the pans
and is easy to clean. Don't forget the often needed
mosquito and bug repellents. Also have burn ointment
and a first aid kit available. Happy barbecuing!

INDEX

PHOTOGRAPHS AND SKETCHES

Erwin A. Bauer
Dick Boyer
George de Gennaro
Hedrich-Blessing
William Hopkins
Charles Kuoni
Roy Mathews
Mike Nelson
Robert Scott
Allen Snook
Frank & Dorothy Williams